FROM CAPE TOWN TO KABUL

This book is written with passion for and deep experience of struggles for women's rights in different parts of the globe. Professor Andrews deals with the vexed issue of the role of local cultures in defining women's rights in both South Africa and Afghanistan. She departs from the traditional western feminist goal of autonomy for women and argues instead for recognition of women's "conditional interdependence". This book is bold and insightful, a rich comparative analysis, with a transformational purpose.

Hilary Charlesworth, The Australian National University, Australia

In this fascinating read, the author addresses the critical complexities of women's rights in transitional societies. Developing the intriguing concept of "conditional interdependence", she challenges feminist conceptualizations based primarily on personal autonomy. Whether in her native South Africa or Afghanistan, progress occurs only with the support of the community of women AND men.

Adrien K. Wing, University of Iowa College of Law, USA

I0130647

From Cape Town to Kabul

Rethinking Strategies for Pursuing Women's Human Rights

PENELOPE ANDREWS
Albany Law School, USA

Routledge
Taylor & Francis Group

LONDON AND NEW YORK

First published 2012 by Ashgate Publishing

Published 2016 by Routledge
2 Park Square, Milton Park, Abingdon, Oxfordshire OX14 4RN
711 Third Avenue, New York, NY 10017, USA

First issued in paperback 2016

Routledge is an imprint of the Taylor & Francis Group, an informa business

British Library Cataloguing in Publication Data
Andrews, Penelope.
 From Cape Town to Kabul : rethinking strategies for pursuing women's human rights.
 1. Women's rights–Afghanistan. 2. Women's rights–South Africa. 3. Women and democracy–Afghanistan. 4. Women and democracy–South Africa.
 I. Title
 323.3'4'09581-dc23

Library of Congress Cataloging-in-Publication Data
Andrews, Penelope.
 From Cape Town to Kabul : rethinking strategies for pursuing women's human rights / by Penelope Andrews.
   p. cm.
 Includes bibliographical references and index.
 ISBN 978-0-7546-7996-7 (hardback : alk. paper)
1. Women's rights–South Africa. 2. Women's rights–Afghanistan. 3. Sex discrimination against women–Law and legislation–South Africa. 4. Sex discrimination against women–Law and legislation–Afghanistan. I. Title.
 K3243.A95 2012
 323.3'4–dc23

2012019358

ISBN 13: 978-1-138-27862-2 (pbk)
ISBN 13: 978-0-7546-7996-7 (hbk)

Contents

Introduction

Writing this book has been a labor of love. The title of the book and its thesis stemmed from my years of advocacy, teaching and scholarship about women's rights, particularly the rights of black South African women and indigenous Australian women. The kernel of the book first took shape in 2004 when I was a visiting scholar at the Rockefeller Center in Bellagio, Italy, surely one of the most spectacular and peaceful places on earth. Any scholar deserves some time in Bellagio!

It is therefore fitting that my first note of thanks goes to the Rockefeller Foundation, for creating the conditions for me to pursue the writing of this book. I had initially hoped that the manuscript would be completed within a year or two after my stint in Bellagio – but various projects precluded this from transpiring. First, I took up a visiting position as the Ariel Sallows Professor of Law and Democracy at the University of Saskatchewan in Saskatoon, Canada, a jewel of a place, albeit somewhat frozen for many months of the year. Over the course of that year I acquired many friends and the time I spent there was very special. I taught a course at the law school on comparative human rights, and organized two conferences: one at the University of Saskatchewan and other at the University of KwaZulu-Natal. The proceedings of the latter conference were published in a volume that I co-edited with Susan Bazilli entitled, *Law and Rights: Global Perspectives on Constitutionalism and Governance.*

In 2007 I left New York and moved to Valparaiso, Indiana, first as a visiting professor at Valparaiso University School of Law, and later joining the faculty on a permanent basis. My years at Valparaiso were wonderful and many on the faculty there became good friends. At Valparaiso I organized a series of conferences. Between 2008 and 2010 I held a joint appointment with Valparaiso and La Trobe University in Melbourne, Australia, tripling my airline mileage but depleting my reserves of energy.

I returned to CUNY School of Law as the Associate Dean for Academic Affairs in 2010. As I submit this manuscript I have just commenced my term as the first female President and Dean of Albany Law School in the capital of New York state.

In addition to thanking the Rockefeller Foundation, several people have to be thanked. First, my support staff at the CUNY School of Law, including Angela Morrison, Maryann Ruggiero, Lisa Smith, and Cathy Larsen. A special thanks also goes to Vicki Hickey. I also thank my research assistants, Margaret Palmer – CUNY Class of 2012, Prathiba Desai – CUNY Class of 2012, and Rachel Sazanowicz – CUNY Class of 2014, all young women who make CUNY School of Law proud, and who will in time become excellent public interest lawyers.

Part of this manuscript was presented over the years at several law schools, including the University of Nebraska (courtesy of Professor Anna Shavers), the Australian National University School of Law (courtesy of Professor Hilary Charlesworth) and the Washington and Lee School of Law (courtesy of Professor Blake Morant – now Dean at Wake Forest School of Law). I am indebted to them for hosting me and enabling me to engage with their intellectual communities.

My gratitude and thanks go to the following individuals: Professor Taunya Banks, a wonderful friend and friendly critic, Ms. Susan Bazilli, who tirelessly and fearlessly advances the rights or women, Professor Heinz Klug, a loving friend, who inspires, Professor Janet Calvo, the most generous and gracious teacher and host and Professor Andrea McArdle, a creative and thoughtful scholar and friend. They have read and commented on versions of this manuscript. A very special thank you is owed to Mr. Napoleon Williams, whose friendship, guidance and support has been a source of joy. He studied the first drafts of many chapters and gave me the benefit of his knowledge and helpful criticisms. I thank the members of the South Africa Reading Group, especially my co-host, Professor Stephen Ellmann, and the members of that group, who in the past two decades have ensured that the legal, constitutional and political project in South Africa remains of interest to Americans. Our regular gatherings are a source of great inspiration and intellectual camaraderie.

My friends and colleagues at CUNY School of Law deserve special mention. They have created the space for me to develop as a teacher, scholar and human rights advocate For that I am grateful. For those whom I have not mentioned individually, I hope that I have honored you by citing your scholarship and its influence on my work. I also thank my sisters, Wendy and Colleen, and my brother Keith, for their love.

I am deeply grateful to the staff and editors at Ashgate for their assistance in getting this manuscript to print: Alison Kirk, Sarah Horsley, Jonathan Hoare, and Barbara Pretty.

I dedicate this book to my dear friend, Ms. Ann Jackson, who at 96 years old has taught me the essence of being a woman, an essence which is at the core fearless.

Penelope Andrews
New York, July 2012

Chapter 1
Setting the Stage:
Transforming Women's Lives

The head-to-toe robe that women in Afghanistan are compelled to wear by the Taliban regime is to many the most overtly sinister symbol of the absolute subjugation of that country's women. It restricts air supply, shuts out the light, inhibits movement, and snuffs out individuality.[1]

The current reality of many South African Muslim women is merely a dream for many of their international counterparts .... They have the right to vote ... an official identity—they own passports .... Their voices can and are being heard ....[2]

South Africa and Afghanistan in Contrast

Contrasting fortunes between women in Afghanistan and women in South Africa have intrigued me for almost a decade. As the two quotations above suggest, the two countries, and the women in them, seemingly have little in common. It is, however, the transition in South Africa, from the release of Nelson Mandela in 1990, to the first democratic elections in 1994, and the transition in Afghanistan, from the NATO invasion in 2002, to the Bonn Agreement later that year, that provides for a review and analysis of the trajectory of gender equality.

Afghanistan, a nation of almost 30 million people, is beset by civil war and foreign occupation. South Africa, with a population of 49 million, is at peace, independent, and for over a decade and a half has made great strides under its new constitution in healing the wounds of war and establishing the rule of law. Moreover, Afghanistan economically is a very poor country, one of the poorest in Asia, with estimated budgetary expenditures in 2010 of approximately $3.3 billion, whereas South Africa is a relatively rich nation, one of the richest in Africa, with estimated budgetary expenditure in 2010 of $126.2 billion.

An estimated 28.1% of the population of Afghanistan is literate (male 43.1% and female 12.6%) but in South Africa approximately 86.0% of the population is literate (male 87.0% and female 85.7%). Differences in religion also seem

1   Liz Sly, *Afghan Women Wage Own War*, CHICAGO TRIBUNE, October 22, 2001.

2   NAJMA MOOSA, UNVEILING THE MIND: A HERSTORY OF THE HISTORICAL EVOLUTION OF THE LEGAL POSITION OF WOMEN IN ISLAM (2004) 152.

extreme. In Afghanistan, 99% of the population is Muslim (Sunni Muslim 80%, Shia Muslim 19%),[3] and ethnically the population is 42% Pashtun, 27% Tajik, 9% Hazara, 9% Uzbek, 4% Aimak, 3% Turkmen, 2% Baloch, and the remainder 4%. In South Africa, the ethnic population is 79.0% Black, 9.6% White, 8.9% Colored, and 2.5% Indian/Asian.[4] Christianity is the dominant religion at 78.0%, with Islam and Hinduism at 1.5% and 1.2% respectively, Judaism at .02%, and 15% of the country claiming to have no religion.[5]

Lastly, South Africa is much more urbanized than Afghanistan, with 62% of its population residing in urban areas, while Afghanistan only has 23% of its population living in urban areas.[6] These differences, though significant, do not tell the whole story. For example, many of the people in both countries are poor. In Afghanistan, the CIA World Factbook lists 36% of the population as below the poverty line, while the corresponding figure for South Africa is 50%.[7] Both, of course, are too high and as these statistics show, large segments of the populations of both countries live in poverty. This fact of poverty is not insignificant with respect to the subject matter of this book, namely women's rights and gender equality. Poverty profoundly impacts the range of options available to women, and severely constrains the ability of poor women to avail themselves comprehensively of a range of legal, social, economic, and political benefits available to women who are affluent or even relatively well-off financially.

Both developing nations are in transition. South Africa is in transition under the impulse for reform generated by the first democratically elected government since 1994 and its constitution. Afghanistan is in transition resulting from pressures for reform generated from the country being under occupation by Western armies, by the need to secure peace internally amongst warring groups and tribes, and by being under a form of superintendence by the United States.

In South Africa, issues of women rights and gender equality came to the fore during the struggle to end the apartheid regime, in drafting a new constitution and creating a representative government, and in efforts to ensure that the

---

3   Both Shia and Sunni Muslims share the fundamental beliefs and basic tenets of Islam, but political differences in the two sects have evolved over time. These differences include those of religious leadership and interpretation of religious texts and practices. Sunni Muslims make up the majority of Muslims globally, but significant minorities may be found in Iran and Iraq. For an explanation *see*: http://www.bbc.co.uk/religion/religions/ islam/subdivisions/sunnishia_1.shtml. See also Dr. Paul Sullivan, *Who Are the Shia?*, HISTORY NEWS NETWORK, April 12, 2004 at: *http://hnn.us/articles/1455.html.*

4   *See* THE CIA WORLD FACTBOOK at: *https://www.cia.gov/library/publications/ the-world-factbook/geos/sf.html* (South Africa) and *https://www.cia.gov/library/ publications/the-world-factbook/geos/af.html* (Afghanistan).

5   *See* SOUTHAFRICA.INFO at: *http://www.southafrica.info/about/people/population. htm#religions.*

6   *See* THE CIA WORLD FACTBOOK, *supra* Note 4.

7   *Ibid.*

promises of the new constitution are kept. In Afghanistan, issues of women's rights first received world attention because of the brutal actions of the prior Taliban government in depriving women of their rights and in taking steps, such as denying them education, that would ensure they would be permanently locked into an inferior status in society, with few or no rights of equality.

Women's rights are in the spotlight in Afghanistan today. In part, this is because Western military intervention in Afghanistan has to some extent created a barrier to the restoration of Taliban excesses against women. In part, it is because United Nations involvement and those of many human rights organizations and other non-governmental organizations are positively motivated to bring Afghanistan into compliance with international norms that further human rights generally and women's rights in particular. And, in part, because consciousness of the wide divide between Afghanistan's recognition and protection of women's rights and that of major developed and developing nations, has spurred homegrown movements in the country that are attempting to ensure that the eventual establishment of peace and end of military occupation will inaugurate a regime in which women's rights are created and protected under the rule of law. Both local groups and international groups are likely to take active roles in monitoring Afghanistan's success in the enforcement of the rights of women.

A Personal Journey and the Subject Matter of This Book

Although born, raised, educated, and trained as a lawyer in South Africa, I have taught law in the last several decades in the United States, Europe, South Africa, Canada, and Australia, as well as presenting lectures and seminars in many other parts of the world. The primary subjects of my lectures and seminars and teaching have been constitutional and human rights law, with special emphasis upon women's rights and the rights of indigenous peoples. The experience I gained in South Africa during the late 1970s and early 1980s in representing victims of apartheid has been invaluable for my teaching, research, and scholarship. As an undergraduate I worked at one of the first legal aid clinics established in South Africa by the pioneering legal aid advocate, Professor David McQuoid Mason. After I graduated I worked at the Legal Resources Center, which was directed by South Africa's pre-eminent public interest lawyer, Arthur Chaskalson, who became the first President of South Africa's Constitutional Court, and later the Chief Justice. The work carried out at the Legal Resources Center was modeled after the pioneering work in civil rights law in the United States of the NAACP Legal Defense and Educational Fund, and other civil rights organizations in the United States.

During that period, legal representation of victims of apartheid and racial discrimination in South Africa was enormously challenging and complicated because there was no constitution at the time guaranteeing equal rights, or protecting against racial, gender, or ethnic discrimination. South Africa, however, had a legal system which, despite overt hostility emanating from most of the judges and outright opposition from government officials, allowed me and my colleagues to obtain significant protection for our clients in the interstices of the law.[8] Individual legal victories were important because they provided building blocks that allowed lawyers, through judicial precedents, to extend the reach of one case to others similarly situated. Even small individual legal victories were an encouragement to a population suffering from apartheid and, along with political actions taken by various opposition groups, churches, and trade unions in South Africa, helped to legitimate the political aspirations of the great majority of the people whose rights were then being denied, and perhaps to indicate the importance of using law to protect the human rights of both the majority and the minority.

It was not merely my past in providing legal representation in South Africa that pushed me into this life-long service of human rights teaching, scholarship, and activism. Just as important, if not far more so, were three other experiences. One was living in South Africa under apartheid and personally experiencing and witnessing the daily humiliation, degradation, suffering, and mistreatment inflicted upon people solely because they were not white and under the political and legal domination of a white ruling class.

A second causative event was witnessing the downfall of the apartheid regime and being friends, colleagues, or acquaintances of some who helped spearhead that effort, and who worked frantically to ensure that the new government would be one of inclusion and based upon a constitution in which the protection of human rights and dignity was firmly embedded. The third cause has been observing over the years how relatively successful the new government, particularly the Mandela government, and the constitution have been in the protection of fundamental human rights for all people and the acclaim South Africa has received for this achievement.

Women and Transition: Raising the Questions

This book will examine the project of gender equality in two very different societies that are pursuing political transformation, but in which both the pursuit of and the meanings of gender equality are highly contested. This book will therefore raise some familiar questions about women's rights and equality. First, how does a society envision and commence the project of gender equality after a brutal history of conflict, dislocation, dispossession, exclusion, distinction, and discrimination? Second, how are the foundations laid, and strategies, particularly legal strategies, adopted and cultivated to best achieve the stated goal of equality? Third, what is the interplay of legal processes with other societal processes, such

---

8   South Africa saw itself as a member of the community of Western legal systems, so the veneer of legality was very important. For a compelling analysis of legal victories under apartheid, *see* RICHARD ABEL, POLITICS BY OTHER MEANS (2002).

as education and culture, in the "gender transformation project"? Fourth, how does a society balance what is perceived as the secular nature of rights enforcement, within a context of deeply entrenched religious mores or "customary norms"?[9] Lastly, how does a society pursue women's rights in the face of enormous economic inequalities, social upheaval, and cultural contestations? Ultimately, this book will consider a central dilemma: the persistence of subordination, disadvantage, and discrimination despite the existence of constitutional and legal protections for women.

This book will draw on the theoretical approaches of feminist and other critical legal schools. It intends to celebrate the many ways in which the feminist legal project has substantially improved the lives of women. This improvement is most pronounced in the more affluent societies, but not entirely so. A cursory glance at both statutory and case law will illustrate the influence of feminist legal theory. But this book will also lament some of the disappointments of the feminist project, most significantly, the failure to capture its truly transformative potential.

The central thesis of this book is to suggest an approach that utilizes conditional interdependence as a conceptual tool to analyze and pursue the rights of women. This approach is predicated on the idea that it is an opportune time to reconsider the way that women's advocates articulate and strive for the human rights of women. This global moment of unprecedented political, social and economic change provides the discursive space for building and expanding upon the achievements of feminist legal advocates, while also considering different and imaginative ways of addressing women's human rights. This may involve the need to rethink widely held truisms, and to jettison some trusted beliefs. For example, even though women's autonomy is highly praised in feminist theory and advocacy, autonomy may not be so treasured in societies where the cultural, religious, economic, and social conditions dictate a great measure of interdependence. In those societies, autonomy as a value may be foreign, even considered hostile, as familial and friendship networks generate considerable reliance on these networks. Similarly, even though reproductive rights, and particularly the right to safe abortions are arguably indispensable to a women's sense of autonomy, freedom, and security, in societies where children are seen as a source of wealth, and where poverty is the national currency, reproductive rights may take on a different flavor.

For the purposes of my central thesis I have coined the term "conditional interdependence" to argue that the way we consider notions of autonomy in the pursuit of women's rights in the affluent countries, mostly in the global north, and also within the elites of the global south, may not be an appropriate paradigm within which to frame women's issues. Instead, I am going to suggest that an approach underpinned by the idea of conditional interdependence is in fact more likely to gain traction and reap greater opportunities for women's rights because

---

9   David Kennedy has referred to international human rights law as essentially a secular construct. *See* David Kennedy, *Losing Faith in the Secular: Law, Religion, and the Culture of International Governance*, in RELIGION AND INTERNATIONAL LAW (Mark W. Janis and Carolyn Evans eds. 2004) 309.

such interdependence is based on the communitarian values that underpin societies like South Africa and Afghanistan. In this book I intend to theorize and develop this idea of conditional interdependence more clearly and expansively.

The perspective of this book is not that all the insights and strategies of feminist advocates be discarded or modified. Rather I argue that in the face of contested approaches to, and interpretations of, women's equality, and especially in the face of cultural uncertainties and entrenched economic, political, and legal inequalities, we rethink what we regard as universal. This requires a reconsideration of not only how we synthesize universal strategies with local needs, but also how local strategies and approaches may influence our conceptions of the universals.

This is not a novel task. These issues have been, and continue to be explored and interrogated by a range of feminist advocates and scholars more talented and thoughtful than I. I am drawing upon my reflections and experience as both a participant in, and an observer of, the political transformation in South Africa since the release of President Mandela in 1990. My observations are also based on my many years as an expatriate in Australia, engaging with the harsh realities of Aboriginal Australians, and particularly Aboriginal women. And they are also premised on my experiences as a long time resident of the United States, where all these questions frequently collide in a society absolutely committed to formal equality, yet riddled with contradictions. In this, my adopted country, where until recently the Speaker of the House was a woman and the Secretary of State is a women, disturbing numbers of women who, in the pursuit of "beauty," choose to mutilate themselves in order to conform to the cultural imperatives of youth and a threadlike slenderness unachievable for the majority female population.

In this book I utilize the South African project of legal transformation as a model for exploring questions of women's rights and equality, and applying them to another contemporary context of transformation, namely, Afghanistan. I suggest that because there has been a formal recognition that women's right to equality has to become part of the democratic constitutional arrangement, South Africa's starting point is a solid one, and that the formal legal arrangements at least ought to be emulated on some level in places like Afghanistan. Certainly as a matter of constitutionalism, formal law, and state policy, this approach might be useful.[10]

---

10   My book attempts to explore the project of gender equality in the two societies through the prism of constitutional drafting, text and interpretation. Its interest lies in exploring what constitutionalism and legal equality may mean for women in the wake of authoritarianism, subjugation and violence. There are other vehicles through which to explore these questions, including comparative analyses of transitional projects through transitional justice mechanisms, or United Nations-sponsored interventions in transitions. Indeed, for a compelling account of transitional societies and gender, *see* ON THE FRONTLINES: GENDER, WAR, AND THE POST-CONFLICT PROCESS (Fionnuala Ni Aolain *et al.* eds. (2011). My focus is on legal transition and the role of constitutionalism and formal legal processes that might lead to equality.

In addition to exploring the questions articulated earlier, this book aims to analyze the tensions between the formal declarations of commitment to gender equality and their ambivalent and lackluster pursuit by newly elected democratic governments. I focus on transitional and newly elected democratic governments because they provide fertile opportunities for assessing and analyzing issues of women's equality and the eradication of all forms of discrimination against women. I center the role of governments not because I believe that only governments can advance the women's rights agenda, but because newly elected governments, in the process of political and legal transformation, are primarily responsible for ensuring the implementation and enforcement of rights.

In many of these "new" democracies, a confluence of factors have created the theoretical and practical spaces for a thorough assessment of rights. Obviously the primary factor is the determination by the citizenry at large, including women, that the old political and legal order should be demolished. In addition, there are external factors, for example, global human rights advocates who have increasingly made the link between human rights and democracy. A significant external factor with respect to women's human rights has been the increasing influence of women's rights activists at the United Nations and other international fora, in which they have placed women's rights on the global human rights agenda.[11]

The issues in this book are analyzed within the context of a wider global debate about women's rights as human rights that crystallized during the last decades of the last century, specifically during the United Nations Decade for Women, from 1975 to 1985, as well as the Fourth World Conference on Women held in Beijing in 1994, the Vienna Conference and the subsequent United Nations Declaration on Violence against Women, and the Beijing Plus 5 and Beijing Plus 10 Program of Action. The Fourth World Conference was by far the most significant United Nations conference for women and indeed one of the most successful United Nations conferences ever, with over 140 governments, regional commissions and associations, United Nations agencies, intergovernmental organizations, and non-governmental organizations in attendance.[12] Women lobbied the governmental delegations extensively and organized a parallel non-governmental conference to coincide with the formal proceedings. The conference produced the Beijing Declaration and Program of Action, a comprehensive global plan to eradicate discrimination against women.[13] At the 1993 Human Rights Conference in

---

11 *See* RECONCEIVING REALITY: WOMEN AND INTERNATIONAL LAW (Dorinda G. Dallmeyer Ed. 1993); *see also* VIOLENCE AGAINST WOMEN UNDER INTERNATIONAL HUMAN RIGHTS LAW (Alice Edwards ed. 2011) and FEMINISM AND ANTIRACISM: INTERNATIONAL STRUGGLES FOR JUSTICE (France Winddance Twine and Kathleen M. Blee eds. 2001).

12 UNITED NATIONS, REPORT OF THE FOURTH WORLD CONFERENCE ON WOMEN, BEIJING 4–15 SEPTEMBER 1995 (1996) at 135–8.

13 BEIJING DECLARATION AND PLATFORM FOR ACTION, at: *http://www.un.org/womenwatch/daw/beijing/platform/*.

Vienna, women activists lobbied extensively in favor of recognizing that violence against women is a violation of human rights. The conference culminated in the Declaration on the Elimination of Violence Against Women—a global blueprint for eradicating violence against women.[14]

This book intends to examine these contradictions and limitations, but it also will pursue the tremendous possibilities for women generated by South Africa's political and legal transformation. Women in transitional societies like Afghanistan may find much that is useful in the South African experience. Indeed, it is arguable that the South African constitutional project may provide some useful pointers to women in an advanced constitutional democracy like the United States, or democracies without Bills of Rights like Australia and New Zealand. In this global interconnected world, as women's rights advocates pursue the goals of gender equality, legal or jurisprudential borrowing becomes an effective strategy.[15] The South African Constitution in fact incorporates this approach by mandating courts to consider international and foreign law in their deliberations.

Structure and Organization of this Book

This book contains seven chapters. In Chapter 2 I elaborate on my approach to reconsidering women's human rights including a consideration of some legal approaches that have been effective in eradicating discrimination against women. This chapter ventures a reconceptualization of theories and approaches that aim to transform women's lives from that steeped in disadvantage and subordination to one premised on equality. In Chapter 3 I outline the global campaign for women's rights commencing in the 1970s and culminating in significant formal legal and policy victories on both national and global fronts. In this chapter I explore the strategies adopted by women's advocates to move women's rights from the margins of political discourse to a central place in law and politics where women's demands for human rights and equality could no longer be ignored.

In Chapter 4 I examine a continuing theme in women's rights advocacy: that of the apparent conflict between harmful and discriminatory cultural norms and practices and the principle of gender equality. The purpose of this chapter is not to recite a litany of the crushing burden of cultural practices in most societies that

---

14   Adopted by the General Assembly in December 1993, GA Resolution 48/104. This Declaration has been implemented on a regional basis as well. *See* DECLARATION OF VIOLENCE AGAINST WOMEN IN THE ASEAN REGION (June 30, 2004) at: *http:// www.asean.org/16189.htm.*

15   *See* D.M. Davis, *Constitutional Borrowing: The Influence of Legal Culture and Local History in the Reconstitution of Comparative Influence: The South African Experience,* INTERNATIONAL JOURNAL OF CONSTITUTIONAL LAW (2003) 181; *see also* Christopher Roederer, *Negotiating the Jurisprudential Terrain: A Model Theoretic Approach to Legal Theory,* 27 SEATTLE UNIVERSITY LAW REVIEW (2003) 385.

continue to plague women, but to suggest a comprehensive approach that may lead to the global eradication of cultural practices that continue to discriminate against and harm women.

In Chapter 5 I outline the major features of South Africa's expansive Bill of Rights, demonstrating how this document in effect vindicates fifty years of global human rights activism. South Africans were fortunate to benefit from these decades of human rights developments—both as markers of possibilities as well as cautionary tales. In other words, South Africans were in the enviable position of selecting what was beneficial from human rights achievements elsewhere, but could also avoid the pitfalls of experiences in other societies. This chapter also traces how South Africa's Constitutional Court is giving effect to the spirit and substance of the Bill of Rights by generating an equality jurisprudence that has increasingly become a model for those pursuing rights for women and other disadvantaged communities and individuals elsewhere.

In Chapter 6 I survey the transformation process in Afghanistan and the attempts by women both inside and outside of Afghanistan to put women's issues on the national agenda. I examine the Afghan Constitution and the possibilities for gender equality incorporated in that constitution, as well as the societal obstacles to attaining equality. Chapter 7 provides a short discussion about moving forward, and the possibilities and obstacles to the pursuit of women's human rights and equality in the twenty-first century.

This book, because of its thematic approach, sweeps with a broad brush. But despite the many generalizations, I hope it captures the complex and multi-layered aspects of women's lives. Ultimately, the purpose for writing this book arises from a need to celebrate women's achievements, however uneven, but also to lament how women continue to labor under disadvantages and discrimination that can be eradicated. By comparing and highlighting the experiences of political and legal transformation in South Africa and Afghanistan, two very different societies, I hope to generate challenging and complex questions regarding the attainment of gender equality. In addition to the questions raised in this book, I have many observations, but no absolute answers, only tentative ones, offered in the spirit of dialogue and engagement

Chapter 2

Reconsidering Women's Rights

As the legal feminist experience makes clear, constitutional choices and their consequences are both highly contingent and historically particular. Where context is so vitally important both to options and to outcomes, the degree to which an historical episode can be generalized is necessarily limited.[1]

I believe the reason the movement for women's equality remains only a partial victory has to do with men. In every arena—in politics, the military, the workplace, professions and education—the single greatest obstacle to women's equality is the behaviors and attitudes of men. I believe that changes among men represent the next phase of the movement for women's equality—that changes among men are vital if women are to achieve full equality. Men must come to see that gender equality is in their interest—as men.[2]

Introduction: Many Questions

The subject of women's rights and gender equality fills countless volumes of books, academic journals, and magazines.[3] The popular media explores the issues, sometimes in depth and not infrequently in a superficial manner. Issues of gender equality and women's rights often get highlighted in news of brutalities committed against women—reports of mass rapes of women in the Congo being an extreme example.[4] Instances of discrimination against discrete groups of women are also highlighted in the media—the enactment of laws banning the veil in public schools in France being another example.[5] Law journals in the United States publishing

---

1   Serena Mayeri, *Constitutional Choices: Legal Feminism and the Historical Dynamics of Change*, 92 CALIFORNIA LAW REVIEW (2004) 755.

2   Michael S. Kimmel, *Why Men Should Support Gender Equality*, WOMEN'S STUDIES REVIEW (Fall 2005) 102 at: *http://lehman.edu/academics/inter/women-studies/documents/why-men.pdf*.

3   *See*, for example, WOMEN'S HUMAN RIGHT'S RESOURCES PROGRAMME, BORA LASKIN LAW LIBRARY at: *http://www.law lib.utoronto.ca/diana/*.

4   *See Congo Mass Rape Comprises 170 Female Victims: U.N. Report*, THE HUFFINGTON POST, August 27, 2011, at: *http//www.huffigntonpost.com/2011/06/24/congo-mass-rape-female-victims-united-nations-_N_883836*.

5   *See Women in Face Veils Detained as France Enforces Ban*, BBC NEWS EUROPE, April 11, 2011 at: *http://www.bbc.co.uk/news/world-europe-13031397*.

articles on women and the law are among the most popular of specialized law journals. The popularity of the articles and interest in their contents have helped to make feminist legal theory an established and important field of study in the law school curriculum. Because of the widespread interest, conferences and symposia on women's rights are held annually in law schools.[6]

Today, recognition of women's rights is common around the globe. The governments of many nations pride themselves on the enactment of laws and the adoption of policies that advance the human rights of women and otherwise promote gender equality. At the United Nations, in the Millennium Declaration of 2000, the attainment of gender equality was proclaimed as one of the primary goals for the twenty-first century. The Declaration exclaimed that "the equal rights and benefits of men and women must be assured."[7]

What is remarkable about this contemporary moment is that a world-wide consensus has been achieved in favor of the fundamental idea that discrimination against women is illegitimate, and that eradication of the discrimination is an urgent priority for all nations.[8] The Convention on the Elimination of All Forms of Discrimination Against Women (CEDAW) has now become one of the most widely ratified of international human rights instruments.[9] It has even been signed by countries where the human rights record on women is abysmal.[10]

---

6   A few examples will suffice. *See JGLS and Cornell Law School Jointly Organize the Second Annual Women and Justice Conference*, BAR & BENCH NEWS NETWORK, October 20, 2011 at: *http://barandbench.com/brief/9/1800/jgls-and-cornell-law-school-jointly-organize-the-second-annual-women-and-justice-conference*; *see also* WOMEN AND THE LAW CONFERENCE, REPRODUCTIVE JUSTICE: EXAMINING CHOICE AND AUTONOMY IN THE NEW MILLENNIUM (2011), at: *http://www.tjsl.edu/conferences/wlc*; and WOMEN AND THE LAW STORIES CONFERENCE, *The Power of Women's Stories II: Examining Women's Role in Law and the Legal System*, April 16, 2010, at: *http://law.scu.edu/womenlawstories/*.

7   RESOLUTION ADOPTED BY THE GENERAL ASSEMBLY 55/2, UNITED NATIONS MILLENNIUM DECLARATION at: *http://www.un.org/millennium/declaration/ares552e.htm*.

8   UNITED NATION'S COMMISSION ON THE STATUS OF WOMEN, at: *http://www.un.org/womenwatch/daw/csw/index.html*.

9   On December 18, 1979, the Convention on the Elimination of All Forms of Discrimination against Women [hereinafter CEDAW] was adopted by the United Nations General Assembly. It entered into force as an international treaty on September 3, 1981 after the twentieth country had ratified it. By the tenth anniversary of the Convention in 1989, almost one hundred nations had agreed to be bound by its provisions. *See http://www.un.org/womenwatch/daw/cedaw/text/econvention.htm*.

10   CEDAW has also been criticized for its weak enforcement mechanism, and the commitment of those governments who have ostensibly signed on to its core provisions. *See* Afra Afsharipour, *Empowering Ourselves: The Role of Women's NGOs in the Enforcement of the Women's Convention*, 99 COLUMBIA LAW REVIEW (1999) 129, and Lisa R. Pruitt and Marta R. Vanegas, *CEDAW and Rural Development: Empowering Women with*

And yet, despite the great success in accomplishing this global consensus, by all accounts, the situation of women around the world has remained dire and wildly uneven.[11] The persistence of this condition has, for the last decade or more, been the focus of study by a number of authors, particularly as to why there has been great difficulty in bringing women's rights and equality to fruition.[12]

With tectonic shifts in politics, history, economics, and legal systems, the dawn of the twenty-first century has given rise to a range of questions related to women's rights concerning how far some women have come, and how distant for some women the reality of equality and dignity provisions of CEDAW remains. Determining obstacles women face in achieving equality and dignity, and identifying the obstacles they have overcome are at the core of the riddle of how to realize gender equality and women's rights.

No One-Fit Solution

For women in different locales and circumstances, the answers will vary. There is no one-size-fits-all solution here. Given the vast cultural, geographic, economic, individual, and other differences which exist amongst women, the appraisal of their overall situation will vary with the differences. However, there are a few common, practical measures which women everywhere can use to gauge the degree to which the women of their class, or locale, have genuine gender equality. They include indicators such as the following: (1) the educational status of women compared to men; (2) whether girls are encouraged in schools to pursue careers in the same way that men are encouraged; (3) whether women earn the same as men for the same kind of work; (4) the nature and extent to which women are employed in jobs for which they are paid less than men or which are regarded as too menial for men to hold; (5) how women are treated in the home; (6) whether the gender of the breadwinner of the household reflects randomness or an underlying bias in the society for one particular gender; (7) whether women are routinely subjected

---

Law from the Top Down, Activism from the Bottom Up, 41 BALTIMORE LAW REVIEW (2011) 263.

11 *See* REPORT OF THE SECRETARY-GENERAL, REVIEW OF THE IMPLEMENTATION OF THE BEIJING DECLARATION AND PLATFORM FOR ACTION, THE OUTCOMES OF THE 23RD SPECIAL SESSION OF THE GENERAL ASSEMBLY AND ITS CONTRIBUTION TO SHAPING A GENDER PERSPECTIVE TOWARDS THE FULL REALIZATION OF THE MILLENNIUM DEVELOPMENT GOALS (February 8, 2010) at: *http://daccess-dds-ny.un.org/doc/UNDOC/GEN/ N09/637/20/PDF/N0963720.pdf?OpenElement.*

12 *See* NICHOLAS KRISTOF AND CHERYL WUDUNN, HALF THE SKY: TURNING OPPRESSION INTO OPPORTUNITY FOR WOMEN WORLDWIDE (2009); *see also* JONI SEAGER, THE PENGUIN ATLAS OF WOMEN IN THE WORLD (2003); and WOMEN, GENDER AND HUMAN RIGHTS: A GLOBAL PERSPECTIVE (Marjorie Agosin ed. 2001).

to violence; (8) the extent of protection women enjoy against violence in their homes, in public places, and private places of employment; (9) whether women have access to credit in the same way that men have; (10) whether women have access to choices regarding reproduction and the overall size of their families; (11) whether women have the right to own property or to have custody of their children; (12) and whether there is in the media and other parts of society an undue focus on women's bodies and looks.

These indicators can be used for comparative purposes as well as in helping to get a handle on the complexities, contradictions, and compromises which women in different societies are forced to tolerate when a particular constitutional, governance, legislative, and policy prescription is undertaken. The variety of options makes writing about women's rights and gender equality rather nuanced. Variety and uncertainty are part of the underlying reality when trying to devise constitutions, laws, policies, and institutions of government that work best for the interests of women. This reality makes it nigh impossible to generalize about African women, Muslim women, Asian women, European women, or indeed many groups of women. Much of what serves the interests of women, in terms of women's rights, will be affected by race, ethnicity, class, geography, sexuality, family status, and a whole other range of variables. So one must be careful in proposing general prescriptions concerning women's rights because there are pitfalls along the way. These pitfalls result from the contextual and limited applicability of perspectives and suggestions for reform.

To be sure, there is a balance to strike between absolute, universal prescriptions and individualized prescriptions based upon locale, class, culture, history, and other discrete factors. It is, however, not an easy balance to strike. Some feminist proponents of women's rights strike off in one direction and others strike off in the opposing direction. For example, in her examination of African women, Rhoda Howard argues that there can be no adequate analysis of the human rights of African women, or improvements made for the effective implementation of laws and policies, without an understanding of the socio-historical and cultural context of women's lives.[13] Presumably, when local women, as opposed to outsiders, participate fully in deciding what rights should be accorded to women in their country, consideration will be given to the socio-historical and cultural contexts of the lives of women there.

But while we must recognize that the identities of "women" are comprised of different aspects, are fluid, are transitional, and are context malleable, focusing solely in this manner is misguided. Women, like people generally, are also definable in terms of what they share in common. This is why South Africa and Afghanistan, though poles apart in many ways, can yet be instructive for one another on the issue of women's rights. The point is to try to identify and protect the dignity of

---

13   Rhoda Howard, *Women's Rights in English-speaking Sub-Saharan Africa*, in HUMAN RIGHTS AND DEVELOPMENT IN AFRICA (Claude E. Welch, Jr. and Ronald I. Meltzer eds. 1984).

women and what constitutes equality of treatment and respect, however differently situated women may be.

Outwardly, a New York female attorney may seem to have nothing in common with a female farm laborer in Sri Lanka. But in paring away at their outward differences, it is realistic to recognize that they are apt to share common expectations and notions of the quality of life they desire and believe they are entitled to have. This will include security of their body when inside or outside the home, protected rights within the family, reproductive freedom, freedom to marry or not, and freedom to reach beyond their present station in life, that is, to live a dignified life potentially equal to those of others.[14] Focusing on such shared expectations, notwithstanding the differences in experiences, shakes up the intellectual notion of a "monolithic them" (for example, Muslim women, poor women, rural women), and conversely, a "monolithic us." If the Sri Lankan woman subsequently became a New York attorney and the New York attorney became a farm laborer in Sri Lanka, their shared expectations would become more evident.

In exploring theories and practices concerning women's rights, both by feminists and others, I have used my homeland, South Africa, as a point of departure and as a model. But in positioning South Africa as a model, I do not suppose for a minute that the course of effectuating women's rights in South Africa is one that can be applied in other countries without making adjustments. Nor do I contend that all has been perfect inside South Africa. A recent development there makes this painfully clear.

On September 5, 2011, the Judicial Services Commission confirmed President Jacob Zuma's choice, Justice Mogoeng Mogoeng of the Constitutional Court, as the next Chief Justice of South Africa. Unhappily, the record and biographies of both President Zuma and now Chief Justice Mogoeng reveal that they have at times exhibited somewhat questionable opinions, behavior, and attitudes concerning women.[15] The Constitutional Court is charged with carrying out the transformative intent of the Constitution and to develop a jurisprudence appropriate for that task,

---

14   These shared expectations about human development and security are explored very thoughtfully by Martha Nussbaum. *See* MARTHA NUSSBAUM, CREATING CAPABILITIES: THE HUMAN DEVELOPMENT APPROACH (2011).

15   For example, President Zuma (before he took office as the President) was tried, and later acquitted of rape in a trial in which the complainant was vilified by the defense attorneys and supporters of the President. *See* Penelope E. Andrews, *Learning to Love after Learning to Harm: Post-Conflict Reconstruction, Gender Equality and Cultural Values*, 15 MICHIGAN STATE JOURNAL OF INTERNATIONAL LAW (2007) 41. President Zuma also has several wives, and at least one child born out of wedlock. *See* Miriam Koktvedgaard Zeitzen, *The Many Wives of Jacob Zuma*, FOREIGN POLICY MAGAZINE, March 12, 2010 at: *http://www.foreignpolicy.com/articles/2010/03/12/the_many_wives_of_jacob_zuma*. The nominee for Chief Justice has a questionable judicial record regarding a series of judgments involving domestic violence and child rape, in which his judgments suggest a surprising lack of understanding of the harm of intimate violence, as well as rape. *See* David Smith, *South Africa Rights Groups Condemn Jacob Zuma's Choice of Top Judge*,

particularly in regards to rights of equality. The choice of a person as Chief Justice whose judicial opinions have at times been arguably dismissive of the respect the Constitution grants to women's rights, bodes poorly for the continuance of that vision with respect to women's human rights.[16] In the short term the appointment of Chief Justice Mogoeng is unlikely to bring about any significant change in the Court's decisions carrying out this transformative mission, although it deals a symbolic blow to it. But in the long term, depending on what other appointments are made to the Court, Chief Justice Mogoeng is likely to have a greater ability to re-direct the transformative mission. Whether he is inclined to do so must, for now, be deemed an unknown.[17]

This recent development in South Africa is but a reminder that in looking at the global picture regarding women's rights, feminist advocates and scholars must give recognition to what has now become evident, namely, that the capacity of law to transform women's lives is a rather complicated one. It is one which is riddled with contradictions and which raises many questions. These complications raise their heads in the literature about women's rights in a global context, and make their writing more protracted.[18] Women in the global North and women in the global South not infrequently have different vantage points from which they view particular generalizations of women's rights.[19] It is not always possible to engage both in candid analysis without eliciting occasions of pity from the former and resentment from the latter, particularly inasmuch as the subject of discussion almost invariably focuses on changes to be made in the lives of the latter and not the former.

Moreover, given the range and multiplicity of women's experiences, roles, status, identities, political philosophies, geographical locations, and other factors, it is not possible to generalize without simplifying, distorting, or exaggerating the plethora of realities of the lives of the women under examination. Nothing is more likely than to adopt perspectives and to draw conclusions that are either

---

THE GUARDIAN, August 25, 2011 at: *http://www.guardian.co.uk/world/2011/aug/25/ south-africa-jacob-zuma-choice-top-judge.*

16   For a summary of the range of opposition to the appointment of Chief Justice Mogoeng, *see http://www.iol.co.za/blogs/carmel-rickard-1.2528.*

17   In Afghanistan as well, President Karzai has not always acted in the interests of women's rights. *See* Jim Sciutto, *Afghanistan President Hamid Karzai Passes Controversial Law Limiting Women's Rights,* ABC NEWS, August 14, 2009 at: *http://abcnews.go.com/ International/story?id=8327666#.T1J8TZjleJo.*

18   *See* INDIRA JAISING, MEN'S LAWS, WOMEN'S LIVES: A CONSTITUTIONAL PERSPECTIVE ON RELIGION, COMMON LAW, AND CULTURE IN SOUTH INDIA (2005); *see also* CATHARINE A. MCKINNON, WOMEN'S LIVES, MEN'S LAWS (2007) and JUDITH A. BAER, OUR LIVES BEFORE THE LAW: CONSTRUCTING A FEMINIST JURISPRUDENCE (1999).

19   CHANDRA TALPADE MOHANTY, FEMINISM WITHOUT BORDERS: DECOLONIZING THEORY, PRACTICING SOLIDARITY (2004).

over-inclusive, under-inclusive, or both. At the heart of this difficulty in capturing the individuality of female population groups around the globe is the tendency to resort ultimately to fashioning narratives of rescue, patronage, despair, and pity. When this happens, one easily loses the intended audience.

Each population group of women is likely to know what constitutes women's rights, or gender equality, when they see it despite inability to provide a comprehensible definition for everyone. Consensus here is fragmented and perhaps ultimately elusive. The model of women's rights in the United States might be seen by those in the United States as best for them and others. Yet, there are many women in the developing world who recoil in horror at some practices of equality in the United States, and vice versa.[20] As mentioned before, it is conceivable that many women outside the West regard what they see as the fruits of women's equality, such as the use of cosmetic surgery, casual sexual dalliances, pornography, wearing of skimpy clothing, and the like, as excessive at best and demeaning at worst. Hence, feminist scholars and advocates have difficulty in agreeing upon a societal model for a universal realization of women's equality.[21] It seems hard to escape the bearing which a woman's status in her society may have upon how she evaluates the meaning of women's rights. Ultimately, this means that it may be relevant for women in any population group, or class, to take into account, when judging what rights they want, official and unofficial practices, policies, cultures, laws, and attitudes prevalent in their society.

I grew up in South Africa during the dark days of apartheid. Today, South Africa is a multi-racial, multi-cultural, multi-ethic, and multi-lingual society. I experienced the long journey the country took from its authoritarian, racist, sexist apartheid past to the contemporary democracy that provides, formally at least, human rights for all South Africans. As this journey has progressed in the past fifteen years, I have become acutely aware of the complexity and challenges that post-conflict societies experience as they negotiate the economic, political, social, and cultural transitions necessary in order for all citizens to benefit from rights and benefits incorporated in formal legal texts, especially in a constitution.

Pursuing human rights for women and creating the conditions for gender equality is at times vexing.[22] Despite decades of general feminist advocacy and of feminist legal advocacy, the gender equality project appears to be incomplete and erratic. It has benefited discrete groups of women in disparate and unequal ways. As I will discuss in Chapter 3, sizeable numbers of women benefited from the court battles in which they invoked equality rights. These beneficiaries include

---

20 For a very thoughtful exploration of these issues *see* UMA NARAYAN, DISLOCATING CULTURES: IDENTITIES, TRADITIONS AND THIRD WORLD FEMINISM (1997).

21 Aziz al-Hibri, *Who Defines Women's Rights? A Third World Woman's Response*, HUMAN RIGHTS BRIEF (1994) at: *http://www.wcl.american.edu/hrbrief/v2i1/alhibr21.htm*.

22 THE UNFINISHED REVOLUTION: VOICES FROM THE GLOBAL FIGHT FOR WOMEN'S RIGHTS (Minky Worden ed. 2012).

women who now serve as judges, government ministers, senior bureaucrats, CEOs, leaders in the academy, or in other powerful societal institutions. There are many places today where the presence of women leaders and supervisors is taken for granted and does not raise an eyebrow.[23]

But then there are places where women are not allowed to drive cars or to go out in public unaccompanied by a male relative. There are places where women do not expect safety and security on the streets or in their homes, and where women cannot make reproductive choices without the input and consent of their husbands.[24] So thinking about women's rights and gender equality in a global context needs to take account of the great range of experiences of women, and the differences in women's status and roles.

In Chapter 1, a number of questions were raised but not fully addressed. Five are particularly important in societies like South Africa and Afghanistan. First, and perhaps foremost, is the vexing issue of how a society can attain true gender equality after a recent history of brutal conflict, dislocations of people, dispossessions of property, exclusions of population groups, the existence of powerful and distinct ethnic groups, and discrimination. In overcoming these formidable obstacles, how can foundations and strategies, particularly legal strategies, be laid for adopting and cultivating the various goals of equality? Third, as this book will emphasize repeatedly, what deference and respect should be shown to culture, and the state of education in the country, in promoting new legal and social norms to advance the "gender transformation project"? Fourth, in countries where there are deeply entrenched religious mores, what balance needs to be struck in erecting and enforcing norms of gender equality which will be perceived by many as having a secular or political basis? Fifth, will advancement of gender equality be set back by preexisting economic inequalities amongst the population and new social upheavals arising from overthrow of the old order?

Conditional Interdependence

In the West, the paradigm of women's equality is generally predicated upon the idea of woman as an independent agent of her own destiny, that is, as an autonomous agent.[25] This view has been contested in perspectives based upon critical race theory, critical legal theory, and postcolonial feminism pursued in many

---

23   Vexen Crabtree, *Which Countries Set the Best Examples?* (2005) at: *http://www.vexen.co.uk/countries/best.html*.

24   *UN Women's First Chief Voices Optimism after Being Named to New Post*, UN NEWS, September 15, 2010 at: *http://www.unwomen.org/2010/09/un-womens-first-chief-voices-optimism-after-being-named-to-new-post/*.

25   Rina Agarwal and Scott M. Lynch, *Refining the Measurement of Women's Autonomy: An International Application of a Multi-dimensional Construct*, 84 SOCIAL FORCES (2006) 2077.

developing countries.[26] The essence of autonomous agency is that it is not fettered by dependency.[27] In regards to gender equality, the way in which many people in the global North, as well as the elites of the global South, think of autonomy, identity, and dignity, may not be the appropriate paradigm within which to frame the concepts for most women, or at least a large plurality, in developing nations.[28] Conditions in affluent nations are so radically different from conditions in poor nations that often it is necessary to reexamine one's underlying assumptions. A term I have coined, namely, "conditional interdependence," is one way to frame a different paradigm for women in developing countries.

The notion of autonomy for women, as viewed in the context of a society where resources are limited, is different when viewed in a context where women enjoy a vast range of options. Even countries that are rich today in resources were not as rich during earlier parts of their history, making both access to resources and the concept of autonomy historically contingent. In countries such as South Africa and Afghanistan, communitarian values underpin the functioning of the traditional society.[29] Typically, in these societies, local people come to the aid of one another and thereby increase access to resources of those who otherwise would be without the resources. When this is taken into account, autonomy for women in poor countries cannot be separated from the conditional interdependence otherwise operative in the society. Accordingly, it is important both to understand and to emphasize the idea of conditional interdependence and its significance.[30]

---

26   *See* e.g., Diana Tietjens Meyers, *Feminism and Women's Autonomy: The Challenge of Female Genital Cutting*, 31 METAPHILOSOPHY (2000) 469.

27   I am using the term as described by Dyson and Moore, namely, "the capacity to manipulate one's personal environment and the ability—technical, social and psychological—to obtain information and to use it as the basis for making decisions about one's private concerns and those of one's intimates." *See* Tim Dyson and Mick Moore, *On Kinship Structure, Female Autonomy, and Demographic Behavior in India*, 9 POPULATION AND DEVELOPMENT REVIEW (1983) 35, 45.

28   *See* Shireen J. Jejeebhoy and Zeba A. Sathar, *Women's Autonomy in India and Pakistan: The Influence of Religion and Region*, 27 POPULATION AND DEVELOPMENT REVIEW (December 2001) 687.

29   *See* KRISTIAN BERG HARPVIKEN, ANNE STRAND AND KARIN ASK, AFGHANISTAN AND CIVIL SOCIETY (2002) at: *http://www.prio.no/sptrans/461921303/Harpviken%20et%20al%2002%20Afghanistan%20and%20Civil%20Society.pdf*. *See also* Barbara Nussbaum, *Ubuntu: Reflections of a South African on Our Common Humanity*, 4 REFLECTIONS (2003) at: *http://barbaranussbaum.com/downloads/reflections.pdf*.

30   Here I am borrowing from critical race feminists, post-colonial feminists, Marxist feminists, and others who have persuasively argued that women in indigenous and other non-Western communities, particularly communities of color, see their rights as linked to the rights of their families and the wider community. *See* SALLY MERRY, HUMAN RIGHTS AND GENDER VIOLENCE: TRANSLATING INTERNATIONAL LAW INTO LOCAL JUSTICE (2006); AYELET SHACHAR, MULTICULTURAL JURISDICTIONS:

Speaking broadly, there are four main aspects of conditional interdependence. First, it highlights a conceptual shift in the theorizing of women's human rights and gender equality. Second, it involves focusing upon the interconnectedness of civil and political rights with economic, social, and cultural rights, since each can enhance or lessen the other by virtue of a transference of resources, or access, from one to the other. To this extent, there is a diminution of the bifurcated approach to human rights. Third, it reinforces the role of men in the project to pursue women's rights, both in supporting gender equality and as active agents, through providing resources and access, in the transformation of women's lives. Fourth, conditional interdependence, with its origin in communitarian traditions, reinforces the idea that the community has a role to play in protecting women, and therefore has a role to play in redressing violations of women's human rights. From here, it is just a short step, at least conceptually, to recognition that a truth and/or reconciliation commission might have relevance in dealing with past violations of women's rights.

Behind the concept of conditional interdependence is the idea that women's rights and gender equality are part of a transformative project that sees women's role and status as central to, and closely inter-related with, the rights and equality claims of all citizens, making women's rights integral to the human rights of all. A caution is in order since conditional interdependence, in the sense used here, is not a subterfuge for the continued subordination and oppression of women. Rather, it is recognition that independence for women is enhanced to the extent interdependence acts as an aid to, and not as a brake upon, what women can achieve.

Understanding conditional interdependence in the context of human rights starts with recognition of how most women live their lives. Due to a range of factors, such as economics, geography, ethnicity, and culture, women in their daily lives often depend upon others in their families or communities to carry out regular tasks. For example, in poor countries such as the Gambia, Nicaragua, and Cambodia, only a few individuals own cars. The owners are almost all males. Moreover, in these countries, public transport is often inadequate for many women to do everyday tasks. To get to the nearest urban centers, they are dependent upon others who have cars. Members of their communities who have cars will often assist them to travel back and forth from the urban centers. Similarly, in South Africa where crimes against women have been rampant and police protection has been inadequate, women depend upon family, friends, neighbors, and others in the community to provide for their security. So this actual interdependence, of relying on others in such a fundamental way, requires a theoretical approach premised on this web of connections. Sometimes, speaking again of South Africa, the protection takes the form of adults in the communities banding together to form neighborhood associations or, where the resources are greater, to employ security guards on the streets or in the neighborhoods. More commonly, women often have

CULTURAL DIFFERENCES AND WOMEN'S RIGHTS (2001); GLOBAL CRITICAL RACE FEMINISM: AN INTERNATIONAL READER (Adrien Wing ed. 2000).

men who are members of the family or neighborhood to accompany them in places where there is a threat of danger.

In developing societies, or during a harrowing transitional period, interdependence in these forms are enablers of women's autonomy and dignity, and thus need to be perceived as potential solutions in the struggle for women's rights. Legal and political activists can work out reforms that utilize the community to help make rights more accessible for women. Women theorists can help in this regard by taking account of differences in status and circumstances of women around the globe, and how those differences, when seen from the perspectives of women affected by them, are relevant to the need for women, in different locales, to determine for themselves how best to bring about the realization of their rights.[31]

Men as Agents of Transformation

Seen from this perspective, conditional interdependence clearly requires recognition that men play a major role in the push for women's equality and human rights. Indeed, the Beijing Platform for Action noted:

> The advancement of women and the achievement of equality between men and women are a matter of human rights and a condition for social justice and should not be seen in *isolation as a women's issue*. They are the only way to build a sustainable, just and developed society. Empowerment of women and equality between women and men are prerequisites for achieving political, social, economic, cultural and environmental security among all peoples.[32]

Just as the struggle to end racism in the U.S.A., or apartheid in South Africa, involved the active engagement of, and collaboration between, blacks, other people of color, and whites, so too men have to be involved as participants in the struggle for women's rights and gender equality.[33]

---

31   Some American women's advocates have raised this as well. As Constance Hilliard notes: "What our troubled planet needs now is not more zealots, but rather more American women willing to engage in authentic, uncontrived dialogue with our sisters abroad. This is precisely because these Third World women may indeed view the world and their place in it quite differently than we do. However much we have to teach to them, sooner or later we will see that we have just as much to learn from them." *See* Constance Hilliard, *Feminists Abroad: Ugly Americans?*, USA TODAY, April 12, 2002 at 15A.

32   THE UNITED NATIONS FOURTH WORLD CONFERENCE ON WOMEN, PLATFORM FOR ACTION at: *http://www.un.org/womenwatch/daw/beijing/platform/plat1.htm* [emphasis added].

33   *See* ENGAGING MEN AND BOYS IN GENDER EQUALITY (United Nations Population Fund, 2011) available at: *https://www.unfpa.org/public/cache/offonce/home/publications/pid/8050;jsessionid=FAFE50AF624F5B8B7948E5AF01F31556.jahia01.*

To be sure, there are differences between racial segregation and discrimination against women. In racially segregated societies, black and white people had only limited engagement with each other. With men and women, however, the engagement is not so limited or distant. They have relationships such as fathers and mothers, daughters and sons, sisters and brothers, spouses, lovers, cousins, and other familial relationships. These bonds and patterns are ancient, and are viewed as vital aspects of the natural world. Moreover, they are sanctioned by most religions in the world. As a result they are very hard to dislodge, and they become embedded in family and community traditions.[34]

The Kenyan gender activist, Njoki Wainana, referring to the key role of men in stemming the HIV/AIDS epidemic, notes:

> There are many compelling reasons for involving men and boys in the struggle for gender equality. For a start, (whether or not, justly, legally legitimately, fairly or appropriately) most men hold the power, authority, control and privileges that are the contention for the gender equality struggle. They must be engaged as they will have to give (up, in, to, away, etc.) something for the struggle to be won. Whether this is to be achieved through persuasion, coercion, political struggle, divine intervention, legislation, socialisation, policy, social revolution or whatever means, they have to be involved.[35]

Chapter 3 will highlight how feminist legal advocates have unsettled the field of legal theory, legal practice, and legal processes, and how women have been very responsive to this unsettling. However, men have not been responsive to the same extent. Interference from ideologies of masculinity has, for many men, blocked receipt of the message, or weakened it. Prevailing ideologies of masculinity operate to reinforce traditional notions of femininity, thereby preventing many men from being in sync with the altered legal landscape of women's rights.[36] Michael Kimmell has made this point very powerfully. He states:

> Men have done very little to prepare for this completely different world. What has not changed are the ideas we have about what it means to be a man. The ideology of masculinity has remained relatively intact for the past three generations. That's where men are these days: our lives have changed dramatically, but the notions we have about what it means to be a man remain locked in a pattern set decades ago, when the world looked very different.[37]

---

34   Denise D. Bielby, *Gender and Family Relations*, in HANDBOOK OF THE SOCIOLOGY OF GENDER (Janet Saltzman ed. 1999) 391.

35   NJOKI WAINANA, THE ROLE OF AFRICAN MEN IN THE FIGHT AGAINST HIV/AIDS (2005) at: *http://www.ww05.org/english3/speech/5.3.NjokiWainana.pdf.*

36   Michael S. Kimmel, *Why Men Should Support Gender Equality*, WOMEN'S STUDIES REVIEW, *supra* Note 2.

37   *Ibid* at 105.

However, it is imperative to conscript men as allies in this project for women's rights and gender equality because legal change is short-lived without cultural and attitudinal change. We know from history that while law is often needed to instigate changes, revolutionary changes in rights must be accompanied by changes in culture, institutions, and attitudes. We see this in the literature on legal efforts to outlaw racism[38] and in the literature to eradicate patriarchy and sexism.[39] In particular, support from "bystanders" and "beneficiaries" are important in bringing about changes in culture, institutions, and attitudes.

Many men, of course, have not been strangers to the movement for women's rights and gender equality. Take, for example, the work of Muhammad Yunus, a Nobel Laureate and the person who in 1976 created the Grameen Bank in Bangladesh to provide loans and other economic opportunities for poor rural people, especially women.[40] He helped women in Bangladesh to achieve autonomy, dignity, and freedom for themselves and to provide support for their families and friends. The model of his bank has been emulated elsewhere. Through his work, poor women in several countries now hold shares in a bank.[41]

Other examples include the Men Stopping Violence Campaign and MensWork in the U.S.A.,[42] the White Ribbon Campaign in the United Kingdom,[43] and the Sonke Justice Network in South Africa.[44] In 2010 the Sonke Justice Network published a report on the campaign by traditional leaders in South Africa to encourage men to strive towards creating healthy communities based on equal partnerships between men and women.[45] These campaigns demonstrate what is possible when men become involved in feminist projects, creating structures, ideas and projects that can be emulated in many societies.

---

38   *See* DERRICK BELL, FACES AT THE BOTTOM OF THE WELL: THE PERMANENCE OF RACISM (1992); *See also* Charles Lawrence III, *The Id, the Ego and Equal Protection: Reckoning with Unconscious Racism*, 1987 STANFORD LAW REVIEW 317 and PATRICIA WILLIAMS, THE ALCHEMY OF RACE AND RIGHTS (1991).

39   Magda Lewis, *Interrupting Patriarchy: Politics, Resistance, and Transformation in the Feminist Classroom*, 60 HARVARD EDUCATIONAL REVIEW (1990) 467; *see also* Mary Becker, *Patriarchy and Inequality: Towards a Substantive Feminism*, UNIVERSITY OF CHICAGO LEGAL FORUM (1999) 21.

40   MUHAMMAD YUNUS, BANKER TO THE POOR (2003).

41   *Ibid.*

42   MENSWORK: ELIMINATING VIOLENCE AGAINST WOMEN at, *HTTP:// MENSWORKINC.COM/*.

43   WHITE RIBBON CAMPAIGN at, *http://www.whiteribboncampaign.co.uk/*.

44   SONKE GENDER JUSTICE NETWORK at: *http://www.genderjustice.org.za/*.

45   SONKE GENDER JUSTICE NETWORK, STORIES OF COURAGE AND LEADERSHIP: SOUTH AFRICAN TRADITIONAL LEADERS SPEAK OUT TO ENGAGE MEN IN CREATING HEALTHY COMMUNITIES (February 2010) at: *http:// www.genderjustice.org.za/*.

Gender Equality and the Pursuit of Social and Economic Rights

In the developing world, talk of gender equality and women's rights, especially in a constitutional context, must go hand in hand with talk of social and economic rights. Nowhere is this more clear than in South Africa. The Bill of Rights embodied in South Africa's Constitution, encompasses civil, political, economic, social, and cultural rights.[46] They are mutually supportive and all are justiciable before South Africa's courts.[47]

The constitutional framework in South Africa signifies that the needs and interests of the poor, who are disproportionately women, were of sufficient national public concern to require incorporation into the Constitution of provisions providing for social and economic rights. These provisions help to ameliorate barriers to the exercise of citizenship rights, they impose affirmative obligations upon the government to help the poor, and they provide additional reasons for the poor to feel that this is their government.[48] As the South African scholar Daniel Brand notes:

> First, courts' adjudication of socio-economic rights claims becomes part of the political discourse, even a medium through which this discourse partly plays out. ... Second, courts also occupy a symbolic, or perhaps more accurately, an exemplary, role with respect to poverty and need discourses—their vocabulary, the conceptual structures they rely on, the rhetorical strategies they employ infiltrate and so influence and shape the political discourses around poverty and need.[49]

Karl Klare has cautioned that the "decision" to "accomplish some significant portion" of the law-making process "through adjudication" is one "fraught with institutional consequences."[50] For women, the ability to gain access to economic resources through litigation opens up great possibilities. For women, especially marginalized women, the Constitution's incorporation of a host of socio-economic rights, and particularly its transformative potential, as outlined in Chapter 5, is an

---

46   CONSTITUTION OF THE REPUBLIC OF SOUTH AFRICA (1996) [hereinafter "CONSTITUTION"] Chapter 2, Section 9-35.

47   *Ibid.* Section 38.

48   Makau wa Mutua, *Hope and Despair for a New South Africa: The Limits of Rights Discourse*, 10 HARVARD HUMAN RIGHTS LAW JOURNAL (1997) 63, 112.

49   D. Brand, *The Politics of Need Interpretation and the Adjudication of Socio-Economic Rights Claims in South Africa*, in THEORIES OF SOCIAL AND ECONOMIC JUSTICE (A.J. Van der Walt ed. 2005) 17, 24.

50   Karl Klare, *Legal Culture and Transformative Constitutionalism*, SOUTH AFRICAN JOURNAL OF HUMAN RIGHTS (1998) 146, 147.

important antidote to the axis of gender subordination: namely, poverty, violence, and custom.[51]

Other scholars have emphasized different consequences of making paramount in law women's rights, in particular, and human rights generally. One group of scholars start their analysis from the circumstance that the prevalence of poverty is a recurring reality for a large part of the world's women.[52] Another group begins, as we will see shortly, with changes in the discourse involving many of the conflicts in the world. This second group will be discussed in the section entitled "Women's Rights are Human Rights."

The first group is concerned about the limitations of rights discourse in the face of economic structures that reinforce economic inequality.[53] Legal scholars such as Upendra Baxi and Boa de Sousa Santos have eloquently argued that the language of human rights has in effect replaced the language of economic redistribution and by doing so has appropriated other ethical discourses.[54] The concern here is that the seductive possibilities generated by litigation for social and economic rights may disproportionately influence communities, especially women, to redirect their attention from non-legal transformative strategies that may in the long run produce deeper and more enduring economic, political, and social justice. This debate is a vigorous one within the contemporary human rights community of scholars and advocates, and is also a hackneyed one reminiscent of the earlier civil rights struggle of the United States.[55] Ultimately this issue relates to the nature of citizenship, and in the choices citizens make in the exercise of their rights.

---

51   I am using the term "custom" very loosely here. It refers to the range of cultural practices and norms that underpin attitudes that embrace notions of female inferiority.

52   *See*, for example, WAPULA NELLY RADITLOANENG, WOMEN, POVERTY AND LITERACY: A CASE STUDY IN BOTSWANA (2010); *see also* RANDY ALBEIDA AND CHRIS TILLY, GLASS CEILINGS AND BOTTOMLESS PITS: WOMEN'S WORK, WOMEN'S POVERTY (1999).

53   *See*, for example, AMARTYA SEN, DEVELOPMENT AS FREEDOM (1999); Makau wa Mutua, *The Ideology of Human Rights*, 36 VIRGINIA JOURNAL OF INTERNATIONAL LAW (1996) 589; Philip Alston, *The Myopia of the Handmaidens: International Lawyers and Globalization*, 8 EUROPEAN JOURNAL OF INTERNATIONAL LAW (1998) 435; and ANDY MCKAY AND POLLY VIZARD, HUMAN RIGHTS AND POVERTY REDUCTION (March 2005) at: *http://www.odi.org.uk/resources/docs/4353.pdf*.

54   Upendra Baxi, *Voices of Suffering and the Future of Human Rights*, 8 TRANSNATIONAL LAW AND CONTEMPORARY PROBLEMS (1998) 125, 147; BOAVENTURA DE SOUSA SANTOS, TOWARD A NEW COMMON SENSE: LAW SCIENCE AND POLITICS IN THE PARADIGMATIC TRANSITION (1995) 266–7.

55   *See* THOMAS E. JACKSON, FROM CIVIL RIGHTS TO HUMAN RIGHTS (2006). *See also* GERALD N. ROSENBERG, THE HOLLOW HOPE: CAN COURTS BRING ABOUT SOCIAL CHANGE? (2008).

Amanda Gouws builds upon this concern in her work to deconstruct the gendered nature of South African citizenship.[56] As will be shown later, the South African Bill of Rights implicitly recognizes such gendered citizenship by incorporating it as an expanded notion of equality. As part of this recognition, South Africa acknowledges, through its Constitution, that constitutional adjudication occurs against a background of disadvantage and discrimination that are deeply embedded in the political, economic, and legal systems.[57] The inevitable consequence is that the legacy of apartheid and sexism will continue into the foreseeable future, and must therefore be a factor in constitutional adjudication.[58] The constitutional text and its interpretation are therefore predicated on a need to derogate purposively from the status quo. As the first President of the Constitutional Court has noted:

> We live in a society in which there are great disparities in wealth. Millions of people are living in deplorable conditions and in great poverty. There is a high level of unemployment, inadequate social security, and many do not have access to clean water or to adequate health services. These conditions already existed when the Constitution was adopted, and a commitment to address them, and to transform our society into one in which there will be human dignity, freedom and equality, lies at the heart of our new constitutional order.[59]

In other words, both text and interpretation are mandated to transform social and economic relations.[60] It is with respect to the implementation of socio-economic rights that the Constitution holds much promise for women. The Constitutional Court's decisions regarding the enforcement of socio-economic rights have shown that these rights can bring meaningful relief to the poorest in the country. These decisions are reviewed in Chapter 5 and include the Constitutional Court decisions regarding the right of access to housing,[61] the right of access to medicine,[62] women's

---

56   *See* UNLINKING CITIZENSHIP (Amanda Gouws ed. 2005).

57   *Government of the Republic of South Africa v Grootboom and Others* (2001) (1) 46 (CC).

58   Penelope E. Andrews, *Imagine All the Women: Power, Gender, and the Transformative Possibilities of the South African Constitution*, in POWER, GENDER, AND SOCIAL CHANGE IN AFRICA AND THE DIASPORA (Muna Ndulo ed. 2009) 213.

59   *Soobramoney v Minister of Health, Kwa Zulu-Natal* (1998) 1 (SA) 765 (CC) at Paragraph 8.

60   Leti Volpp has also explored this issue of gendered citizenship in the context of the headscarves debate in France. *See* Leti Volpp, *The Culture of Citizenship*, 8 THEORETICAL INQUIRIES IN LAW (2007) 571.

61   *Government of the Republic of South Africa v Grootboom supra* Note 57.

62   *Minister of Health and Others v Treatment Action Campaign and Others* 2002 (5) SA 721 (CC).

right to inherit property under African customary law,[63] and the proprietary consequences of divorce under African customary law as compared to divorces under South African law.[64]

Gender and the TRC

South Africa's Truth and Reconciliation Commission (TRC) has been heralded internationally as a pioneering project and has been lauded almost universally by human rights advocates.[65] Indeed, in the literature referencing racial reconciliation and restorative justice, the TRC looms large. Whether it is the iconic image of Bishop Tutu shepherding an emotionally-laden process through difficult political and legal territory, or the comforting images of victim and perpetrator engaging in a dance of forgiveness and remorse, the TRC is mostly regarded globally as a pre-eminent exercise in national forgiveness of crimes against humanity.[66]

Within South Africa, however, the assessment of the TRC is much more contested, its limitations have been scrutinized and criticized in detail, and some, especially victims, have expressed deep misgivings about the TRC.[67]

Most commentators, however, have concluded that South Africa could not have moved forward as a functioning democracy if the TRC had not been

---

63 *Bhe & Others v The Magistrate, Khayelitsha*, 2005 (1) SA 581 (CC), at 594–600, 621–2; *Shibi v Sithole & Others* 2005 (1) SA 580 (CC) (S. Afr.); *South African Human Rights Commission and Women's Legal Center Trust v President of the Republic of South Africa and Minister for Justice and Constitutional Development* 2005 (1) SA 580 (CC) (S. Afr.). The Court combined the three cases since they all concerned the question of intestate succession under African customary law. [Hereafter *Bhe & Others v The Magistrate.*]

64 *See Gumede (Born Shange) v President of the Republic of South Africa & Others* 2009 (3) BCLR 243 (CC).

65 *See* MARTHA MINOW, BETWEEN VENGEANCE AND FORGIVENESS: FACING HISTORY AFTER GENOCIDE AND MASS VIOLENCE (1998); *see also* ERIC K. YAMAMOTO, INTERRACIAL JUSTICE, CONFLICT AND RECONCILIATION IN POST CIVIL-RIGHTS AMERICA (1999).

66 Margaret (Peggy) Maisel, *Have Truth and Reconciliation Commissions Helped Remediate Human Rights Violations against Women? A Feminist Analysis of the Past and Formula for the Future*, 20 CARDOZO JOURNAL OF INTERNATIONAL AND COMPARATIVE LAW (2011) 143, 153.

67 In fact, a group of TRC-designated victims and others filed a lawsuit in the United States against corporations including General Motors, IBM, and Citibank. This lawsuit is a direct result of their dissatisfaction with the TRC. It is ironic that the purpose of establishing the TRC was to emphasize the principles of restorative justice in lieu of the more traditional notions of punitive justice, as typified by lawsuits. *See* Penelope E. Andrews, *Reparations for Apartheid's Victims: The Path to Reconciliation?*, 53 DE PAUL LAW REVIEW (2004) 1155.

established.[68] Its creation was a political compromise. Its role, although limited, has been significant within the broader project of transformation. A major problem with the TRC, however, was how it dealt with the issue of gender equality. The work of the TRC was extremely damaging insofar as it gave short shrift to the plight of women who had been victims of apartheid.[69]

The definition of victim in the enabling Act of the TRC in effect excluded from its ambit millions of women who daily were subjected to the degradations of apartheid, including the destruction of family life through the operation of the pass law or the migrant labor system.[70] In addition the lethal cocktail of apartheid masculinities exposed women to systemic violence, both in the public and private sphere.[71]

The number of victims certified by the TRC was 22,000.[72] This was a rather tiny amount in the light of the 300 years plus of colonialism, and forty years plus of apartheid. The TRC, for the most part, focused on men and the violations to which they had been subjected.[73]

The TRC only took notice of the sufferings of women, as persons in their own rights, after women started lobbying the TRC. The women complained that major abuses of women had occurred under apartheid but that these abuses were not being considered by the TRC.[74] The response of the TRC was to initiate three days of women's hearings. Until then, the women who appeared before the TRC Committee were largely seen as "secondary victims."[75] In other words, they testified as mothers, wives, and sisters, referencing the suffering of their male

---

68   COMMISSIONING THE PAST: UNDERSTANDING SOUTH AFRICA'S TRUTH AND RECONCILIATION COMMISSION (Deborah Posel and Graeme Simpson eds. 2002); ANTJE KROG, THE COUNTRY OF MY SKULL: GUILT, SORROW AND THE LIMITS OF FORGIVENESS IN THE NEW SOUTH AFRICA (1998).

69   Margaret (Peggy) Maisel, *Have Truth and Reconciliation Commissions Helped Remediate Human Rights Violations against Women? supra* Note 66 at 153.

70   *Ibid* at 155.

71   *See* Adrien Katherine Wing and Eunice P. de Carvalho, *Black South African Women: Toward Equal Rights*, 8 HARVARD HUMAN RIGHTS JOURNAL (1995) 57, 59.

72   Paul Lansing and Julie C. King, *South Africa's Truth and Reconciliation Commission: The Conflict between Individual Justice and National Healing in the Post-Apartheid Age*, 15 ARIZONA JOURNAL OF INTERNATIONAL AND COMPARATIVE LAW (1998) 753, 766.

73   Margaret (Peggy) Maisel, *Have Truth and Reconciliation Commissions Helped Remediate Human Rights Violations against Women? supra* Note 66 at 155.

74   *See* BETH GOLDBLATT AND SHIELA MEINTJES, GENDER AND THE TRUTH AND RECONCILIATION COMMISSION: A SUBMISSION TO THE TRUTH AND RECONCILIATION COMMISSION (1996), available at: *http://www.justice.gov.za/ trc/hrvtrans/submit/gender.htm.*

75   Margaret (Peggy) Maisel, *Have Truth and Reconciliation Commissions Helped Remediate Human Rights Violations against Women? supra* Note 66 at 159.

relatives. As one observer noted, the TRC located women in the "private realm as supporters of men," but not in the public realm as "resisters of oppression."[76]

The women who testified before the TRC in the three-day hearings complained about a whole host of issues, including the fact that the media did not regard their testimony, as compared to the testimony of men, as noteworthy or important. Some female witnesses were labeled by the media as the "crying team" of the Commission.[77]

Women also complained that three days of hearings were not sufficient to fully investigate the range of human rights violations to which women had been subjected. Because sexual violence against women had been committed both by the apartheid government and the liberation movement in exile, probably there was a measure of discomfort about these public revelations, especially since very senior men of power and influence were in danger of being exposed. But there were also limitations upon the women with regards to complaints they were willing to press. These limitations stemmed from fear that, in a patriarchal and religious country like South Africa, very graphic details about sexual violations would render the women vulnerable to ridicule and contempt.[78]

In its final report, the TRC emphasized the need for national reconciliation and the creation of a human rights culture.[79] The report, however, did not address the systemic nature of violence against women in South Africa. This was a signal failure of the TRC. In fact, the TRC's process was one that was sanitized insofar as it failed to deal sufficiently with the various ways in which women were oppressed.[80]

Several factors may have contributed to this omission. One possible factor was the inability of society at large to properly appreciate the role of women in the popular struggle against apartheid and in the liberation movements. No doubt, this is related to the difficulty many in these movements then experienced in accepting

---

76   Lynn Graybill, *The Contribution of the Truth and Reconciliation Commission toward the Promotion of Women's Rights in South Africa*, 24 WOMEN'S STUDIES INTERNATIONAL FORUM (2001) 1, 4.

77   Pumla Gobodo-Madikizela, *Women's Contributions to South Africa's Truth and Reconciliation Commission*, WOMEN WAGING PEACE POLICY COMMISSION, vii (2005) at: *http://www.womenwagingpeace.net/content/articles/SouthAfrica/TJFullCaseStudy. pdf.*

78   *Ibid.*

79   FINAL REPORT OF THE TRUTH AND RECONCILIATION COMMISSION, Vol. 6 (2003) at: *http://www.info.gov.za/otherdocs/2003/trc/.*

80   How the TRC Failed Women in South Africa: A Failure That Has Proved Fertile Ground for the Gender Violence Women in South Africa Face Today, KHULUMANI.NET, October 3, 2011 at: *http://khulumani.net/truth-a-memory/item/527-how-the-trc-failed-women-in-south-africa-a-failure-that-has-proved-fertile-ground-for-the-gender-violence-women-in-south-africa-face-today.html.*

the role of women as autonomous political agents.[81] This difficulty mirrors the societal vision of women as secondary partners, whether in the home or in public places. It therefore is not surprising that it would extend to the role of women in the popular anti-apartheid movement and the liberation struggle. Another likely factor was the failure by the TRC to appreciate sufficiently the quantitative and qualitative nature of violence against women in the form of sexual violence, other forms of violence, and sexual harassment. The failure of the TRC to address violence against women in its processes also deprived women advocates of a valuable opportunity to confront, before the TRC, apartheid sexualized violence in a comprehensive manner.[82]

In Afghanistan, a new constitutional regime was adopted without instituting a transitional justice mechanism that would enable national reconciliation in the way that South Africa's TRC attempted. This may prove to have been a major oversight, although it is still not too late given the continued warfare in that country. Indeed newspaper reports in January 2012 state that the Taliban has established offices in Qatar, and it is not too far-fetched to imagine a mechanism like the TRC being established in Afghanistan in the future.[83] Women in Afghanistan, who have been brutalized, subjugated, and oppressed, need a vehicle in which to articulate the harms to which they have been subjected as a matter of course. Not having something like South Africa's TRC that would address injustices suffered by women may impede some of the progress Afghanistan needs to bring about gender equality and women's rights.[84]

To be sure, the TRC was not a panacea for overcoming all legacies of trauma and brutality. But the TRC format is one that enables a society to identify explicitly the harms that have been caused to victims, that gives victims a public space within which to air their pain, and that forces the general public to come to terms with the nature and extent of harm and pain endured by vast numbers of the citizenry.[85]

---

81   *See* Anne McClintock, *"No Longer in a Future Heaven": Women and Nationalism in South Africa*, 51 TRANSITION (1991) 104.

82   How the TRC Failed Women in South Africa, *supra* Note 80.

83   *See Hamid Karzai, Afghanistan President, Welcomes Taliban Office in Qatar*, THE HUFFINGTON POST, January 4, 2012 at, *http://www.huffingtonpost.com/2012/01/04/ hamid-karzai-taliban-office-qatar_n_1183089.html*.

84   Rashida Manjoo, the U.N. Rapporteur on Violence Against Women, discusses this question in some detail. *See* Rashida Manjoo, *The South African Truth and Reconciliation Commission: A Model for Gender Justice?* UNITED NATIONS RESEARCH INSTITUTE FOR SOCIAL DEVELOPMENT (November 2004).

85   *See* TRUTH AND RECONCILIATION COMMISSION, *INTERIM REPORT* (June 1996), Section 4: Committee Reports available at: *http://www.justice.gov.za/trc/ report/finalreport/Volume%205.pdf*.

Women's Rights are Human Rights?

Today the language of universal human rights is accepted, if not always in substance, as the norm that should govern global cooperation. Since the passage of the Universal Declaration of Human Rights in 1948, the proliferation of United Nations treaties, conventions and declarations dedicated to human rights reflect this new world order of rights. The celebration of fifty years of "global governance" in 1995 and the much heralded report on global governance reflect an optimistic and confident global arrangement and the supposed global consensus of shared values.[86]

The Portuguese scholar, Boaventura de Sousa Santos, is a member of the second group of scholars to which reference was made previously. He has stated that human rights has achieved a kind of primacy amongst norms, that the language of human rights is "the language of progressive politics," and that it confidently provides an "emancipatory script" for those seeking redress from unjust and abusive regimes.[87] Another scholar of this vein, Upendra Baxi, the Indian human rights scholar, refers to the discourse of human rights as seeking to "supplant all other ethical languages."[88]

Of course this optimistic edifice masks a more sinister period in world history, one not necessarily typified by international strife but rather often typified by intra-national conflicts which devastate the population within a nation, sometimes as many as millions of people.[89] In these conflicts, many of which have occurred over the last several decades, whole communities sometimes fare dismally, but women and children are often the most vulnerable. Many women often experience injury based on their gender. For them, the international human rights framework exists as a distant, arcane construct.[90]

---

86 OUR GLOBAL NEIGHBORHOOD: THE REPORT OF THE COMMISSION ON GLOBAL GOVERNANCE (1995). But note critique of the global human rights movement, MAKAU MATUA, HUMAN RIGHTS: A POLITICAL AND CULTURAL CRITIQUE (2008).

87 Boaventura de Sousa Santos, *Toward a Multicultural Conception of Human Rights*, in *INTERNATIONAL HUMAN RIGHTS LAW IN A GLOBAL CONTEXT* (Felipe Gómez Isa and Koen Feyter eds. 2009) 97.

88 Upendra Baxi, *Voices of Suffering and the Future of Human Rights*, *supra* Note 54.

89 Nils Peter Gleditsch *et al.*, *Armed Conflict 1946–2001: A New Dataset*, 39 JOURNAL OF PEACE RESEARCH (2002) 615.

90 *See* various HUMAN RIGHTS WATCH, SOLDIERS WHO RAPE, COMMANDERS WHO CONDONE: SEXUAL VIOLENCE AND MILITARY REFORM IN THE DEMOCRATIC REPUBLIC OF CONGO (2009); HUMAN RIGHTS WATCH, SWEPT UNDER THE RUG: ABUSES AGAINST DOMESTIC WORKERS AROUND THE WORLD (2006); HUMAN RIGHTS WATCH, STRUGGLING TO SURVIVE: BARRIERS TO JUSTICE FOR RAPE VICTIMS IN RWANDA (2004).

The edifice of global governance and international human rights law have spawned three general issues related to women's human rights. The first issue is whether governments have created, or are capable of creating, structures and institutions needed to enforce, protect, and promote the rights of its citizens. The second issue is the basket of concerns that arise from invoking law to handle a host of political, social, and economic issues. Some have termed this the globalization of law or the "judicialization of politics."[91] The problem is mostly present where constitutional or high courts, or courts generally, have the final say in the meaning and interpretation of constitutional texts. In these societies, large sectors of civil society focus their struggles on legal ones, utilizing courts to pursue a range of interests in the name of human rights.[92]

The third issue is a variant of the concern expressed by scholars such as Boaventura de Sousa Santos. This concern revolves around the extent to which human rights has become the dominant language for dealing with political, economic, and social struggles. Some have in particular observed that ever since the collapse of communism and the destruction of the Berlin Wall in 1989, the language of rights has emerged to replace the language of policies about redistribution.[93] Of course, the collapse of communism also was interpreted as victory of the free market, and it could be said that the victory of the free markets coincides with, or reflects, the tendency of political, economic, and social struggle to revolve around the recognition and enforcement of legal rights, rather than redistribution of wealth and resources.[94]

Contemporary political discourse, and indeed political developments on the ground globally, reflect the hegemony of liberal democracy as the dominant political paradigm. This paradigm is imbued with its own version of legal formalism, one predicated on constitutionalism and the rule of law. Its most profound manifestation is in the primacy afforded to written constitutions, or at the least, to the idea of constitutional governance.[95] Boaventura de Sousa Santos, in particular, argues that this version of legal formalism, namely constitutional governance, has effectively resulted in the "judicialization of politics," the reality that legal institutions and processes of conflict resolution, or legal ordering of societal relationships, are now hegemonic.[96]

---

91   Boaventura de Sousa Santos, *Toward a Multicultural Conception of Human Rights*, *supra* Note 87.

92   *See* GERALD ROSENBERG, THE HOLLOW HOPE, *supra* Note 55.

93   Gwen Brodsky and Shelagh Day, *Beyond the Social and Economic Rights Debate: Substantive Equality Speaks to Poverty*, 14 CANADIAN JOURNAL OF WOMEN AND THE LAW (2002) 184, 197.

94   *Ibid.*

95   *See* Ran Hirschl, *The Political Origins of the New Constitutionalism*, 11 INDIANA JOURNAL OF GLOBAL LEGAL STUDIES (2004) 71.

96   Boaventura de Sousa Santos, *Toward a Multicultural Conception of Human Rights*, *supra* Note 87.

South Africa exhibits the most recent reflection of this tendency: arguably the conviction amongst some that the revolution there was largely a legal one. The most influential processes prior to the elections there in 1994 were constitutional negotiations. It was the pens of lawyers that gave the nation its new legal and political order, albeit at the behest of politicians who brokered the substance of the final documents, primarily the new constitution.[97] But globally, the proliferation of quasi-legal and legal regulatory agencies and human rights bodies, specifically to administer and enforce the new dispensation of human rights, reflects a bureaucratization of human rights enforcement and its legalistic culture.[98]

The global developments that have led to the channeling of political aspirations and conflict resolution through the prism, and conscription, of legal mechanisms and legal processes are overall very positive and quite laudatory. But what this legal edifice obscures are underlying economic and social inequalities which fall outside the confines of legal solutions. These inequalities are best addressed through the processes of political and economic enfranchisement. It is these extra-legal processes which ultimately empower people both at the ballot box and in the ordinary encounters of their lives.[99]

The processes are especially important because many marginalized and poor people do not have access to courts and lawyers. They do, however, have some opportunities, though often limited, to engage with their elected representatives, either individually or through a range of civil organizations. For them, the idea of representative democracy and participatory democracy creates the discursive space in which to pursue their rights as citizens with representatives who are political accountable to them.[100]

Holding government accountable by holding elected officials accountable is an important part of the struggle. It is not being cavalier about the struggle or the significance of legal rights. Rather, it is a reminder that the formal edifice of rights can easily obscure underlying structural problems which law cannot cure. Where, as for example in the United States, a huge proportion of the population, including a disproportionately large number of people of color, has effectively disregarded the electoral process, that population has ceded its ability to advance their social and economic interests.[101]

---

97   *See* SIRI GLOPPEN, SOUTH AFRICA: THE BATTLE OVER THE CONSTITUTION (1997).

98   Cesare P.R. Romano, *The Proliferation of International Judicial Bodies: The Pieces of the Puzzle*, 31 NEW YORK UNIVERSITY JOURNAL OF INTERNATIONAL LAW AND POLICY (1999) 709, 709–10.

99   *See* GERALD ROSENBERG, THE HOLLOW HOPE, *supra* Note 55.

100   *Ibid.*

101   ANDREW HACKER, TWO NATIONS: BLACK AND WHITE, SEPARATE, HOSTILE, UNEQUAL, (1992) and WILLIAM JULIUS WILSON, TRULY DISADVANTAGED: THE INNER CITY, THE UNDERCLASS AND PUBLIC POLICY (1990).

Another problem looms large in the ability of developing nations to provide structures and institutions adequate for protecting the rights and interests of their citizens. A traditional rights-based approach situates the state as the major provider of rights. However, many of these nations, because of lack of finances, have in the past found themselves subject to demands of the International Monetary Fund and the World Bank.[102] These international finance bodies have forced many countries to restructure their economies, thereby severely constraining their ability to help economically marginalized groups, particularly women, with deleterious consequences. The latest global economic downturn has exacerbated these problems.[103]

In summary, conditional interdependence calls for a shift in the conceptualizing of women's human rights. This shift might include the idea of designing a transitional mechanism, such as a Truth and Reconciliation Commission, which would highlight injustice and violence against women, and provide a vehicle through which the society as a whole might commit itself to pursuing rights and dignity for women. Such a shift certainly involves the conscription of men as agents of transformation, for without the active participation of men the pursuit of women's human rights is often thwarted. Such a shift involves an appreciation of the interconnectedness of political, economic and social rights, and the centrality of women's rights as human rights. In the final analysis, a conceptual shift involving these modifications may allow for an approach based on conditional interdependence to further the pursuit of women's human rights and equality, and result in meaningful change for women who are often marginalized even with legal and policy change designed to benefit them.

---

102   JOSEPH E. STIEGLITZ, GLOBALIZATION AND ITS DISCONTENTS (2001).

103   *See* INDIRA SINHA, GLOBAL FINANCIAL MELTDOWN AND WORKING WOMEN'S RIGHTS – WITH SPECIAL REFERENCE TO DEVELOPING COUNTRIES, PAPER PRESENTED AT 2010 ANNUAL MEETING OF AMERICAN POLITICAL SCIENCE ASSOCIATION at: *http://papers.ssrn.com/sol3/papers.cfm?abstract_ id=1642054. See also* Sher Verick, *Who Is Hit Hardest during a Financial Crisis? The Vulnerability of Young Men and Women to Unemployment in an Economic Downturn,* ILO/IZA DISCUSSION PAPER NO. 4359 (2009) at: *http://papers.ssrn.com/sol3/papers. cfm?abstract_id=1455521.*

Chapter 3

The Global Legal Campaign for Women's Rights

The temperance of a man and of a woman, or the courage and justice of a woman, are not ... the same; the courage of a man is shown in commanding, of a woman in obeying. And this holds of all other virtues ....[1]

Feminist analysis is like friendship: an ongoing process of deepening complexity, interactive, contradictory, insightful, emotional, enlightening, challenging, conflicted.[2]

Feminist Legal Advocates

The victory in South Africa over apartheid andthe successful transition to a constitutional democracy protecting and promoting human rights and dignity was primarily a victory by the people of South Africa, their extraordinary leaders, and organizations dedicated to ending apartheid, particularly the Congress of South African Trade Unions, the South African Council of Churches, the liberation movements in exile, namely the African National Congress and the Pan-Africanist Congress, and a range of anti-apartheid civil society organizations.[3] However, international factors were crucial too, such as a general international campaign to end apartheid, spearheaded by the United Nations and anti-apartheid organizations in Europe, Australia, and the United States, as well as solid support for the liberation movements by the Scandinavian governments, and governments in Africa and the former Soviet-bloc countries. In addition, particularly commencing in the 1970s, the global campaign for women's rights and gender equality, and the general work of feminist legal theorists and advocates worldwide, also played a part in the transition. As such, international constituencies share the credit, though

---

1   THE BASIC WORKS OF ARISTOTLE 1143, POLITICA, cited in Catharine Hantzis, *Is Gender Justice a Completed Agenda*, 100 HARVARD LAW REVIEW (1987) 690, 697.

2   Nancy E. Dowd, *Introduction*, FEMINIST LEGAL THEORY (Nancy E. Dowd and Michelle S. Jacobs eds. 2003) 5.

3   *See* ANTHONY W. MARX, LESSONS OF STRUGGLE: SOUTH AFRICAN INTERNAL OPPOSITION 1960–1990 (1992); *see also* RICK ABEL, POLITICS BY OTHER MEANS: LAW IN THE STRUGGLE AGAINST APARTHEID (2002).

not the predominant credit, for the positive political, social, economic, legal, and constitutional developments in South Africa.[4] These international factors are likely to have positive effects in Afghanistan as well, perhaps even more pronounced, as that state struggles to obtain peace, an effective constitutional democracy, and means for ensuring the protection of human rights, especially women's human rights.[5]

I now turn to a consideration of these intertwined factors, the international campaign and feminist legal theory and advocacy, as a backdrop to the examination that will be undertaken later of Afghanistan and South Africa's constitutional frameworks and what they have meant for the protection and advancement of women's rights.

The feminist legal movement and the global campaign for women's rights are ideological and political structures that have been available and active in helping to secure women's rights and gender equality everywhere.[6] The feminist legal movement has its genesis, in part, in the civil rights movement in the United States of the 1960s, and, in part, from a more general movement in Western democracies like the United States, Australia, and Europe during the nineteenth and twentieth centuries for the right of women to vote, to pursue an occupation, to be economically and socially independent, and to be recognized as a separate person under the law.[7]

The global campaign for women's rights also had its origin in two parts. One was the framework of covenants, treaties, conferences, and agreements that followed upon the establishment of the United Nations and its Charter. Key here were first, the Universal Declaration of Human Rights, adopted by the U.N. General Assembly in 1948,[8] and second, the International Covenant on Civil and Political Rights, adopted by the U.N. General Assembly in 1966 and in force beginning 1976,[9] and the International Covenant on Economic, Social and Cultural Rights, adopted by the General Assembly in 1966 and in force beginning 1976.[10] These documents established the legitimacy of the global campaign for human rights,

---

4   *See* HAKAN THORN, ANTI-APARTHEID AND THE EMERGENCE OF A GLOBAL CIVIL SOCIETY (2006).

5   These issues are explored in Chapter 6.

6   CATHERINE ESCHLE AND BICE MAIGUASHCA, MAKING FEMINIST SENSE OF THE GLOBAL JUSTICE MOVEMENT (2010).

7   BUILDING FEMINIST MOVEMENTS AND ORGANIZATIONS: GLOBAL PERSPECTIVES (Lydia Alpizar *et al.* eds. 2007).

8   At: *http://www.un.org/en/documents/udhr/.*

9   Adopted and opened for signature, ratification and accession by General Assembly resolution 2200A (XXI) of 16 December 1966, entry into force 23 March 1976, in accordance with Article 49; at: *http://www2.ohchr.org/english/law/ccpr.htm.*

10   Adopted and opened for signature, ratification and accession by General Assembly resolution 2200A (XXI) of 16 December 1966, entry into force 3 January 1976, in accordance with Article 27; at: *http://www2.ohchr.org/english/law/cescr.htm.*

including women's rights, and provided an organizing structure for promoting and defending human rights and support networks.

The second part of the genesis of the global campaign was the rise of numerous non-governmental organizations (NGOs) around the world whose inspiration comes from fulfilling the mission of the United Nations in promoting peace, civil and political rights, economic, social, and cultural rights, and promoting the universality of peace and of these human rights overall.[11]

The global feminist campaign has had the most profound effect in advancing women's rights and gender equality and in providing succor to activists in developing countries who are fighting for women's rights and women's interests.[12] The feminist legal movement has had a powerful effect as well, though not on the same scale. Both parts of the feminist global movement, and their feminist legal counterparts, have established influential frameworks for analyzing issues of women's rights and have been critical in educating women, as well as men, of the necessity for making women's rights and gender equality a fundamental component of society, government, and laws.[13] Both parts of the feminist movement have been useful in getting people and governments to accept, and understand, that it is not enough simply to promulgate laws committed to gender equality, but it is also important to enforce them.[14] In addition, the realization of such rights require the removal of barriers, including cultural or traditional practices, that materially infringe, as a practical matter, upon the effective exercise of those rights.[15]

I now turn to the feminist legal movement and the more general feminist movement, noting, however, that the review is not intended to be comprehensive or definitive. The focus is a general outline exploring gains of the global feminist movement in a chronological order. Others have explored the issues in great depth, capturing the complexity and nuance.[16]

---

11   *See* PETER WILLETTS, NON-GOVERNMENTAL ORGANIZATIONS IN WORLD POLITICS (2010); *see also* CIVIL SOCIETIES AND SOCIAL MOVEMENTS: DOMESTIC, TRANSNATIONAL AND GLOBAL (Ronnie D. Lipschutz ed. 2006).

12   *See*, for example, CATHARINE A. MACKINNON, ARE WOMEN HUMAN? AND OTHER INTERNATIONAL DIALOGUES (2006); *see also* WOMEN'S RIGHTS, HUMAN RIGHTS: INTERNATIONAL FEMINIST PERSPECTIVES (Julie Peters and Andrea Wolper eds. 1994).

13   WOMEN'S RIGHTS, HUMAN RIGHTS: INTERNATIONAL FEMINIST PERSPECTIVES *Ibid.*

14   CONSTITUTING EQUALITY: GENDER EQUALITY AND COMPARATIVE CONSTITUTIONAL LAW (Susan H. Williams ed. 2011).

15   REBECCA J. COOK AND SIMONE CUSACK, GENDER STEREOTYPING: TRANSNATIONAL LEGAL PERSPECTIVE (2009).

16   *See* Serena Mayeri, *Constitutional Choices: Legal Feminism and the Historical Dynamics of Change* 92 CALIFORNIA LAW REVIEW (2004) 755; *see also* WOMEN'S ACTIVISM AND GLOBALIZATION: LINKING LOCAL STRUGGLES AND TRANSNATIONAL POLITICS (Nancy A. Naples and Manisha Desai eds. 2002); GLOBAL CRITICAL RACE FEMINISM: AN INTERNATIONAL READER (Adrien

Of the many social and political movements of the mid to the late twentieth century, the so-called second wave of feminism was surely one of the most significant. Organizing and lobbying on all five continents, increasingly aided and abetted by the liberating possibilities of the innovative communications technology, especially the internet, women's voices in the political realm were no longer muted. The last few decades saw concerted efforts by women activists across the globe to bring women's issues from the margins of political and legal discourse to a place where women's concerns and priorities were at least recognized.[17]

The progress of feminist theory and women's activism in the past few decades has been exciting, rancorous, emotional, and innovative. Feminist legal theory and women's activists have embraced competing narratives of rights, resulting in a rich and creative body of feminist legal theory that has forced the law to embrace the concerns of women.[18]

Confronting Formal Equality

As scholars and advocates celebrate nearly four decades of feminist agitation, it is worth recalling the well orchestrated campaigns to effect changes in the political and legal spheres across all continents. The 1960s and 1970s witnessed the emergence of a groundswell of legal scholarship and activism providing impetus for the emerging legal struggle for equality and non-discrimination, and responding to the policy and legal successes and setbacks in past struggles. Betty Friedan's path-breaking book, *The Feminine Mystique*, had just been published,[19] very much building on Simone De Beauvoir's 1949 book on women as the "second sex."[20] Further campaigns included the Freedom Rides of 1992 to encourage minority voting and to promote young people's, especially young women's, interests in feminism, and the pro-choice campaigns by NARAL Pro-Choice America, for example, the March for women's lives in 2004.[21]

Wing Ed. 2000); SUSAN DELLER ROSS, WOMEN'S HUMAN RIGHTS: THE INTERNATIONAL AND COMPARATIVE LAW CASEBOOK (2008).

17   RETHINKING EQUALITY PROJECTS IN LAW: FEMINIST CHALLENGES (Rosemary Hunter ed. 2008).

18   *See*, for example, FATIMA SADIQUI AND MOHA ENNAJI, WOMEN IN THE MIDDLE EAST AND NORTH AFRICA: AGENTS OF CHANGE (2011); *see also* Brooke Ackerly and Jacqui True, *Back to the Future: Feminist Theory, Activism, and Doing Feminist Research in an Age of Globalization*, 33 WOMEN'S STUDIES INTERNATIONAL FORUM (2010) 464.

19   BETTY FRIEDAN, THE FEMININE MYSTIQUE (1963).

20   SIMONE DE BEAUVOIR, THE SECOND SEX (1949).

21   Robin Toner, *A Call to Arms by Abortion Rights Groups*, NEW YORK TIMES, April 22, 2004 at: *http://www.nytimes.com/2004/04/22/politics/22MARC.html?pagewanted=all*.

In developed Western nations in North America, in the European Union, and Australia, the impact of feminist activism is well known.[22] What feminist jurisprudence has accomplished is remarkable. It has unsettled the field of legal theory, transformed many areas of domestic law, and forced the law to accommodate the actual experiences of women. For example, in the United States the advocacy of Professor Catherine McKinnon provided the foundation for the subsequent development of the law of sexual harassment.[23] Similarly, in Canada and in Australia, Professors Mary Jane Mossman and Margaret Thornton analyzed the discrete experiences of women in the legal profession and their roles in developing the principle of gender equality.[24]

A cursory glance at the areas of criminal law (particularly rape and domestic battery), family law, constitutional law, and tort law, reveals the impact of feminist jurisprudence. For example, the innovative scholarship of Professors Leslie Bender and Joyce McConnell has influenced the way that tort law is taught and practiced in the United States, and particularly the way that the law interprets women's experience of harm.[25] They have advocated for an interpretation of tort law beyond individual harms, to one of group systemic injury. In addition, in many jurisdictions, mandatory arrest policies are in place for rape, as well as domestic violence.[26]

One also sees the impact of feminist legal theory in the areas of immigration and refugee law, for example, where the discrete experiences of women, for example as rape victims in war, or those subjected to government condoned private violence, are increasingly seen as grounds for political asylum. Here the work of Professor Audrey Macklin in Canada, and Professor Siobhan Mullally in Ireland are apposite, both calling for legal approaches in the area of refugee law that accommodate the gendered power dynamics that lead women to seek

---

22   *See* WOMEN AND THE LAW: STORIES (Elizabeth M. Schneider and Stephanie M. Wildman eds. 2010); AUSTRALIAN FEMINISM: A COMPANION (Barbara Caine *et al.* eds. 1999); BRITISH FEMINISM IN THE 20TH CENTURY (Harold L. Smith ed. 1990).

23   CATHERINE A. MACKINNON, THE SEXUAL HARASSMENT OF WORKING WOMEN: A CASE OF SEX DISCRIMINATION (1979).

24   MARY JANE MOSSMAN, THE FIRST WOMEN LAWYERS: A COMPARATIVE STUDY OF GENDER, LAW AND THE LEGAL PROFESSIONS (2006); MARGARET THORNTON, DISSONANCE AND DISTRUST: WOMEN IN THE LEGAL PROFESSION (1996).

25   Leslie Bender, *An Overview of Feminist Torts Scholarship*, 78 CORNELL LAW REVIEW (1993) 575; Joyce McConnell, *Beyond Metaphor: Battered Women, Involuntary Servitude and the Thirteenth Amendment*, 4 YALE JOURNAL OF LAW AND FEMINISM (1992) 207.

26   Michelle J. Anderson, *Marital Immunity, Intimate Relationships, and Improper Inferences: A New Law on Sexual Offenses by Intimates*, 54 HASTINGS LAW JOURNAL (2003) 1465, 1468–73; *see also* Julie Goldscheid, *Gender-Motivated Violence: Developing a Meaningful Paradigm for Civil Rights Enforcement*, 22 HARVARD WOMEN'S LAW JOURNAL (1999) 123.

protection in foreign countries.[27] In the United States, some notable court victories have been obtained for female asylum applicants. For example, in two successful claims for asylum, rape and domestic violence respectively were seen as grounds for asylum.[28]

Certainly in countries of the global North, although male bias persists in the law, the situation of women, particularly those in the middle and upper classes, has improved dramatically in the past few decades, and this change is a direct result of feminist law reform efforts.[29]

But of course not all women (in these Western nations) have benefited in the same way. The twin processes of racism and poverty have rendered legal victories somewhat pyrrhic to a significant proportion of poor women and women of color.[30] Despite great advances in human rights protections in these countries, lesbian women, despite gains in some areas, perpetually remain subject to heterosexual preferences and orthodoxies that marginalize their experiences and reduce their freedoms. In her work Professor Ruthann Robson has articulated how the law should consider the perspectives of lesbian women, either as subjects of historical discrimination and/or neglect, or as agents of their own destiny.[31]

This is the situation also with women who suffer from mental and physical disabilities, that is, they suffer both as a result of their disabilities and from deeply ingrained prejudicial notions of what constitutes femininity. Disability has historically been a social marker, and chronic illnesses such as chronic fatigue syndrome and anorexia have often been dismissed by doctors and in the medical

---

27   *See* Audrey Macklin, *Cross-Border Shopping for Ideas: A Critical Review of United States, Canadian, and Australian Approaches to Gender-Related Asylum Claims*, 13 GEORGIA IMMIGRATION LAW JOURNAL (Fall 1998) 25; *see also* Siobhan Mullally, *Migrant Women Destabilizing Borders: Citizenship Debates in Ireland*, in INTERSECTIONALITY AND BEYOND: LAW, POWER AND THE POLITICS OF LOCATION (Emily Grabham, Davina Cooper, Jane Krishnadas and Didi Herman eds. 2009).

28   *See Reina Izabel Garcia-Martinez v John Ashcroft, Attorney General* 371 F.3d 1066 (9th Cir. 2004); *see also In re Alvarado* No. A73753922 (United States Board of Immigration Appeals, 20 September 1996) at: *http://www.unhcr.org/refworld/docid/3f8fb4774.html*.

29   *See* generally ANN SCALES, LEGAL FEMINISM: ACTIVISM, LAWYERING AND LEGAL THEORY (2006); *see also* CATHARINE A. MCKINNON, SEXUAL HARASSMENT OF WORKING WOMEN: A CASE OF SEX DISCRIMINATION (1979).

30   *See* Jenny Rivera, *The Violence Against Women Act and the Construction of Multiple Consciousness in the Civil Rights and Feminist Movements*, 4 JOURNAL OF LAW AND POLICY (1996) 463; *see also* Nekima Levy Pounds, *Beaten by the System and Down for the Count: Why Poor Women of Color and Children Don't Stand a Chance Against U.S. Drug Sentencing Policy*, 3 UNIVERSITY OF ST. THOMAS LAW JOURNAL (2006) 464.

31   Ruthann Robson, *Assimilation, Marriage, and Lesbian Liberation*, 75 TEMPLE LAW REVIEW (Winter 2002) 710; Ruthann Robson, *Convictions: Theorizing Lesbians and Criminal Justice*, in LEGAL INVERSIONS (Didi Herman and Carl Stychin eds. 1995) 180.

literature as "women's illnesses."[32] Professor Arlene Kanter, the founder and Director of the Disability Law and Policy Program at Syracuse University College of Law has spent her career advocating for inclusion and equality for those with disabilities, including women with disabilities.[33]

Still, one may feel a certain degree of satisfaction from the circumstance that the legal imagination and legal reality at least now formally embrace the notion of women's equality, however disparate and unevenly implemented that notion may be.

Neither feminists generally nor feminist legal theorists and advocates in the global North have been satisfied with fighting for women's rights only in the Western democracies or other developed nations. Many of these Western feminists[34] have used their resources to challenge prevailing international legal theories and policies. One target has been what is perceived as the male bias of international law and the major institutions of international law, especially the United Nations. For example, the definition of "refugee" in the international treaty on refugees often overlooks the specific persecution that women suffer.[35] Similarly, the enforcement of the major international instrument that focuses on human trafficking often results in women being treated as criminals, and not victims of human trafficking.[36] Another target by feminist international legal scholars, like Professors Hilary Charlesworth and Christine Chinkin, has been the lack of a sufficiently vigorous enforcement of international law with respect to human rights law, and a lack of sufficient gender sensitivity at the United Nations. In particular, Charlesworth, Chinkin, and other scholars have insisted upon a restructuring of United Nations enforcement mechanisms and procedures, including the appointment of women at

---

32   *See* M. Bell, *Re/Forming the Anorexic "Prisoner": Inpatient Medical Treatment as the Return to Panoptic Femininity*, 6 CULTURAL STUDIES AND CRITICAL METHODOLOGIES (2006) 282; *see also* K. Barron, *The Bumpy Road to Womanhood*, 12 DISABILITY AND SOCIETY (1997) 223.

33   At: *http://www.law.syr.edu/deans-faculty-staff/profile.aspx?fac=72.*

34   I use the term "Western feminist" very loosely. I am referring to those constituencies of women, mostly White, who reside in the U.S.A., Europe, Canada and Australia. They are largely schooled in the Judeo-Christian tradition.

35   Article 1 of the U.N. CONVENTION RELATING TO THE STATUS OF REFUGEES created in July of 1951 and amended in January 1967 by the PROTOCOL RELATING TO THE STATUS OF REFUGEES defines a refugee as "Any person owing to a well-founded fear of being persecuted for reasons of race, religion, nationality, membership of a particular social group or political opinion, is outside the country of his nationality and is unable or, owing to such fear, is unwilling to avail himself of the protection of that country; or who, not having a nationality and being outside the country of his former habitual residence as a result of such events, is unable or, owing to such fear, is unwilling to return to it."

36   Robert Booth, *Human Trafficking Victims Will Not Be Treated as Criminals*, THE GUARDIAN, July 3, 2011; *Cambodia: Young Trafficking Victims Treated as Criminals*, HUMAN RIGHTS WATCH, June 22, 2002, at: *http://www.hrw.org/news/2002/06/22/cambodia-young-trafficking-victims-treated-criminals.*

middle and senior levels,[37] thereby ensuring more gender sensitivity in the U.N.'s overall operations.

Although feminists acting in these regards, namely global feminists, purport, to a greater or lesser extent, to represent the world's women, there are, of course, vast economic, geographical, cultural, and social differences between women in the world in which they live and women in the developing world. Even within the countries in which they live, namely the more affluent developed countries of the global North, there are great economic disparities amongst women, especially between the feminists themselves, a somewhat elite group, and the bottom half of the female population. An economic divide also exists amongst many women living in urban and rural areas.[38] This divide often results in significant disparities in education, opportunities for political involvement, the ability to partake of cultural activities, and the freedom to exercise full legal rights for women. In the face of these differences between women in developed and developing nations, these global women activists have adhered to their program of advocating and organizing a collective mobilization of women against gender inequality, patriarchy, and male domination, in all its various forms and guises.[39]

Not all feminist theorists and activists reside in developed nations. Indeed, a critical mass of feminist theorists and activists are now from developing nations, with the numbers swelling every year.[40] They have joined rank with Western feminists in a large number of endeavors. Unlike their Western counterparts, a significant percentage of these feminist theorists and activists come from poor countries in which the nationalist struggle for independence or for democracy under the rule of law is an ongoing enterprise.[41] They also successfully lobbied, in conjunction with Western feminists, the United Nations to make it pursue women's rights more vigorously around the globe, a major strategic victory.[42]

---

37   These issues are explored in a seminal article, Hilary Charlesworth *et al.*, *Feminist Approaches to Law*, 85 AMERICAN JOURNAL OF INTERNATIONAL LAW (1991) 613.

38   UNIFEM, PROGRESS OF THE WORLD'S WOMEN (2005).

39   I am not suggesting here that this mobilization has not been fraught with conflict, disagreement, and dissension. Much anger has been unleashed in the various global women's campaigns—and continues to be—as women engage in battles of representivity, voice, transparency, and other issues that are raised in this book.

40   *See*, for example, THE GENDER FACE OF ASIAN POLITICS (Azaar Ayaz and Andrea Fleschenberg eds. 2009); KUMKUM ROY, THE POWER OF GENDER AND THE GENDER OF POWER (2011); AMINA MAMA, BEYOND THE MASKS: RACE, GENDER AND SUBJECTIVITY (1995).

41   WOMEN'S MOVEMENTS IN THE GLOBAL ERA: THE POWER OF LOCAL FEMINISMS (Amrita Basu ed. 2010).

42   My chronological account should not be interpreted as suggesting that women activists in the poorer countries took their political and activist cues from Western feminists. Rather, women in colonial and other undemocratic societies were very engaged political actors, in which the eradication of gender discrimination was assumed (albeit falsely) to be part of the national liberation struggle. So their liberatory impulses were not just directed

They continue to organize on a host of fronts, and form coalitions in order to amplify their efforts.[43]

One important consequence of the activities of these feminist advocates from developing nations has been the energizing of women activists everywhere and of non-governmental organizations (NGOs) in the cause of women's rights as well as in causing the proliferation in the number of NGOs themselves.[44]

Through the individual and combined efforts of these NGOs, governments have been forced to take up gender issues despite a reluctance to do so. One might say these NGOs have "engendered" organs of civil society, which is to say they now have a component whose mission is centered on women's rights.[45] Examples of such activism abound: for example, the major international human rights NGOs like Amnesty International and Human Rights Watch all have significant programs that focus on women's issues.[46] In addition, groups like Equality Now, Women for Women International, and the Global Fund for Women were established to focus entirely on women's issues.[47]

The result of this activism has meant that despite formidable obstacles in many parts of the world to respecting women's equality itself, there now exists a highly organized, politically astute, articulate, and vocal group of women activists worldwide who have committed themselves to eradicating the vestiges of sex discrimination and subordination, not only within their borders, but on a global scale.[48]

In recognition of the importance at the beginning of the twenty-first century of gender equality at the global level, the Millennium Development Goals (MDGs), endorsed in 2000 by every member nation of the United Nations as part of the Millennium Declaration, call on governments to "promote gender equality and

---

against sexism and patriarchy—but against the whole super-structure of suppression and subordination. One such example was the struggle against the eradication of apartheid in South Africa.

43　*See* WOMEN'S MOVEMENTS IN THE GLOBAL ERA, *supra* Note 41.

44　VANAJA DHRUVARAJAN AND JILL VICKERS, GENDER, RACE AND NATION: A GLOBAL PERSPECTIVE (2002).

45　SALLY ENGLE MERRY, HUMAN RIGHTS AND GENDER VIOLENCE: TRANSLATING INTERNATIONAL LAW INTO LOCAL JUSTICE (2006); JUTTA M. JOACHIM, AGENDA SETTING, THE U.N. AND NGOs: GENDER VIOLENCE AND REPRODUCTIVE RIGHTS (2007); STRUGGLES FOR SOCIAL RIGHTS IN LATIN AMERICA (Susan Eva Eckstein and Timothy P Wickham-Crowley eds. 2002).

46　*See http://www.amnestyusa.org/our-work/issues/women-s-rights* and *http://www.hrw.org/category/topic/women.*

47　*See www.equalitynow.org, www.womenforwomen.org,* and *www.globalfundforwomen.org.*

48　*See* GLOBAL CRITICAL RACE FEMINISM, *supra* Note 16; *see also* GENDERING THE STATE IN AN AGE OF GLOBALIZATION: WOMEN'S MOVEMENTS AND STATE FEMINISM IN POSTINDUSTRIAL DEMOCRACIES (Melissa Hausmann *et al.* eds. 2007).

empower women."[49] Although the awaited major review of the MDGs by world leaders in New York in September 2005 was disappointing, gender equality remained an important global goal.

The pursuit and achievement of gender equality as important aspirational goals have been strengthened through the active participation of regional political entities. For example, the Southern African Development Community, in a major declaration, namely, the 2008 Protocol on Gender and Development, commits itself to a comprehensive plan of action that sets out specific targets and timeframes for achieving gender equality.[50] The Protocol includes as well comprehensive monitoring and evaluation mechanisms for measuring progress on gender equality. One target includes a commitment by all state parties that sign on to the document to "endeavor, by 2015, to enshrine gender equality and equity in their Constitutions and ensure that these rights are not compromised by any provisions, laws or practices."[51] Similarly, the Protocol provides that state parties to the Protocol shall strive, by 2015, to set aside at least fifty percent of "decision-making positions in the public and private sectors" to women.[52]

The European Union too has endeavored to improve the conditions of European women in a host of areas. Earlier in 2011, the Directorate-General for Internal Policies of the European Parliament and the Parliament's Committee on Gender Equality requested an evaluation and assessment of the compatibility of European Union law with that of the Convention on the Elimination of All Forms of Discrimination Against Women (CEDAW), with the aim of implementing CEDAW within the European Union legal framework.[53] Across the globe, we now see dozens of feminist activists who are now cabinet ministers, diplomats, and high-level political leaders.[54]

The active pursuit of gender equality is reflected in five major global initiatives that have the possibility of transforming women's lives. They are first, the Convention on the Elimination of All Forms of Discrimination Against Women (CEDAW),[55] which sets out to delineate the rights that women are entitled to in all

---

49   UNITED NATIONS MILLENNIUM DECLARATION, Resolution Adopted by the General Assembly, 8 September 2000 at: *www.un.org/millenium/declaration/ares552e.htm.*

50   SADC PROTOCOL ON GENDER AND DEVELOPMENT (2008), at: *http://www.sadc.int/key-documents/protocols/protocol-on-gender-and-development/.*

51   *Ibid.* Part Two, Article 4.

52   *Ibid.* Part Three, Article 12 (1).

53   HOW COULD THE CONVENTION ON THE ELIMINATION OF ALL FORMS OF DISCRIMINATION AGAINST WOMEN BE IMPLEMENTED IN THE EU LEGAL FRAMEWORK? (2011) at: *http://www.europarl.europa.eu/document/activities/cont/2011 07/20110725ATT24656/20110725ATT24656EN.pdf.*

54   A few examples will suffice: Angela Merkel, Chancellor of Germany, Hillary Clinton, United States Secretary of State, Ellen Sirleaf Johnson, President of Liberia, and Aung San Suu Kyi, Burmese opposition politician.

55   CEDAW, *supra* Chapter 1, Note 23.

spheres of life, and mandates governments to work towards the attainment of those rights. Second, the Vienna Declaration on Violence Against Women, which notes in its Preamble its concern for "various forms of discrimination and violence, to which women continue to be exposed all over the world." [56] The Declaration reinforces what CEDAW provides for,[57] but states further:

> Gender-based violence and all forms of sexual harassment and exploitation, including those resulting from cultural prejudice and international trafficking, are incompatible with the dignity and worth of the human person, and must be eliminated. This can be achieved by legal measures and through national action and international cooperation in such fields as economic and social development, education, safe maternity and health care, and social support.[58]

Third, the Beijing Program and Platform for Action (including Beijing Plus Five and Beijing Plus Ten), build on the decades leading to the Fourth World Conference on Women in Beijing in 1995, and serve to reinforce the global commitment to the continued pursuit of women's rights and gender equality.[59] Fourth, the United Nations Millennium Development Plan adopted in 2000 targets gender equality as one of its goals. Finally, Security Council Resolution 1325 reiterates the important role of women in peace-building and nation-building, and their key roles as equal partners in the transitions to democracy.[60]

At the end of this chapter I highlight a women's human rights timeline, which chronologically charts the contours of the pursuit and promotion of women's human rights.

---

56 DECLARATION ON THE ELIMINATION OF VIOLENCE AGAINST WOMEN, G.A. Res. 48/104, U.N. Doc. A/RES/48/104 (December 20, 1993).

57 Chapter 18 of the Declaration states: "The human rights of women and of the girl-child are an inalienable, integral and indivisible part of universal human rights. The full and equal participation of women in political, civil, economic, social and cultural life, at the national, regional and international levels, and the eradication of all forms of discrimination on grounds of sex are priority objectives of the international community."

58 DECLARATION ON THE ELIMINATION OF VIOLENCE AGAINST WOMEN, *supra* Note 56.

59 THE UNITED NATIONS FOURTH WORLD CONFERENCE ON WOMEN, PLATFORM FOR ACTION at: *http://www.un.org/womenwatch/daw/beijing/platform/plat1.htm.*

60 RESOLUTION 1325, Adopted by the Security Council on October 31, 2000 at: *www.un.org/events/res_1325e.pdf.*

Feminist Methodologies

Feminist legal theorists have generated concepts and methodologies that provide a way of viewing the world. This empowers individuals and civil society groups with the capability to adopt tactics and strategies to help transform institutions, particularly where they impact negatively on women's equality.[61]

Feminist legal theorists provide methods of exploring laws, policies, and practices that center the experiences and interests of women. Indeed, feminist "explorations" in this regard have been likened to an "archaeological dig."[62] In elaboration, Professor Hilary Charlesworth, the Australian international lawyer, has stated that "there are various layers of practices, procedures, symbols, and assumptions to uncover and different tools and techniques may be relevant at each level."[63] Feminist theoretical explorations therefore involve a search for silences in law and omissions of the law; these correlating with the gendered experiences of women.

A prominent technique of feminist legal theorists has involved dissolution of the false dichotomy between the public and the private sphere insofar as recognizing and protecting women's rights are concerned. For example, they have demonstrated how private harms frequently inflicted upon women by men or by society are the types of harms which deserve to be recognized as worthy of general public opprobrium and punishment, and therefore are harms for which laws should provide redress.[64]

This perspective is the impetus behind the campaigns to outlaw marital rape and domestic battery, and for mandatory arrests in cases of domestic violence. For feminist legal theorists, treating such acts as "private" ones between the woman and man rather than as public acts entailing criminality results in the demeaning, subordination, and impoverishment of women and their roles in society, as well as to reward male criminality.[65]

This, however, is not to say that feminist legal advocates are always in agreement on how to draw the line between the public and private. Differences surface from time to time. Such differences have become serious in communities where governments have been oppressive and abusive towards them and suspicion

---

61   *See*, for example, MARTHA CHAMALLAS, INTRODUCTION TO FEMINIST LEGAL THEORY (2003); *see also* CRITICAL RACE FEMINISM: A READER (Adrien Wing ed. 1997); FEMINIST LEGAL THEORY, *supra* Note 2, and CATHARINE A. MC KINNON, TOWARD A FEMINIST THEORY OF THE STATE (1989).

62   Hilary Charlesworth, *Feminist Methods in International Law*, in FEMINIST LEGAL THEORY, *supra* Note 2 at 78.

63   *Ibid.*

64   BETTY W. TAYLOR, SHARON RUSH AND ROBERT J. MUNRO, FEMINIST JURISPRUDENCE, WOMEN AND THE LAW: CRITICAL ESSAYS, RESEARCH AGENDA, AND BIBLIOGRAPHY (1997).

65   *Ibid.*

of the police and government authority is rife. An example is the situation with Aboriginal women in Australia where despite widespread private violence against women (from their husbands and intimate partners) mandatory arrest policies appear particularly draconian in the face of documented deaths in police custody and other instances of maltreatment of Aboriginal males in the criminal justice system.[66] Similarly, in South Africa, where suspicion of the police lingers in the face of extensive police abuse during apartheid, feminists insisting on removing the divide between the public and the private as a practical matter face difficulties, even though the South African Constitution outlaws private violence against women.[67]

On a different plane, feminist legal theorists have worked consistently to challenge assumptions about femininity and masculinity. They have insisted that law, its institutions, and legal processes be used to expose and eviscerate the underlying societal assumptions and prejudices bolstering these categories and perpetuating the subordination of women and discrimination against women.[68]

Divergent and critical voices amongst feminist legal theorists have attempted to ensure that the feminist legal project remain unified and inclusive, by encouraging and incorporating the many voices of women. In this they have found common cause with women challenging racism and other forms of discrimination and who demand that these struggles intersect and engage with the struggle against sexism.[69] These demands represent the "multi-racial" and "multi-ethnic" voices of women within the feminist movement who have insisted that the category "woman" be constantly challenged. These feminist advocates also wish to ensure an embrace of other indicators of a women's identity, including class, race, sexual orientation, geography, religion, disability, and culture.[70]

For a feminist legal analysis, context is central to analyzing issues of women's rights in all situations. Thus, critical feminist theorists, including third world feminists and feminists of color, have in their writing emphasized the need to

---

66   Penelope E. Andrews, *Violence against Aboriginal Women in Australia: Redress from the International Human Rights Framework*, 60 ALBANY LAW REVIEW (1997) 917.

67   Penelope E. Andrews, *Violence against Women in South Africa: The Role of Culture and the Limitations of the Law*, 8 TEMPLE POLITICAL AND CIVIL RIGHTS LAW REVIEW (1999) 425.

68   *See*, for example, REBECCA J. COOK AND SIMONE CUSACK, GENDER STEREOTYPING: TRANSNATIONAL LEGAL PERSPECTIVES, *supra* Note 15; *see also* Paula Ruth Gilbert, *Discourses of Female Violence and Societal Gender Stereotypes*, 8 VIOLENCE AGAINST WOMEN (2002) 1271.

69   CHANDRA TALPADE MOHANTY, FEMINISM WITHOUT BORDERS: DECOLONIZING THEORY, PRACTICING SOLIDARITY (2004).

70   *See* Hope Lewis, *Embracing Complexity: Human Rights in Critical Race Feminist Perspective*, 12 COLUMBIA JOURNAL OF GENDER AND LAW (2003) 510; *see also* Penelope E. Andrews, *Globalization, Human Rights Critical Race Feminism: Voices from the Margins*, 3 JOURNAL OF GENDER, RACE AND JUSTICE (2000) 373 and Tracy E. Higgins, *Ant-Essentialism, Relativism, and Human Rights*, 19 HARVARD WOMEN'S LAW JOURNAL (1996) 89.

examine, in each circumstance, the role of culture as part and parcel of the process of ascertaining the nature and extent of rights women require to overcome realities that otherwise threaten to leave them defenseless.[71]

Cultural impact, however, is not always readily apparent. Accordingly, many critical feminist legal theorists have proposed that the cultural realities in which women live are matters that must be unfolded, layer by layer, using as criteria the goal of achieving gender equality. Put another way, they have reminded women's rights advocates not to treat culture as a domain separate and independent from the claims of rights women seek, at least not if they want to attain equality for women.[72] Investigating how culture impinges upon the scope of women's ability to act must parallel investigations of what rights women have, should have, and do not have. Only in this parallel pursuit, the argument goes, is it possible to obtain the liberation of women, establish a realistic sense of women's identity, and attain gender equality, as a practical matter. With this approach, a given aspect of culture might be determined to have, depending on the conditions, a liberating effect rather than a cabining effect, or vice versa.[73]

An interesting example of this can be found in the writings of Louise Halper, the late American legal scholar. She examines this issue in a thoughtful analysis of the discourses of Islam and feminism in Iran.[74] Although recognizing the heavy burdens that women in Iran still bear as a consequence of the imposition of Islamic law after the Islamic revolution in 1979, Halper traces how Iranian women have nevertheless been able to engage strategically with the ruling class to pursue equality in education, access to employment, and access to reproductive health care. Halper believes, as a result, that there is much currency in the idea that a specific type of "Islamic feminist" has emerged in Iran, with developments for women in Iran a key indicator of such feminism.[75]

Halper's approach is just one of the various ways in which different feminist legal theorists have generated rich and innovative approaches to uncovering layers

---

71   *See* Antoinette Sedillo Lopez, *Women's Rights as Human Rights: Intersectional Issues of Race and Gender Facing Women of Color*, 28 SOUTHERN UNIVERSITY LAW REVIEW (2001) 279; *see also* Stephanie Walterick, *The Prohibition of Muslim Headscarves from French Public Schools and Controversies Surrounding the Hijab in the Western World*, 20 TEMPLE INTERNATIONAL AND COMPARATIVE LAW JOURNAL (2006) 251.

72   Vasuki Nesiah, *Toward A Feminist Intersectionality: A Critique of U.S. Feminist Legal Scholarship*, 16 HARVARD WOMEN'S LAW JOURNAL (1993) 189.

73   Stephanie Walterick, *The Prohibition of Muslim Headscarves from French Public Schools and Controversies Surrounding the Hijab in the Western World, supra* Note 71.

74   Louise Halper, *Law and Women's Agency in Post-Revolutionary Iran*, 28 HARVARD JOURNAL OF LAW AND GENDER (2005) 85.

75   *Ibid.*

of context in which culture is intertwined with the issue of female subordination or female empowerment.[76]

Isabelle Gunning's approach includes another direction, one that questions whether the sense of superiority of some Western feminists, particularly feminists in the United States, leads to a faulty diagnosis of issues of women's empowerment, rights, and dignity.[77] She boldly suggests that United States feminists engage in "world traveling," by which she means that they should adopt an empathetic and humble approach to analyzing the conditions of women considered as "other." She exhorts her feminist colleagues to recognize the context of women's oppression elsewhere and to construct a transformative vision of equality that eschews degrading stereotypes about "civilized us" and "barbaric them."[78]

Angela Harris has adopted a somewhat similar theme. She cautions against a narrow essentialism that unquestioningly universalizes and homogenizes women's experiences, without regard to other important markers of women's identity like race and class.[79] Taunya Banks and Leslye Obiora have expanded upon this theme, arguing for a contextual approach to equality that embodies the multifaceted aspects of women's identities, and recognizes that such identities are fluid, constantly evolving, and at times contradictory.[80]

Another approach taken by some feminist legal theorists is to attack the very concept of a hierarchy of human rights. Instead, they call for an integrated approach to all layers of rights.[81] They insist upon eviscerating the divide between civil and political rights, that is, the so-called first-generation rights, on the one hand, and economic, social, and cultural rights, that is, the so-called second-generation rights, on the other hand. With great force and conviction, they argue that the

---

76   *See*, for example, Megan Davis, *The Globalisation of International Human Rights Law: Aboriginal Women and the Practice of Aboriginal Customary Law*, in FEMINIST PERSPECTIVES FOR THE NEW MILLENNIUM (Maureen Cain and Adrian eds. 2007) 137.

77   Isabelle Gunning, *Arrogant Perception: World Traveling and Multicultural Feminism: The Case of Female Genital Surgeries*, 23 COLUMBIA HUMAN RIGHTS LAW REVIEW (1992) 189.

78   *Ibid.*

79   Angela Harris, *Race and Essentialism in Feminist Theory*, 42 STANFORD LAW REVIEW (1990) 581.

80   Taunya Banks, *Toward a Global Critical Feminist Vision: Domestic Work and the Nanny Tax Debate*, 3 JOURNAL OF GENDER, RACE AND JUSTICE (1999) 1; Leslye Amede Obiora, *New Skin, Old Wine: (En)gaging Nationalism, Traditionalism, and Gender Relations*, 28 INDIANA LAW REVIEW (1995) 575. Professor Dianne Otto has also called for this approach. *See* Dianne Otto, *Rethinking the Universality of Human Rights Law*, 29 COLUMBIA HUMAN RIGHTS LAW REVIEW (1997) 1.

81   *See* Sandra Liebenberg, *The Value of Freedom in Interpreting Socio-Economic Rights*, 1 ACTA JURIDICA (2008) 149; *see also* Charlotte Bunch, *Women's Rights as Human Rights: Toward a Re-Vision of Human Rights*, 12 HUMAN RIGHTS QUARTERLY (1990) 486.

right to free speech deserves no greater respect than the right to health; each being predicated on the existence of the other.[82]

As is well known, second generation rights are not nearly as well integrated into the existing international frameworks requiring the reporting, evaluation, and monitoring of human rights violations. Group rights are even further lower in the hierarchy. Women's rights seem to partake at times of the quality of first generation rights and at other times of the quality of second generation rights. The argument of these feminists is basically that if women's lives are to be protected, then such distinctions must be eliminated.[83]

Feminist legal scholars have been adept at pointing out how the regulatory field, international law, and particularly the major regulatory body, the United Nations, has failed women by consistently ignoring their needs through its enforcement documents, procedures, enforcement mechanisms, and administration—in short the formal edifice of international law and the United Nations and its umbrella organizations.[84] These advocates continue to expose international law's patriarchal edifice. Changing the edifice will be an uphill battle, but it is arguable that gender equality is seen as a necessary goal and has been given the formal nod in previously recalcitrant quarters. One very hopeful development at the United Nations has been the establishment of the office of U.N. Women, led by the former President of Chile, Michelle Bachelet.[85] On September 14, 2010, the U.N. Secretary-General Ban Ki-Moon appointed Ms. Bachelet as Under-Secretary-General for U.N. Women. This new United Nations body for gender equality and the women's empowerment merged four agencies and offices: the U.N. Development Fund for Women, the Division for the Advancement of Women, the Office of the Special Adviser on Gender Issues, and the U.N. International Research and Training Institute for the Advancement of Women.[86] Other recent positive developments include the range of international conferences focusing on women's rights. These include the Beijing Conference and the Platform for Action in 1995, the Vienna Conference that preceded it in 1993, and the Population and Development Conference in Cairo

---

82   ENGENDERING HUMAN RIGHTS: CULTURAL AND SOCIO-ECONOMIC REALITIES IN AFRICA (Obioma Nnaemeka and Joy Ezeilo eds. 2005).

83   FAREDA BANDA, WOMEN, LAW AND HUMAN RIGHTS: AN AFRICAN PERSPECTIVE (2005); ALICE KESSLER-HARRIS, IN PURSUIT OF EQUITY: WOMEN, MEN, AND THE QUEST FOR ECONOMIC CITIZENSHIP IN 20TH CENTURY AMERICA (2001).

84   Hilary Charlesworth and Christine Chinkin, *Feminist Approaches to International Law, supra* Note 37.

85   *See* UNWOMEN.ORG, EXECUTIVE DIRECTOR at: *http://www.unwomen.org/ about-us/directorate/executive-director//*.

86   This new body became operational on January 1, 2011. *See http://www.un.org/en/ globalissues/women/*.

in 1994. One can therefore argue the international law landscape for feminist activists appears more amenable to change for women.[87]

Lesbian legal theory as exemplified by the work of Ruthann Robson has challenged the heterosexual orthodoxy of mainstream feminism and has generated a multi-layered theory of equality that eschews mere formal equality to one that embraces a more substantive version.[88]

Feminist theorists have come in several guises under divergent labels: cultural feminists, dominance theorists, socialist feminists, radical feminists, post-modernists, post-colonial feminists, and critical race feminists. Considering these many different approaches, it seems that there is a rather reductionist quality in labeling them all under the umbrella of Western feminists. It could be argued that these different approaches to women's equality represent such divergences in interpretation and strategy, that they in fact are different kinds of feminists and that sweeping them into one definition obscures their very real differences, both in theory and in practice.[89]

This issue raises interesting questions, but is outside the scope of this chapter. The different schools of feminists are mentioned to indicate the richness of the body of feminist legal theory and the creative approaches taken by the many feminisms to pursue the rights of women.[90]

---

87 HUMAN RIGHTS OF WOMEN: NATIONAL AND INTERNATIONAL PERSPECTIVE (Rebecca Cook ed. 1994).

88   *See* Ruthann Robson, *Assimilation, Marriage and Lesbian Liberation, supra* Note 31; *see also* Ruthann Robson, *Making Mothers: Lesbian Legal Theory and the Judicial Construction of Lesbian Mothers*, 22 WOMEN'S RIGHTS LAW REPORTER (2000) 15 and Ruthann Robson, *To Market, to Market: Considering Class in the Context of Lesbian Legal Theories and Reforms*, 5 UNIVERSITY OF SOUTHERN CALIFORNIA JOURNAL OF LAW AND WOMEN'S STUDIES (1995) 173.

89   These divergences in theory reflect the divergence and multifaceted reality of women's lives. They reflect the fact that a woman may be the President, or a Supreme Court judge, but she is just as likely to be a victim of trafficking or domestic violence. Women's achievement may be a cause for celebration, but the lack of achievement may provide a cause for concern. *See* Esther Vicente, *Feminist Legal Theories: My Own View From a Window in the Caribbean*, 66 REVISTA JURIDICA UNIVERSIDAD DE PUERTO RICO (1997) 211.

90   For a comprehensive analysis of these different schools of feminism, a small sampling is provided: UMA NARAYAN: DISLOCATING CULTURES: IDENTITIES, TRADITIONS AND THIRD WORLD FEMINISM (1997); FOR LESBIANS ONLY: A SEPARATIST ANTHOLOGY (Sarah Hoagland and Julia Penelope eds. 1988); THIS BRIDGE CALL MY BACK: WRITINGS BY RADICAL WOMEN OF COLOR (Cherrie Moraga and Gloria Anzaldua eds. 1981); FEMINISM AND POSTCOLONIAL THEORY: A READER (Reina Lewis and Sara Mills eds. 2003); VALENTINE M. MOGHADAM, GLOBALIZING WOMEN: TRANSNATIONAL FEMINIST NETWORKS (2005).

The next few pages will explore the achievements of global feminists by focusing on the four major initiatives undertaken by the United Nations to pursue women's equality.[91]

CEDAW

CEDAW adopted in 1979 by the U.N. General Assembly, is the most important global document relating to women's rights.[92] Consisting of a preamble and thirty articles, it defines in detail what constitutes discrimination against women and sets up an agenda for national action to end such discrimination. Many countries have adopted several of CEDAW's provisions in their national laws outlawing discrimination against women. For example, Australia's Sex Discrimination Act passed in 1986 has incorporated many of CEDAW's principles.[93]

CEDAW defines discrimination against women as,

> ... any distinction, exclusion or restriction made on the basis of sex which has the effect or purpose of impairing or nullifying the recognition, enjoyment or exercise by women, irrespective of their marital status, on a basis of equality of men and women, of human rights and fundamental freedoms in the political, economic, social, cultural, civil or any other field.[94]

This definition encompasses a broad definition of equality although the comparison with men—"on the basis of equality of men and women"—has generated substantial debate.[95] This debate mostly revolves around notions of sameness and difference, and of the proper accommodation of women's unique experiences in the assessment of equality.[96] This is most pronounced around women's reproductive capacity and the status of pregnancy in the definition of equality.

---

91   With respect to the implementation of international law and different feminist approaches, *see* R. Christopher Preston and Ronald Z. Ahrens, *United Nations Convention Documents in Light of Feminist Theory*, 8 MICHIGAN JOURNAL OF GENDER AND LAW (2001) 1.

92   CEDAW, *supra* Chapter 1, Note 23.

93   SEX DISCRIMINATION ACT OF 1984.

94   CEDAW, *supra* Chapter 1, Note 23.

95   *See*, for example, CAROLINE A. FORELL AND DONNA M. MATTHEWS, A LAW OF HER OWN: THE REASONABLE WOMAN AS A MEASURE OF MAN (2000); *see also* AT THE BOUNDARIES OF LAW: FEMINISM AND LEGAL THEORY (Martha Albertson Fineman and Nancy Sweet Thomadsen Eds. 1990).

96   *See* Nancy Levit, *A Different Kind of Sameness: Beyond Formal Equality and Antisubordination Principles in Gay Legal Theory and Constitutional Doctrine*, 61 OHIO STATE LAW JOURNAL (2000) 867.

Governments that sign CEDAW commit themselves to undertake a series of measures to end discrimination against women in all forms, including the incorporation of the principle of gender equality in their legal system, and the abolition of all gender discriminatory laws. Governments also undertake to provide effective machinery, for example, national and local institutions that pursue the protection of women's rights and equality.[97]

CEDAW encapsulates equality in both the public and private spheres and includes a panoply of civil and political rights, as well as social, cultural, and economic rights. These include the right to vote as well as the right to education, health, and employment. Governments agree to "take all appropriate measures" to ensure that women can enjoy all their human rights and fundamental freedoms.[98] These include active measures against trafficking and other forms of economic exploitation of women.[99]

Significantly, CEDAW affirms the reproductive rights of women and targets culture and tradition as influential forces shaping gender roles and family relations.[100] Countries that have ratified or acceded to CEDAW are legally bound to put its provisions into practice. They are also committed to submit national reports, at least every four years, on measures they have taken to comply with their treaty obligations. More governments have signed on and ratified CEDAW than almost any other international legal instrument. Not surprisingly, these signatures reflect a symbolism that unfortunately has not translated into consistent substantive changes for the majority of the world's women.[101]

Vienna Declaration on Violence Against Women

It is the Vienna Declaration that pushed the problem of violence against women to the forefront of the struggle for women's human rights.[102] In 1993, the United Nations at its World Conference on Human Rights in Vienna recognized the specificity of women's rights as part of the international human rights agenda.[103] At the closure of the conference, the Vienna Declaration specifically identified

---

97 Sally Engle Merry, *Constructing a Global Law: Violence against Women and the Human Rights System*, 28 LAW AND SOCIAL INQUIRY (FALL 2003) 941, 944.

98 CEDAW, *supra* Chapter 1, Note 23, Part I, Article 2(E).

99 *Ibid.* Part I, Article 6.

100 *Ibid*, Part I, Article 5.

101 *See* Jennifer T. Sudduth, *CEDAW's Flaws: A Critical Analysis of Why CEDAW Is Failing to Protect a Woman's Right to Education in Pakistan*, 38 JOURNAL OF LAW AND EDUCATION (2009) 563.

102 *See* Katherine M. Franke, *Gendered Subjects of Transitional Justice*, 15 COLUMBIA JOURNAL OF GENDER AND LAW (2006) 813.

103 UN GENERAL ASSEMBLY DECEMBER 1993, 85TH PLENARY MEETING, DECLARATION ON THE ELIMINATION OF VIOLENCE AGAINST WOMEN.

the "human rights of women" as "an inalienable, integral and indivisible part of universal human rights."[104] The Declaration goes on to state that "the full and equal participation of women in political, civil, economic, social and cultural life, at the national, regional and international levels, and the eradication of all forms of discrimination on the grounds of sex are priority objectives of the international community."[105] The Declaration also condemns "[g]ender-based violence and all forms of sexual harassment and exploitation," and calls upon the General Assembly to "adopt a draft declaration on violence against women."[106] The Draft Declaration adopted by the United Nations General Assembly in 1994 noted that "violence against women is an obstacle to the achievement of equality."[107] The Declaration also recognized both the legal and extra-legal measures required to stem violence against women, encouraging governments to focus on education and to adopt steps to modify cultural and social patterns that give rise to prejudice and odious stereotypes that perpetuate violence against women.[108]

The Beijing Declaration and Platform for Action

The Beijing Declaration, adopted at the Fourth World Conference on Women in 1995, undertakes to "advance the goals of equality, development and peace for all women" across the globe, noting the diversity of women's experiences and the uneven progress towards gender equality.[109] The Declaration is expansive—embracing principles of equality and dignity and building on human rights instruments since the adoption of the Charter of the United Nations and the Universal Declaration of Human Rights.[110]

The Declaration embraces a range of civil and political rights as well as a host of social and economic rights including the right to health and access to resources.[111] The Declaration particularly notes the eradication of poverty as a precondition for the pursuit of gender equality, as well as the elimination of violence against women.[112] Although highly aspirational in substance, the Declaration pre-empts

---

104   *Ibid* at 18.

105   *Ibid.*

106   *Ibid.*

107   *Ibid.*

108   *Ibid.*

109   BEIJING DECLARATION AND PLATFORM FOR ACTION, FOURTH WORLD CONFERENCE ON WOMEN, 15 SEPTEMBER 1995, A/CONF.177/20 (1995) AND A/CONF.177/20/ADD.1 (1995).

110   *Ibid.*

111   *Ibid.*

112   *Ibid.*

the Beijing Platform for Action, which prescribes concrete steps that governments need to take to ensure that the commitments in the Declaration can be achieved.[113]

The Platform for Action has been revisited in two major international meetings to assess the progress that countries have made towards achieving the goals outlined in the Beijing Declaration. In both the Beijing Plus 5 as well as the Beijing Plus 10 meetings, women activists applauded the steps that had been taken to ensure equality for women, but they also highlighted the disappointingly little progress that had been made in many countries, particularly the poorer countries.[114]

These four major initiatives by no means capture the range of activities relating to the pursuit of women's rights and gender equality at the global level. But they do capture the flavor of the trajectory at the global level, and continued advocacy on the part of women advocates to ensure the centrality of women in the United Nations human rights processes. Many more initiatives are mentioned in the timeline at the end of this chapter. They include Resolution 1993/46, which was adopted on March 8, 1993 by the United Nations High Commissioner for Human Rights, and which calls for a greater integration of the rights of women into the mainstream of United Nations human rights mechanisms.[115] The following year, in 1994, the International Conference on Population and Development in Cairo, despite major controversies, reaffirmed women's and girls' rights to autonomy with respect to reproductive choices.[116]

Two important initiatives regarding violence against women include U.N. Security Council Resolution 1325, which calls for the active engagement of women in peace and security, including their role in decision making.[117] In addition, the judgment of Judge Navi Pillay in the International Criminal Tribunal in Rwanda's decision to declare rape as a war crime generated a significant conceptual shift in the way that the international community regards crimes against women during

---

113 *Ibid.*

114 FIVE-YEAR REVIEW OF THE IMPLEMENTATION OF THE BEIJING DECLARATION AND PLATFORM FOR ACTION (BEIJING + 5) HELD IN THE GENERAL ASSEMBLY, 5–9 JUNE 2000 at: *http://www.un.org/womenwatch/daw/followup/beijing+5.htm*; TEN-YEAR REVIEW AND APPRAISAL OF THE IMPLEMENTATION OF THE BEIJING DECLARATION AND PLATFORM FOR ACTION AND THE OUTCOME OF THE TWENTY-THIRD SPECIAL SESSION OF THE GENERAL ASSEMBLY HELD DURING THE FORTY-NINTH SESSION OF THE CSW, FROM 28 FEBRUARY TO 11 MARCH 2005, at: *http://www.un.org/womenwatch/daw/review/english/49sess.htm*.

115 OFFICE OF THE HIGH COMMISSIONER FOR HUMAN RIGHTS, INTEGRATING THE RIGHTS OF WOMEN INTO THE HUMAN RIGHTS MECHANISMS OF THE UNITED NATIONS (March 8, 1993) at: *www.amun.org/undocs/chr_1993_46.pdf*.

116 REPORT OF THE INTERNATIONAL CONFERENCE ON POPULATION AND DEVELOPMENT (October 18, 1994), at: *http://www.un.org/popin/icpd/conference/offeng/poa.html*.

117 RESOLUTION 1325 (2000) Adopted by the Security Council at its 4213th meeting, on October 31, 2000 at: *http://www.un.org/events/res_1325e.pdf*.

times of conflict,[118] and laid the foundations for the codification of sexual and gender crimes as war crimes and crimes against humanity in the Rome Statute of the International Criminal Court.[119]

Women's Continuing Goals and Aspirations

Many of the goals demanded by women on the global level remain aspirational.[120] However, the script for women's emancipation and equality, no longer written only by Western feminists peddling a brand of essentialist politics, is now multi-authored. In short, the trenchant claims of universalism continue to be challenged and modified to accommodate competing visions of human rights interpretation and enforcement.[121] But the challenges to universality cannot hide the universal realities of women's lives.[122]

---

118   *The Prosecutor v Jean-Paul Akaysu* (Trial Judgment) ICTR-96-4-T, September 2, 1998.

119   ROME STATUTE OF THE INTERNATIONAL CRIMINAL COURT, UN Doc. A/Conf. 183/9 entered into force on July 1, 2002, at: *http://untreaty.un.org/cod/icc/statute/ romefra.htm*. Article 7 of the Statute provides as follows:

"Crimes against humanity: For the purpose of this Statute, 'crime against humanity' means any of the following acts when committed as part of a widespread or systematic attack directed against any civilian population, with knowledge of the attack:

... (g) Rape, sexual slavery, enforced prostitution, forced pregnancy, enforced sterilization, or any other form of sexual violence of comparable gravity;

(h) Persecution against any identifiable group or collectivity on political, racial, national, ethnic, cultural, religious, gender as defined in paragraph 3, or other grounds that are universally recognized as impermissible under international law, in connection with any act referred to in this paragraph or any crime within the jurisdiction of the Court;

... (2) For the purpose of paragraph 1:

... (f) 'Forced pregnancy' means the unlawful confinement of a woman forcibly made pregnant, with the intent of affecting the ethnic composition of any population or carrying out other grave violations of international law. This definition shall not in any way be interpreted as affecting national laws relating to pregnancy;

... (3) For the purpose of this Statute, it is understood that the term 'gender' refers to the two sexes, male and female, within the context of society. The term 'gender' does not indicate any meaning different from the above."

120   David L. Neal, *Women as a Social Group: Recognizing Sex-Based Persecution as Grounds for Asylum*, 20 COLUMBIA HUMAN RIGHTS LAW REVIEW (1988) 203, 223–4.

121   *See* Makau wa Mutua, *Savages, Victims, and Saviors: The Metaphor of Human Rights*, 42 HARVARD INTERNATIONAL LAW JOURNAL (2001) 201; *see also* Douglas Lee Donoho, *Autonomy, Self-Governance, and the Margins of Appreciation: Developing a Jurisprudence of Diversity within Universal Human Rights*, 15 EMORY INTERNATIONAL LAW REVIEW (2001) 391.

122   *See* Penelope E. Andrews, *Women's Human Rights and the Conversation Across Cultures*, 67 ALBANY LAW REVIEW (2003) 609.

The lesson for women, from the history of the Canadian Charter process, to the South African constitutional process, to the Rwandan transitional process, and the Afghan constitutional process, is that incorporating gender equality provisions in the Constitution is a complicated, frustrating, difficult, and stressful course of action.[123] Political and constitutional negotiations lead to alliances made and broken, friendships formed and friendships ruined, hopes raised and hopes dashed, endless sleepless nights, much conflict, and many fights.

But this process is essentially the easy part. Once gender equality is incorporated in the constitution, the hard work commences; work that has to do with enforcement, regulation, and the need to pursue a lasting culture of rights. South Africa illustrates this problem most acutely. In that country, with the most admirable and expansive Constitution and Bill of Rights, and a constitutional jurisprudence that has the potential to be transformative, far too many women's lives continue to be wretched. This is reflected in national statistics on poverty and economic inequality, violence against women, and a devastating HIV/AIDS epidemic.[124]

Another example of the fissure between the formal guarantee of rights and their implementation on the ground is to be found in Australia, a country with one of the highest standards of living in the world. There the situation of far too many indigenous women resemble those of women in the poorer global south.[125]

So the challenges today are somewhat different than what they were decades ago. But in some ways they are similar. We still have countries in the world where women do not have the right to vote, where they are systematically erased from public life, and where the most egregious kinds of abuses are seen as normal. In these countries, formal legal requirements of full citizenship are still some way off.[126]

But for those women who live under constitutional frameworks or legal regimes that promise equality, there is a different challenge, namely, how to translate that legal equality into political, social, and economic equality.[127] This means addressing poverty that is the reality of far too many women, particularly

---

123   *See* Adrien K. Wing and Samuel P. Nielson, *An Agenda for the Obama Administration on Gender Equality: Lessons from Abroad*, 107 MICHIGAN LAW REVIEW (2009) 124; E. Diane Pask, *Canadian Family Law and Social Policy: A New Generation*, 31 HOUSTON LAW REVIEW (1994) 499; Jennifer Kristen Lee, *Legal Reform to Advance the Rights of Women in Afghanistan within the Framework of Islam*, 49 SANTA CLARA LAW REVIEW (2009) 531.

124   UNITED NATIONS CHILDREN'S FUND STATISTICS REPORT: SOUTH AFRICA at: *http://www.unicef.org/infobycountry/southafrica_statistics.html*.

125   UN PERMANENT FORUM OF INDIGENOUS PEOPLES, REPORT ON THE STATE OF THE WORLD'S INDIGENOUS PEOPLES, 2009 U.N. Doc ST/ESA/328.

126   UN WOMEN, IN PURSUIT OF JUSTICE: PROGRESS OF THE WORLD'S WOMEN 2011–2012 at: *http://progress.unwomen.org/wp-content/uploads/2011/06/EN-Summary-Progress-of-the-Worlds-Women1.pdf*.

127   WOMEN MAKING CONSTITUTIONS (Alexandra Dobowolsky and Vivian Hart eds. 2004); *see also* AT THE BOUNDARIES OF LAW, *supra* Note 95.

in Africa, but also elsewhere. It is undisputed that poverty carries with it all kinds of collateral consequences: women forced into prostitution, being trafficked, disproportionately impacted by the HIV/AIDS epidemic, and suffering total and utter desperation and subjugation.[128]

It means addressing the systemic and widespread violence that women are subjected to as a matter of course, whether it is in the war-torn Congo, where girls and women are routinely captured as sex slaves or raped in alarming numbers, or in Pakistan where women who marry against their family wishes are brutally assaulted or murdered, or in Kenya where the rape of young girls is seen as a cure for HIV/AIDS, or immunization against the virus.[129] It also means addressing the run of the mill violence perpetrated on women in the U.S.A., where a ubiquitous cosmetic surgery industry results in widespread harm from breast augmentation surgeries, liposuction, and other medical procedures carried out in a culture that continues to insist that women conform to a retrogressive stereotype.[130]

It means addressing the cultural norms and practices that continue to subjugate women. Culture should be a sword where rampant assimilation demands a bland sameness—and should be fiercely protected. But culture should not be a shield to subjugate a society's female members.

With the rise of fundamentalisms everywhere—whether it's the evangelized movement in the U.S.A., Uganda, or elsewhere, Islamic fundamentalists, or their Hindu or Jewish counterparts, it is time we push hard for a gender fundamentalism, a term used by Mary Anne Case.[131] This gender fundamentalism, whilst recognizing

---

128   *See* Janie A. Chuang, *Rescuing Trafficking from Ideological Capture: Prostitution Reform and Anti-Trafficking Law and Policy*, 158 UNIVERSITY OF PENNSYLVANIA LAW REVIEW (2010) 1655, 1659.

129   Katy Glassboro, *Forced Marriage Appeal May Influence ICC*, INTERNATIONAL JUSTICE - ICC ACR ISSUE 123, August 6, 2007 at: *http://iwpr.net/report-news/forced-marriage-appeal-may-influence-icc*; Khalid Tanver, *Family Suspected Of Electrocuting Pakistani Bride*, MSNBC.COM, January 23, 2011, at: *http://www.msnbc.msn.com/id/41220289/ns/world_news-south_and_central_asia/t/family-suspected-electrocuting-pakistani-bride/#.tybxncoq324*; UNAIDS, VIOLENCE AGAINST WOMEN AND GIRLS IN THE ERA OF HIV/AIDS A SITUATION AND RESPONSE ANALYSIS IN KENYA (June 2006) at: *http://data.unaids.org/pub/report/2006/20060630_gcwa_re_violence_women_girls_kenya_en.pdf*.

130   *See, Demand for Surgery Rebounds by almost 9%*, AMERICAN SOCIETY FOR AESTHETIC PLASTIC SURGERY, April 4, 2011 at: *http://www.surgery.org/media/news-releases/demand-for-plastic-surgery-rebounds-by-almost-9%25* (stating that almost 9.5 million cosmetic procedures were done in the U.S. in 2010 and the most frequently performed procedure was breast augmentation). *See also* RHIAN PARKER, WOMEN, DOCTORS AND COSMETIC SURGERY: NEGOTIATING THE "NORMAL" BODY (2010) and SUSAN M. ZIMMERMAN, SILICONE SURVIVORS: WOMEN'S EXPERIENCE WITH BREAST IMPLANTS (1998).

131   Mary Anne Case, *Feminist Fundamentalism on the Frontier between Government and Family Responsibility for Children*, UTAH LAW REVIEW (2009) 382 at: *http://epubs.*

our differences steeped in history, geography, race, ethnicity, class, and other indicators, must not equivocate at all when it comes to eradicating the continued subordination of women.

In thinking about a global onslaught against women's subordination and a constant commitment to women's rights and gender equality, it may be worth recalling that powerful and effective global force for change that was the anti-apartheid movement. Activists committed to the eradication of apartheid lobbied, protested, agitated, and generally raised hell to undermine and finally dismantle apartheid.[132] Similarly, it may be worth considering ways that the global community may garner its energies to eradicate what Rebecca Cook has termed "gender apartheid."[133]

To capture the analysis pursued in this chapter, an international women's rights timeline is provided in Table 1.

Table 1   International Women's Rights Timeline

Year	Event	Link
1985	Third World Conference on Women	*http://www.earthsummit2002.org/toolkits/ women/un-doku/un-conf/narirobi-2.html*
1993	Vienna Declaration and Program of Action	*http://www.unhchr.ch/huridocda/huridoca. nsf/(symbol)/a.conf.157.23.en*
	Adoption of the Declaration on the Elimination of Violence Against Women	*http://www2.ohchr.org/english/law/ eliminationvaw.htm*
	U.N. Commission on Human Rights adopts Resolution 1993/46 on March 8, aimed at integrating the rights of women into mainstream U.N. human rights mechanisms	*www.amun.org/undocs/chr_1993_46.pdf*
1994	International Conference on Population and Development in Cairo—a major step forward for women's and girls' rights to control their own bodies	*http://www.un.org/popin/icpd/conference/ offeng/poa.html*

continued

---

utah.edu/index.php/ulr/article/viewFile/173/146.

132   HAKAN THORN, ANTI-APARTHEID AND THE EMERGENCE OF A GLOBAL CIVIL SOCIETY (2006). *See also* ADRIAN GUELKE, RETHINKING THE RISE AND FALL OF APARTHEID: SOUTH AFRICA AND WORLD POLITICS (2005).

133   Rebecca J. Cook, *The Elimination of Sexual Apartheid: Prospects for the Fourth World Conference on Women*, 5 ASIL ISSUE PAPERS ON WORLD CONFERENCES (1995) 3.

Year	Event	Link
1995	Fourth World Conference on Women where the Beijing Declaration and Platform for Action (BPFA) was adopted	*http://www.un.org/womenwatch/daw/beijing/*
	The World Summit for Social Development in Copenhagen where women mobilized to ensure that women's issues are on the global agenda	*http://www.un.org/documents/ga/conf166/ aconf166-9.htm*
1998	International Criminal Tribunal in Rwanda declares rape a war crime: *The Prosecutor v. Jean-Paul Akayesu (Trial Judgement)*, ICTR-96-4-T, International Criminal Tribunal for Rwanda (ICTR), 2 September 1998	*http://www.unhcr.org/refworld/ docid/40278fbb4.html*
2000	U.N. Security Council Resolution 1325 on Women in Conflict	*www.un.org/events/res_1325e.pdf*
	U.N. Millennium Declaration was adopted. It provides specifically: • Freedom. Men and women have the right to live their lives and raise their children in dignity, free from hunger and from the fear of violence, oppression or injustice. Democratic and participatory governance based on the will of the people best assures these rights. • Equality. No individual and no nation must be denied the opportunity to benefit from development. The equal rights and opportunities of women and men must be assured.	*http://www.un.org/millennium/declaration/ ares552e.htm*
	Five Year Review of Beijing Declaration and Platform for Action	*http://www.un.org/womenwatch/daw/ followup/beijing+5.htm*

Year	Event	Link
2002	Rome Statute enters into force and codifies sexual and gender crimes as war crimes and crimes against humanity	*http://www.icc-cpi.int/NR/rdonlyres/ EA9AEFF7-5752-4F84-BE94- 0A655EB30E16/0/Rome_Statute_English.pdf*
	Women's International War Crimes Tribunal on Japan's Military Sexual Slavery held to prosecute WWII abuses against women	*http://www1.jca.apc.org/vaww-net-japan/ english/womenstribunal2000/Judgement.pdf*
2005	Ten Year Review of Beijing Platform for Action where women successfully defeated U.S. proposal for anti-abortion amendment to the Declaration	*http://www.un.org/womenwatch/daw/Review/ english/49sess.htm*
2008	U.N. Security Council Resolution 1820 which for the first time recognized sexual violence in conflict as a matter of international peace and security	*http://www.unifem.org/gender_issues/ women_war_peace/unscr_1820.php*
2010	15 Year Review of Beijing Platform for Action	*http://www.un.org/womenwatch/daw/ beijing15/index.html*
	Millennium Goals Review Summit	Progress Chart: *http://unstats.un.org/unsd/mdg/Resources/ Static/Products/Progress2010/MDG_ Report_2010_Progress_Chart_En.pdf* MDG 2010 Report: *http://www.un.org/millenniumgoals/pdf/ MDG%20Report%202010%20En%20 r15%20-low%20res%2020100615%20-.pdf* The Summit's Outcome Document: *http://content.undp.org/go/cms-service/ download/asset?asset_id=2802060*
2011	Creation of U.N. Women	*www.unwomen.org*

Chapter 4
Culture and Women's Rights:
A Continuing Dilemma

A woman in a veil is protected like a pearl in an oyster shell.[1]

We know about knives that can heal: the knife that saves the life of a baby in distress, the knife that cuts the cancerous growths in our breasts, the knife that straightens our spines .... But we also know about other knives: the knife that cuts off our toes so that our feet will fit into elegant shoes, ... the knife that slices our labia in episiotomies and other forms of genital mutilation ... And now we are coming to know the knives and needles of the cosmetic surgeon —the knives that promise to sculpt our bodies, to restore our youth, to create beauty out of what was ugly and ordinary ....[2]

Introduction

The opening quotations in this chapter offer contrasting perspectives on the image of women's bodies as seen through the prisms of different cultural norms. The diametrically opposed views of women's bodies expressed therein highlight cultural differences that can easily become manifest in a nation's laws, social structure, and political system, thereby rendering acute how fraught the debates around culture and women's rights can be. Of the pantheon of issues that affect any discussion regarding the rights of women, surely it is the uneasy relationship between the demands of cultural identity and belonging, on the one hand, and the demands of human rights and dignity of women, on the other hand, that are paramount.

Whether human rights advocates are engaged in an analysis regarding the symbolism of the wearing of the veils in public spaces and weighing whether governments ought to ban such wearing, or engaged in assessing whether polygamy and cultural practices such as dowry are consistent with respect for women's rights, human rights advocates often experience a genuine tension. This tension involves two established iconic aspects of the human rights movement,

---

1   AZAR NAFISI, READING LOLITA IN TEHRAN (2003) 200.

2   Kathryn Pauly Morgan, *Women and the Knife: Cosmetic Surgery and the Colonization of Women's Bodies*, in NAGGING QUESTIONS: FEMINIST ETHICS IN EVERYDAY LIFE (Dana E. Bushnell ed. 1995) 306, 311.

namely, the right of nations, communities and individuals to cultural autonomy and the rights of women to equality.

This issue is not limited to women living in developing nations. Here in the United States, the culture is immersed in visions of women that are racially tinged, reflecting preferences for white beauty standards.[3] Moreover, that vision incorporates too much the legacy of the role of women in terms of their domestic roles.[4] These visions persist despite the achievement of tremendous gains in equality in the United States for women, as evidenced by demographic, economic, and social statistics.[5] The normalcy of this situation is taken for granted and generates very little debate, thereby aiding the perpetuation of the cultural stereotype of the ideal woman.[6]

Chapter 3 earlier examined how feminist legal theorists and women activists began the transformation of the formal edifice of law to incorporate the many varied concerns and experiences of women. It also revealed how global collaborative efforts have led to successful campaigns to improve the lives of women in the legal system and through governmental policy. A lingering concern of women around the world is the relationship between culture and women's equality. These concerns are taken up in this chapter. This perennial question of the relationship and impact of women's rights to and on cultural traditions and value, continues to re-surface whenever reform is sought in legal and extra-legal processes and practices that discriminate against women and that aid their subordination.

'Culture' Confronts the Global Feminist Campaign

The issue of harmful cultural practices in the context of women's rights gained prominence during the 1990s when a global movement was organized to outlaw the practice of female genital surgeries in parts of Africa.[7] During highly publicized campaigns of the activities of these global activists, a large number of whom were United States feminists, many third world, particularly African feminists, became

---

3   *See* KATHY PEISS, HOPE IN A JAR: THE MAKING OF AMERICA'S BEAUTY CULTURE (2011). *See also* Lucinda Finley, *Feminist Jurisprudence*, 1 COLUMBIA JOURNAL OF GENDER AND LAW (1991) 5.

4   For an interesting comparative perspective on these issues, *see* DIVIDING THE DOMESTIC: MEN, WOMEN AND HOUSEHOLD WORK IN CROSS-NATIONAL PERSPECTIVE (Judith Treas and Sonja Drobnic eds. 2010).

5   *See* Hanna Rosin, *The End of Men*, THE ATLANTIC, July/August 2010 at: *http://www.theatlantic.com/magazine/archive/2010/07/the-end-of-men/8135/*.

6   EVE ENSLER, THE GOOD BODY (2004); ROBIN TOLMACH LAKOFF AND RAQUEL L. SCHERR, FACE VALUE: THE POLITICS OF BEAUTY (1984).

7   Meredith Aherne, *Olowo v Ashcroft: Granting Parental Asylum Based on Child's Refugee Status*, 18 PACE INTERNATIONAL LAW REVIEW (2006) 317, 320 (referring to the 1999 US AID forum on FGM),

alarmed. This alarm surfaced not because of disagreement with the ultimate goal of eradicating an obviously egregious practice, but because many women activists, especially those in the global South, had reservations about tactics utilized in the campaigns.[8] Reflecting this alarm, eight African feminists in 1993 wrote a letter to the *New York Times* complaining about an Op-ed article on Alice Walker's film and novel, *Possessing the Secret of Joy*, condemning the practice of female genital surgeries.[9] In addition to writing the book, Alice Walker also produced a documentary, entitled *Warrior Marks*, based on her experiences of investigating the practice of female genital surgeries in West Africa.[10] As an alternative to the 'Alice Walker' approach, the eight African feminists emphasized the effective campaigns to outlaw female genital surgeries conducted by women in several African countries in collaboration with village elders and religious leaders.[11]

Other global campaigns by feminist activists of the global North denouncing a range of traditional, cultural, or religious practices have also been criticized for their tactics, in particular the projection of evangelism invoking the narrative of rescue.[12] This narrative, a recurrent theme in relations between West and East and between North and South, has as its principal ingredient the notion that women in non-Western societies need to be rescued from unfeeling, primitive, barbaric, and oppressive cultural practices imposed upon them by their fellow citizens. This theme, or narrative, resonates in much of the scholarship and activism of feminist advocates from the developed world.[13]

These campaigns to combat and end cultural practices that are indeed harmful and discriminatory, very often failed to appreciate the full circumstances in which a particular community's traditions and laws operated and functioned to sustain

---

8   Christine J. Walley, *Searching for "Voices": Feminism, Anthropology and the Global Debate over Female Genital Operations*, 12 CULTURAL ANTHROPOLOGY (1997) 403.

9   Seble Dawit and Salem Mekuria, *The West Just Doesn't Get It*, NEW YORK TIMES, December 7, 1993, at A27.

10   ALICE WALKER, WARRIOR MARKS: FEMALE GENITAL MUTILATION AND THE SEXUAL BLINDING OF WOMEN (1996). The film of the same name was produced in 1993.

11   In contrast to the response to Alice Walker's endeavors, in 2004, Ousmane Sembène, the Senegalese film director, produced a film, *Moolade*, that criticized female genital surgeries in West Africa. *Moolade* was acclaimed at the African Film Festival in New York, and was praised for its indictment of the practice. This may be a result of his status as a respected African artist, or it may be that by 2004 eradicating the practice has acquired global consensus.

12   *See*, for example, THE POLITICS OF SURVIVAL IN SUB-SAHARAN AFRICA (Gwendolyn Mikell ed. 1997); *see also* Leti Volpp, *Feminism v Multiculturalism*, 101 COLUMBIA LAW REVIEW (2001) 1181.

13   Ratna Kapur, *The Tragedy of Victimization Rhetoric: Resurrecting the "Native" Subject in International Post-Global Feminist Legal Politics*, 15 HARVARD HUMAN RIGHTS JOURNAL (2002) 1.

the communities.[14] These cultural practices, in many instances, had their genesis in the complexities and contradictions of interactions of law, status, relationships, identity, traditions, and community. The global campaigns tended, however, to ignore the nuanced and complex nature of the individual's existence, development, and engagement as a function of these interactive processes.[15]

Perhaps not surprisingly, the campaigns generated from the global North paid scant or little attention to the efforts by women in those societies who worked hard to eradicate or ameliorate the harmful cultural practices, while at the same time trying to change the cultural norms which supported them. This was particularly true of the intensive efforts conducted by women in Africa, as well as by men, to outlaw the practice of female genital surgeries.[16] It has been a severe shortcoming of the scholarship and literature of feminist campaigns in the West to overlook, ignore, and not credit the industry, persistence, and bravery of local women in the global South to transform their lives by meeting head-on the arrayed forces behind these cultural practices. The result has been the creation of tensions in which human rights advocates from the global South accuse their counterparts in the global North of cultural arrogance and insensitivity.[17]

The colonial legacy of imperial ventures, anthropological theories, and excessive religious zeal, and a hyperactive sense of mission to bring Christianity and civilization to indigenous communities, have provided the justification for this narrative of rescue and salvation in which the cultures and traditions of non-Western peoples are always to be put under incriminating scrutiny, and rendered suspect as something exotic or oriental.[18] This proved true for non-Western peoples under colonial rule, when missionaries and colonial administrators regarded the civilizing mission as destiny, and proved equally true when non-Western peoples were the beneficiaries of developmental assistance. During the colonial period, the pejorative notion of the "other," that is, the colonized individuals, was a parallel

---

14   For a thoughtful analysis focusing on the Alice Walker campaign, *see* Joseph McLaren, *Alice Walker and the Legacy of African-American Discourse on Africa*, in THE AFRICAN DIASPORA: AFRICAN ORIGINS AND NEW WORLD IDENTITIES (Isadore Okpewhu *et al.* eds. 1999) 525.

15   *See* Kathleen Mahoney, *Theoretical Perspectives on Women's Human Rights and Strategies for Their Implementation*, 21 BROOKLYN JOURNAL OF INTERNATIONAL LAW (1996) 799, 832.

16   *See* MARIE-HELENE MOTTIN-SYLLA AND JOELLE PALMIERI, CONFRONTING FEMALE GENITAL MUTILATION: THE ROLE OF YOUTH AND ICTS IN CHANGING AFRICA (2011); *see also* Marc Lacey, *African Women Gather to Denounce Genital Cutting*, NEW YORK TIMES, February 6, 2003 at: *http://www.nytimes.com/2003/02/06/world/african-women-gather-to-denounce-genital-cutting.html*.

17   *See* Ratna Kapur, *The Tragedy of Victimization Rhetoric: Resurrecting the "Native" Subject in International Post-Global Feminist Legal Politics*, *supra* Note 13.

18   EDWARD SAID, ORIENTALISM (1979).

narrative used for justifying the underlying values and practices of colonialism.[19] This "other" was an object of scorn, but also an object of paternalism and patronage. This duality is reflected in the reaction of the colonial authorities to the practice of polygamy in Africa, where it is noted that the polygamous husband:....

> had too much land, leisure and sex. Instead of working for an employer, as was his proper destiny, he battened in ease on the labor of his wives. African women, said the colonists, were hardly better off than slaves.[20]

Invocation of this parallel narrative allowed relationships fostered between colonizer and colonized to range between outright hostility and benign caring, but always one where colonial authority was dominant.[21] Karen Blixen's character in the popular 1980s movie, "Out of Africa," masterfully captured the essence of the relationship in her constant references to "my Kikuyu."

Postcolonialism, Law and Development

Ironically, during the period of decolonization in the 1960s and the growth of fledgling democracies, a wave of Westerners, mostly United State, lawyers, and legal scholars arrived with all sorts of ideas on how to create a legal system and thereby establish the rule of law to support the emergent goals of liberation and democracy, and thus realize new found political possibilities.[22] I say this was ironic because the arrivals generated accusations of a new form of colonialism.[23]

The trend and arrivals intensified during the 1980s, when one after another democracy-labeled project was established in countries making a transition from

---

19   Deborah M. Weissman, *The Human Rights Dilemma: Rethinking the Humanitarian Project*, 35 COLUMBIA HUMAN RIGHTS LAW REVIEW (2004) 259. "Colonialism has characteristically invoked Manichean dichotomies to justify the exercise of power over alien peoples, of civilization and enlightenment on one side, and barbarism and backwardness on the other. Colonizers assigned themselves the task of uplifting 'uncivilized' people who represented 'the negation of values', and set out to transform norms of the colonized cultures to correspond to the standards of morality as conceived in the world of the colonizer." *Ibid* at 267.

20   HAROLD JACK SIMONS, AFRICAN WOMEN: THEIR LEGAL STATUS IN SOUTH AFRICA (1986) 15, 21–2.

21   EDWARD SAID, ORIENTALISM, *supra* Note 18.

22   B. Seidman, *Law and Development: A General Model*, 6 LAW AND SOCIETY (1972) 311.

23   David Trubek and Marc Galanter, *Scholars in Self-Estrangement: Some Reflections on the Crisis in Law and Development Studies in the United States*, 1974 WISCONSIN LAW JOURNAL REVIEW (1974) 1062.

colonialism, or subjugation, to independence and democracy.[24] The efforts were highly profiled in places like Latin America, Eastern Europe, and many parts of Africa.[25] The rush of Western lawyers was inspired by a desire to assist lawmakers and lawyers in newly independent states in carrying out their goal of developing and installing modern constitutions and laws consistent with maintenance of a modern democratic state. These Western lawyers, the first arrivals of the future human rights brigades, were keen supporters of transforming the entire legal, political, and social institutions that previously existed in the countries.[26]

Widely referred to as "law and development scholars" they were, in the main, heartened by legal victories achieved in the United States civil rights movement. They saw these successes not only as positive but also as models of how the legal systems of developing nations should function. That they had power and influence in developing nations that far exceeded what they could exercise in their own countries, probably contributed to an attitude of arrogance and superiority. They eschewed law's positivist trappings and viewed the legal system as integrally related to the development project.[27]

In an article highlighting the role of the law and development scholars in the developing world, Jean Zorn, an American legal scholar, commented:

> They viewed the introduction of Western law into the Third World as a modernizing and beneficent act. To these American lawyers, impelled by a terrible innocence not only of the Third World, but of their own society as well,.. Western law.. would promote individual freedom, expand citizens' participation in government and in the shaping of their own lives, and enhance social equality.[28]

Their enthusiastic embrace of Western law as the model by which developing nations were to be reconstitute, coincided with what became a pattern in post-colonial governments. This was one of fatally subordinating indigenous traditional law to the needs of modernization, as they saw it, and/or relegating indigenous traditional law to second-rate status in a dual legal framework incorporating both modern laws and indigenous traditional law.[29]

---

24   *See*, PROMOTING THE RULE OF LAW ABROAD (Thomas Carothers ed. 2006).

25   *Ibid.*

26   David Trubek and Marc Galanter, *Scholars in Self-Estrangement*, *supra* Note 23.

27   Jean C. Zorn, *Lawyers, Anthropologists and the Study of Law: Encounters in the New Guinea Highlands*, 15 LAW AND SOCIAL INQUIRY (1990) 271, 285–6.

28   *Ibid.*

29   Martin Chanock thoughtfully explores these themes in his scholarship. *See*, for example, MARTIN CHANOCK, LAW, CUSTOM AND SOCIAL ORDER: THE COLONIAL EXPERIENCE IN MALAWI AND ZAMBIA (1998) and MARTIN CHANOCK, THE MAKING OF SOUTH AFRICAN LEGAL CULTURE 1902–1936: FEAR, FAVOUR AND PREJUDICE (2007); *see also* Nonso Ukato, *Law Enforcement*

The primary goal, and need, of newly independent governments was national unification. Upsetting traditional laws in any form or trying to uproot cultural practices of traditional communities was complicated beyond belief. It also proved, in many instances, to be premature or too sensitive for the public scrutiny if national cohesion was to be preserved.[30]

Yet, the need to modernize was an imperative for a post-colonial government. Thus tensions developed in these countries as they sought ways to ameliorate the conflict between the needs of a modern system of laws and their people's attachment to traditional law and customs.[31] To avoid destabilizing the country while taking steps to escape this Hobson's choice, many newly-elected governments often appointed commissions of inquiry to make recommendations to the government. Frequently, however, these recommendations were shelved, particularly when their implementation was fraught with danger.[32]

In the interim, there has been several decades of activism for recognition and self-determination on the part of indigenous peoples, creating a whole set of new issues with respect to the treatment of indigenous traditional law and custom.[33] Certain cultural traditions and practices are deeply embedded in the lives of indigenous groups and thus remain highly contested and complex. Talk of eliminating them can engender very passionate debates. Increasingly, adherents to old practices know that the practices appear incongruous to many inside and outside their society, particularly as they relate to women.[34]

Many adherents of course know from government officials and national news programs that the practices are deemed by the United Nations, leading Western nations, and human rights groups to contradict the newly accepted principles of human rights, dignity, and equality. Similarly, they are aware of often repeated

---

in Postcolonial Africa: Interfacing Indigenous and English Policing in Nigeria, IPES WORKING PAPER NO 7, May 2007 at: *WWW.IPES.INFO/WPS/WPS%20NO%207.PDF.*

30   Martin Chanock, *Cutting and Sewing: Goals and Means in the Constitutionalist Project in Africa,* in LAW AND RIGHTS: GLOBAL PERSPECTIVES ON CONSTITUTIONALISM AND GOVERNANCE (Penelope Andrews and Susan Bazilli eds. 2008) 47.

31   *See* MARTIN CHANOCK, LAW, CUSTOM AND SOCIAL ORDER, *supra* Note 29.

32   *See* TASLIM OLAWALE ELIAS, THE NATURE OF AFRICAN CUSTOMARY LAW (1956) at 3 (citing Commissions of Inquiry in many African states including Nigeria, Uganda, Kenya and others).

33   *See* Ofelia Schutte, *Indigenous Issues and the Ethics of Dialogue in Latcrit Theory,* 54 RUTGERS LAW REVIEW (2002) 1021.

34   *See* Karen Knop, *Examining the Complex Role of Women,* 15 EUROPEAN JOURNAL OF INTERNATIONAL LAW (2004) 395, 398.

claims that the practices are particularly noxious because they discriminate against and disadvantage women.[35]

Governments, in contending with the legions of such adherents, picture themselves as being caught between a conflict between the traditions of large segments of their population and the demand to vigorously enforce women's rights emanating from liberal subgroups of their population and from international groups. Seeing this as a lose--lose situation, they often resort to compromises that incorporate aspects of both sides of the contradictory demands. The South African situation, which will be dealt with in greater detail in Chapter 5, provides an impressive example of compromise.

Governments have been very creative and resourceful in attempting to accommodate the contradictory demands. They have tried to create a win--win solution by paying respects to both sets of demands but placing management of the conflict under judicial supervision so as to provide a controlled outlet for raising and settling disputes on the conflicting claims. South Africa is a prime example of a nation which pursued this approach. Indeed, it may be deemed one of the originators of such an approach. As we will see later in Chapter 5, what South Africa achieved was to find a way to constitutionally protect indigenous and religious laws and custom while making them subject to equality and dignity rights provided in other clauses of the constitution.

"Competing" Narratives of Liberation: Nationalism and Feminism

Chapter 5 discusses the transition processes in South Africa. Without getting too far ahead of the issues raised in that chapter, it should be kept in mind that tensions in South Africa, which surfaced in the aftermath of the end of the apartheid regime regarding indigenous traditions and women's rights, have not disappeared. Though muted and managed, they are alive and kicking, reflecting locally the contemporary global patterns of conflicts between women's rights and indigenous laws and custom.[36]

Around the world, women activists are embroiled in rancorous debates regarding culture and rights. The tensions, however, are not just between men and women but are amongst women as well. Men and women are on both sides of the divide, the conflict pitting traditionalists against feminists irrespective of gender.[37]

---

35 *See* Karima Bennoune, *Secularism and Human Rights: A Contextual Analysis of Headscarves, Religious Expression, and Women's Equality under International Law*, 45 COLUMBIA JOURNAL OF TRANSNATIONAL LAW (2007) 367.

36 Penelope E. Andrews, *Who's Afraid of Polygamy? Exploring the Boundaries of Family, Equality and Custom in South Africa*, 2 UNIVERSITY OF UTAH LAW REVIEW (2009) 351.

37 Muna Ndulo, *African Customary Law, Customs, and Women's Rights*, 18 INDIANA JOURNAL OF GLOBAL LEGAL STUDIES (2011) 87.

The rise of a global women's rights movement has coincided with the rise of movements by indigenous peoples, and other minorities, for recognition of traditional cultural, and other derivative, rights and values. The confluence of these movements has heightened the level of conflict surrounding culture and the human rights movement.[38]

Tension between the two movements has been on full display in conferences at the United Nations for years. At the 1995 Beijing Women's Conference, the most significant United Nations sponsored conference on women yet held, the language in the Platform for Action was watered down because of this conflict.[39] Although the Platform designated women's human rights as paramount, a price was exacted for the designation. The price paid, a concession made to induce acceptance of women's rights and reduce fears of venerable traditions being overthrown, was explicit recognition in the Platform of the "significance of national and religious particularities and various historical cultural and religious backgrounds."[40]

This outcome could perhaps have been foreseen from the clashes that occurred at the United Nations Population Conference held in Cairo in 1994.[41] There, the Vatican joined forces with several Muslim governments to counter the use of human rights principles such as individualism and autonomy as trump cards for imposing Western values upon the rest of the world.[42] By the time of the 1995 Beijing Women's Conference, the opposition had become sufficiently strong to attain the previously mentioned recognition in the Platform for Action. This, however, should not be taken as creating insurmountable problems for women's rights because, as I stated earlier and will discuss later, the South African Constitution has structured a fruitful method of bridging the divide by placing under judicial supervision the management of the conflict.[43]

On the positive side, during these last several decades, it can be said, as a general proposition, that a global consensus has emerged on the nature of the proper theoretical edifice of human rights law and policy. Across a range of population

---

38   *See* Penelope E. Andrews, *Striking The Rock: Confronting Gender Equality in South Africa*, 3 MICHIGAN JOURNAL OF RACE AND LAW 307 (1998).

39   UNITED NATIONS REPORT OF THE FOURTH WORLD CONFERENCE ON WOMEN BEIJING, 4–15 SEPTEMBER 1995 (1996).

40   *Ibid*, Chapter 2, 9.

41   *See* C. Alison McIntosh and Jason Finkle, *The Cairo Conference on Population and Development: A New Paradigm?*, 21 POPULATION AND DEVELOPMENT REVIEW (1995) 223.

42   *See* Meredith Marshall, *United Nations Conference on Population and Development: The Road to a New Reality for Reproductive Health*, 10 EMORY INTERNATIONAL LAW REVIEW (1996) 441; *see also* Jennifer Jewett, *The Recommendations of the International Conference on Population and Development: The Possibility of the Empowerment of Women in Egypt*, 29 CORNELL INTERNATIONAL LAW JOURNAL (1996) 191.

43   *See* Nomtuse Mbere, *The Beijing Conference: A South African Perspective*, 16 SAIS REVIEW 1 (1996) 167.

groups, constituencies, and locations, the concept of protecting individual rights has come to be seen as a necessary precondition for good governance.[44]

In the wake of this understanding, and not infrequently because of harmful consequences that ensue from being too absolutist about it, there has also emerged a growing belief that the welfare of a country may depend upon making economic, social, and cultural rights somewhat competitive with the primacy accorded to civil and political rights. To varying degrees, and dependent upon the country, the interdependence of these rights has won acceptance.[45] In a country like South Africa, as well as elsewhere, the right to dignity is seen as integral to the human rights project.[46] None of this, however, eliminates the conflict between rights and culture.[47] One reason why the conflict remains is that respect for cultural traditions and custom is often perceived as itself being a sort of right, hence the pressure to have the Platform for Action note "significance of national and religious particularities and various historical cultural and religious backgrounds."[48]

Reconciling women's rights with the perceived need of indigenous peoples to maintain respect for their traditions and custom, is not always the principal conflict with which the movement for women's rights must contend. Since the demise of colonialism and the late twentieth-century rise in the developing world of the modern democratic constitutional state, the movement for women's rights has also collided with two contemporary movements, namely, the struggle against racism and the struggle for self-determination.[49]

---

44   OFFICE OF THE UNITED NATIONS HIGH COMMISSIONER FOR HUMAN RIGHTS, GOOD GOVERNANCE PRACTICES FOR THE PROTECTION OF HUMAN RIGHTS (2007), *1 at: www.ohchr.org/Documents/Publications/GoodGovernance.pdf.*

45   *See* Catherine Powell and Jennifer Lee, *Recognizing the Interdependence of Rights in the Anti-Discrimination Context through the World Conference against Racism,* 34 COLUMBIA HUMAN RIGHTS LAW REVIEW (2002) 235; *see also* Dianne Otto, *Holding up Half the Sky: But for Whose Benefit?: A Critical Analysis of the Fourth World Conference on Women,* 6 AUSTRALIAN FEMINIST LAW JOURNAL (1996) 9.

46   CONSTITUTION OF SOUTH AFRICA [Hereinafter "THE CONSTITUTION"], Chapter 2, Section 10.

47   Arguably these issues have been central to the modern global human rights project. They may have been attached to different labels over time, for example, first and third world, individualism versus communitarianism, traditional versus modern. In fact, these issues have been debated for some time. In the words of Canadian law professor, Rebecca Cook: "How can universal human rights be legitimized in radically different societies without succumbing to either homogenizing universalism or the paralysis of … relativism." Rebecca J. Cook, *Human Rights of Women,* in HUMAN RIGHTS OF WOMEN: NATIONAL AND INTERNATIONAL PERSPECTIVES (Rebecca Cook ed. 1994); *See also* MARTHA C. NUSSBAUM, SEX AND SOCIAL JUSTICE (1999) 35–42.

48   UNITED NATIONS REPORT OF THE FOURTH WORLD CONFERENCE ON WOMEN BEIJING, 4–15 SEPTEMBER 1995. Chapter 2, 9.

49   *See,* for example, Ruth L. Gana, *Which "Self"? Race and Gender in the Right to Self-Determination as a Prerequisite to the Right to Development,* 14 WISCONSIN

The context in which the conflict with these two struggles occurred, however, differs from the context in which the women's rights movement is confronted by the conflicts around the question of culture. The latter is one of continual conflict and accommodation whereas the conflict regarding the struggles against racism and for self-determination was essentially one of whether one struggle was to be given priority over the other. For example, during both the civil rights movement in the United States and the anti-apartheid democratic movement in South Africa, the question arose whether the fight to achieve women's equality should be subordinated, until the struggle for racial equality, in the United States, and the struggle for democracy and majority political control, in South Africa, were achieved.[50]

During recent years, a number of South African writers have described how the negotiators for a new democratic state and constitution, including the now-ruling African National Congress (ANC), at times seemed to treat the issue of gender equality almost as an afterthought.[51] Ultimately, however, South Africa avoided this fate and created a constitution which, in addition to embracing pluralism, contains the strongest protections for gender equality to be found in the world. Other developing nations grappling with the problem of providing a constitutional framework embracing pluralism and protecting indigenous communities, religious minorities, and other historically marginalized communities, should not use the supposed conflict between gender equality and cultural rights as an excuse to waver from securing gender equality. South Africa provides a model for accommodating these diverse interests within a unitary constitutional framework.

Enacting constitutional provisions for human rights, equality, and individual freedoms is the most dramatic way in which a nation can signal its rejection of the legacies of colonialism, authoritarianism, and dictatorship and is a precondition for the construction of a democratic constitutional state.[52] Historically, it

---

INTERNATIONAL LAW JOURNAL (1995) 133, 137.

50 *See* Sheila Meintjies, *The Women's Struggle for Equality during South Africa's Transition to Democracy*, 30 TRANSFORMATION (1996) 47; *see also* REILAND RABAKA, AGAINST EPISTEMIC APARTHEID: W.E. DU BOIS AND THE DISCIPLINARY DECADENCE OF SOCIOLOGY (2010) at 192 *and* Gemma Tang Nain, *Black Women, Sexism and Racism: Black or Antiracist Feminism?*, 37 FEMINIST REVIEW (1991) 1.

51 *See* Gay Seidman, *Feminist Interventions: The South African Gender Commission and "Strategic" Challenges to Gender Inequality*, 2 ETHNOGRAPHY (2001) 219. *See also Candidate List Outburst a Reminder of ANC's Gender Equality Policy*, SABC NEWS. COM, April 24, 2011 at: *http://www.sabc.co.za/news/a1/d4948ee66288f210VgnVCM1 0000077d4ea9bRCRD/'Candidate-list-outburst-a-reminder-of-ANC's-gender-equality-policy'-20110424*.

52 MEENA K. BHAMRA, THE CHALLENGES OF JUSTICE IN DIVERSE SOCIETIES: CONSTITUTIONALISM AND PLURALISM (2011); Adeno Addis, *Constitutionalizing Deliberative Democracy in Multilingual Societies*, 25 BERKELEY JOURNAL OF INTERNATIONAL LAW (2007) 117.

has been typical for a developing nation to have been ruled by a hegemonic, homogenous, ethnic group. This dominion ends, at least formally, when the nation adopts constitutional provisions as described above, and the rise of women and marginalized minorities as partners in governance begins. This is what makes the South African constitution an important model for creating democratic, pluralistic government without relegating women to traditional roles of inferiority. The South African model, though one of many, is a good example of how the modernist project of democratic constitutionalism can be made to function as a collective guarantor of women's rights, religious freedom, and autonomy for indigenous people, with conflicts resolved through a constitutional framework.[53]

Universality in Different Cultural Contexts

So far, I have been arguing that the creation of a new nation in the aftermath of the end of colonialism and the concomitant eruption of nationalism need not result in the subordination of women as a means of establishing a pluralistic society. Now, I want to turn to the different though related issue of the universality of human rights claims notwithstanding the imperatives of cultural contexts and cultural realities.[54] Here, too, however, the question of women's rights is fundamental, but less in the context of direct demands that women's rights be subordinated to nationalism and the independence movement, and more in the context of beliefs and assertions that respect for culture entails, in a human rights framework, freezing the status quo in the roles of women. This issue has aroused heated claims and impassioned responses.

Katha Pollitt makes this point, strident to some, when she says:

> That cultural-rights movements have centered on gender is a telling fact about
> them. It's related to the way in which nationalism tends to identify the nation with

---

53   *See* Rhoda Kadalie, *Constitutional Equality: The Implications for Women in South Africa,* 2 SOCIAL POLITICS (1995) 208; *see also* Justice Yvonne Mokgoro, *Constitutional Claims for Gender Equality in South Africa: A Judicial Response,* 67 ALBANY LAW REVIEW (2003) 565 *and* FEMINIST CONSTITUTIONALISM: GLOBAL PERSPECTIVES (Beverley Baines *et al.* eds. 2012).

54   As Abdullah Ahmed An-Naim and Francis Deng observe: "Are we being romantic and are we unnecessarily complicating the process of universalizing the cause of human rights, or are we presenting a cultural challenge for all members of the human family and their respective cultures that can help shape the lofty ideals of universal human rights? And could such worldwide involvement in itself lead to a realization of the universality of human dignity, which is the cornerstone of international human rights? Or would it be more practical to assume that some cultures are just not blessed with these human ideals, and that the sooner they recognize this and try to adjust and live up to the challenge presented by the pioneering leadership of those more endowed with these lofty values, the better for their own good and for the good of humanity." HUMAN RIGHTS IN AFRICA: CROSS-CULTURAL PERSPECTIVES (Abdullah Ahmed An-Naim and Francis Deng eds. 1990).

the bodies of its women: they are the ones ....conceptualized as the producers of babies for the fatherland and keepers of the hearth for the men at the front .... How far would an Algerian immigrant get ... if he refused to pay the interest on his Visa bill on the grounds that Islam forbids interest on borrowed money? Everyone understands that money is too important to be handed out in this whimsical fashion. Women and children are another story.[55]

In trying to justify their attempts at freezing the status quo cultural roles of women, opportunistic male politicians, and their conservative supporters, have attempted to create a false "tension" between human rights generally and cultural norms by spreading fears of a global feminist imperialist movement.[56] Reinforcing their static conception of culture and ignoring the dynamism of culture, including the dynamic ways in which women throughout history have altered their cultural context, is just a blind way of being impervious to the notion that shifting cultural norms and their accommodation occur all the time, for both men and women.[57] When these politicians engage in the discourse of women's rights, they seek merely to imprison women in a frozen time by insisting on a view of culture devoid of the resilience which has been the hallmark of culture since time immemorial.[58]

Human rights advocates in general, and feminist advocates in particular, see through this charade. They know that shifts in cultural norms, as theory and as practice, occur all the time. Scholars and activists like Katha Pollitt have made an important contribution to the women's movement with their insight about the dynamic quality of women's cultural roles and their evolution. This insight undermines the erroneous notion that culture functions in an unproblematic, seemingly natural manner that is unencumbered by the constraints of political, economic, social, and other factors, and thereby destroys the claim of these opportunists that indigenous or traditional cultures operate in a kind of cocoon shielded and isolated, unlike that of

Western culture. In truth, both Western culture and indigenous culture are constantly evolving, and are, at the core, dynamic.

Katha Pollitt's quotation above is, as I said, very insightful. She voices legitimate sentiments regarding the hypocrisy surrounding the discourse of culture,

---

55   Katha Pollitt, *Whose Culture?*, in IS MULTICULTURALISM BAD FOR WOMEN? (Joshua Cohen *et al.* eds. 1999) 27.

56   *See* Hannibal Travis, *Freedom or Theocracy? Constitutionalism in Afghanistan and Iraq*, 3 NORTHWESTERN JOURNAL OF INTERNATIONAL HUMAN RIGHTS (2005) 1 at: *http://www.law.northwestern.edu/journals/jihr/v3/4.*

57   *See* ARZOO OSANLOO, THE POLITICS OF WOMEN'S RIGHTS IN IRAN (2009); *see also* WOMEN AND LAND IN AFRICA: CULTURE, RELIGION AND REALIZING WOMEN'S RIGHTS (L. Muthoni Wanyeki ed. 2003).

58   *See* Sibongile Ndashe, *Challenges to Litigating Women's Right to Inheritance*, 14 INTERIGHTS BULLETIN (2004) 154; *see also* Rana Husseini, *Enforcing Laws against "Honor" Killings in Jordan*, 14 INTERIGHTS BULLETIN (2004) 157.

identity, rights, and autonomy, and specifically as they pertain to the principle of gender equality. Pollitt is not the only Western observer who has provided this analysis. Martha Nussbaum, in her book, states:

> Cultures are not museum pieces, to be preserved intact at all costs. There would appear, indeed, to be something condescending in preserving for contemplation a way of life that causes real pain to real people.[59]

These critiques by Western feminists have served two important educational functions, namely, educating women about women's cultural roles and unifying women politically and socially in facilitating joint campaigns that have generated tremendous benefits for women, particularly in the global South.[60] One, for example, has been the campaign to eradicate the practice of female genital surgeries.[61] Another has been campaigns to highlight the plight of rape victims in war-torn zones of the world.[62]

It has not, however, been just Western scholars and advocates making the claim that cultural norms are not static, and the related claim that harmful and discriminatory cultural norms and practices must not be frozen but rather should be outlawed.

Take, for example, the cultural practice of "bride price."[63] In February, 2004, a campaign was commenced in Kampala, Uganda, to discourage and ban this practice. The campaign, however, was not initiated by Western feminist activists. Rather, it was organized by Mifumi, a women's organization in rural Uganda, and women from Uganda, Kenya, Tanzania, Nigeria, Ghana, Senegal, Rwanda, and South Africa.[64] They met to discuss strategies to outlaw the practice. They recognized that this practice was harmful to women, discriminatory against them, and therefore was not to be kept on life support, but rather was to be prohibited.

These campaigns are important vehicles to highlight the pain and suffering of women in the global South, particularly those in Africa. They have now made

---

59   MARTHA NUSSBAUM, SEX AND SOCIAL JUSTICE, *supra* Note 47 at 37.

60   UN WOMEN 2012 WORLD DEVELOPMENT REPORT ON GENDER EQUALITY AND DEVELOPMENT, at: *http://go.worldbank.org/CQCTMSFI40*.

61   Celia Duggar, Senegal Curbs a Bloody Rite for Girls and Women, NEW YORK TIMES, October 15 2011 at: *http://www.nytimes.com/2011/10/16/world/africa/movement-to-end-genital-cutting-spreads-in-senegal.html?_r=2*.

62   *See*, for example, WOMEN FOR WOMEN INTERNATIONAL'S CAMPAIGN IN THE DEMOCRATIC REPUBLIC OF CONGO at: *http://www.womenforwomen.org/global-initiatives-helping-women/help-women-congo.php*, and COPERMA at: *http://www.crosiersincongo.com/1/cic/around_the_country.asp?artid=7218*.

63   Variously entitled *lobolo, bohari and lobala*, these terms refer to the practice whereby a prospective groom will pay the father of the bride a certain sum of money to validate the marriage. In traditional societies the payments mostly consisted of a goat or a cow.

64   For more about the project, *see http://www.mifumi.org/*

their way into the foreign policy lexicon of the developed world, especially the United States, where concerns about women's rights have influenced government policy.[65] However, it is one thing for developed nations to advocate the primacy of women's rights over harmful and discriminatory cultural practices and another thing for them to adopt the right policy and action towards it. Typically, the instant reaction is to deny foreign aid.[66] But depriving a poor developing nation of needed financial aid as a way of intersecting with women's concerns does not always benefit women. One example was the Bush government's Global Gag Rule[67] making foreign aid dependent on abortion and other contraceptive choices not being offered or discussed at family planning clinics financed with United States funds. This action was totally destructive of women's rights in developing economies.[68]

Turning the Cultural Lens Inwards

It may be worth considering another perspective, from treating culture in developing nations as an ice storage for women's roles, to how Western societies, including human rights groups in the West, often portray themselves and characterize the circumstances of women in those societies. Here, I am addressing the 'rescue' notion.

The global campaigns for the rights of women and the solidarity that they generate are laudable. But what has emerged over time has been a certain pathology on the part of Western feminists about the need to rescue women from barbaric patriarchal laws and practices in the non-Western world.[69] In this zeal to rescue, whole populations of women are denied agency in these communities and

---

65   US AID, WOMEN AND CONFLICT AN INTRODUCTORY GUIDE FOR PROGRAMMING (2007) at: *pdf.usaid.gov/pdf_docs/PNADJ133.pdf*, or *US AID'S WEBSITE FOR GENDER EQUALITY AND WOMEN'S EMPOWERMENT at: http://www. usaid.gov/our_work/cross-cutting_programs/wid/.*

66   *See* Peter Juul, *Advancing Women's Rights Is Progressive Foreign Policy*, CENTER FOR AMERICAN PROGRESS at: *http://www.americanprogress.org/issues/2011/06/ hillary_womens_rights.html*; *see also* Serra Sippel, *Women's Health and Rights: Why US Foreign Policy Matters*, THE HUFFINGTON POST, November 22, 2010 at: *http://www. huffingtonpost.com/serra-sippel/womens-health-and-rights_b_786804.html.*

67   The Global Gag Rule was established by executive order by President Bush on the day he took office in 2001. The Rule denies United States family planning financial aid to organizations that advocate for or provide abortion services to women, even when they use private funds raised elsewhere.

68   *The War On Women*, NY TIMES EDITORIAL, February 25, 2011 at: *http://www. nytimes.com/2011/02/26/opinion/26sat1.html.*

69   *See* Vasuki Nesiah, *Toward a Feminist Intersectionality: A Critique of U.S. Feminist Legal Scholarship*, 16 HARVARD WOMEN'S LAW JOURNAL (1993) 189; *see also* Carla Power, *The Politics of Women's Head Coverings*, TIME MAGAZINE, July 13, 2009 at: *http://www.time.com/time/magazine/article/0,9171,1908306,00.html.*

not seen as having autonomous roles. This is because the rescue imperative, and narrative, often obscures the vital role of local women activists. As a consequence, particularly with regard to odious cultural practices and norms, the impetus is one that is only directed outwards towards the conditions in the developing country, not inwards to somewhat parallel conditions inside the developed nations from which the Western feminist activists hail.[70]

What occurs to women inside Western society, and here I refer specifically to American society, becomes immune from criticism. What is often lacking is attention to culturally sanctioned discrimination in the U.S.A.[71] For example, feminist publications have paid considerable attention to cultural practices that violate international human rights norms. The focus of much of this literature is almost always on non-Western communities, with examples like polygamy, honor killings, female genital surgeries, and the veil. These practices continue to be the focus of vigorous campaigns and highly contested debates about their harmful and discriminatory effects on women.[72]

Western feminists, however, appear to be loath to focus their intellectual lenses on their own societies, in which negative cultural stereotypes persist and in which privatized violence against women is widespread.[73] For example, the popularity of a range of cosmetic surgeries, such as breast augmentation, face lifts, and liposuction, thrives in the cultural environment in the United States, a cultural environment which demands that women conform to a particular feminine stereotype.[74] Similarly, in the United States, young girls, at pre-puberty stages, are displayed in all manner of ways as sexual objects in magazines, advertisements, and beauty contests. But these conditions often do not come under the glare of feminist human rights actors, although they are receiving increasing attention.[75]

---

70   L. Amede Obiora, *Bridges and Barricades: Rethinking Polemics and Intransigence in the Campaign against Female Circumcision*, CASE WESTERN RESERVE LAW REVIEW (1997) 275.

71   Eve Ensler is one of the most imaginative critics of the female obsession with body image. Her humorous observations in THE GOOD BODY, *supra* Note 6, piercingly outlines the contours of this obsession on a global scale.

72   Nicholas Kristof, *The Women's Crusade*, NEW YORK TIMES, August 17, 2009 at: *http://www.nytimes.com/2009/08/23/magazine/23Women-t.html?pagewanted=all.*

73   Callie Marie Rennison, *Intimate Partner Violence, 1993–2001*, UNITED STATES DEPARTMENT OF JUSTICE, BUREAU OF JUSTICE STATISTICS, CRIME DATA BRIEF (February 2003) at: *http://www1.umn.edu/aurora/pdf/Rennison%20BJS.pdf.* [About 588,490, or 85% of victimizations by intimate partners in 2001 were against women.]

74   According to a report compiled by the American Society for Aesthetic Plastic Surgery, in 2003 approximately 8.3 million cosmetic procedures were performed in the U.S.A. The top five surgical procedures were liposuction, breast augmentation, eyelid surgery, rhinoplasty and breast reduction. *See* Report at *http://my.wemmd.com/content/Article/82/97313.htm.*

75   *See*, for example, PATRICE OPPLIGER, GIRLS GONE SKANK: THE SEXUALIZATION OF GIRLS IN AMERICAN CULTURE (2008), *see also* Mikaela

And in an area vital to women's health and welfare, health care services and medical insurance plans that have covered payments for Viagra, a pill to enhance erections for males, appear not to have covered payments for contraceptives pills and devices for women. This is now slowly changing as a direct result of women's advocacy.[76] Recently, the United States federal government has announced that this will change under the new health law passed in 2010.[77] This was a result of agitation by feminist groups.[78]

It is an open secret that human rights groups do not regard cosmetic surgeries performed on women in the U.S.A. as in any way comparable to the kinds of surgeries performed on young girls and women in Africa, such as genital surgeries.[79] The blinders are put on by adopting the narrative that cosmetic surgery is not harmful but rather is beneficial. Moreover, the argument goes that cosmetic surgery is voluntary. The argument proceeds in two steps. First, it is claimed that the surgery enhances a woman's beauty or youthful appearance, and second, that as opposed to girls who are circumcised, cosmetic surgery results from a woman's active, independent choice.[80]

But just like the harmful, often lethal results of female genital surgeries, these cosmetic surgeries can and do result in infection, bleeding, facial nerve injury, blindness, and sometimes even death.[81] Moreover, the surgeries occur in a cultural milieu of subversive coercion, "camouflaged by a language of choice, fulfilment

---

Conley, *Toddlers, Tiaras, and Thigh-High Boots: 3-Year-Old Hooker's Outfit*, ABCNEWS. COM, September 8, 2011 at: *http://abcnews.go.com/blogs/health/2011/09/08/toddlers-tiaras-and-thigh-high-boots-3-year-olds-hooker-outfit/*.

76 Geraldine Sealey, *Erections Get Insurance: Why Not the Pill?*, ABC NEWS, June 9, 2002 at: *http://abcnews.go.com/US/story?id=91538#.Ty74HiOQ324*.

77 *Obama Administration: Health Insurers Must Cover Birth Control with No Co-Pays*, AP/HUFFINGTON POST, October 1, 2011 at: *http://www.huffingtonpost. com/2011/08/01/obama-birth-control-health-insurance_n_914818.html*.

78 Cecile Richards, *Birth Control Coverage a Victory for Women's Health*, January 21, 2012 at: *http://mustafashen.com/2012/01/21/cecile-richards-birth-control-coverage-a-victory-for-womens-health/*.

79 But *see* Marianne Mollman, *The Deeply Rooted Parallels between Female Genital Mutilation and Breast Implantation*, RH REALITY CHECK, January 10, 2012 at: *http:// www.rhrealitycheck.org/article/2012/01/04/female-genital-mutilation-breast-implantation-why-do-they-happen-and-how-do-we-st*. For a compelling analysis of the comparison, *see* Isabelle R. Gunning, *Global Feminism at the Local Level: Criminal and Asylum Laws Regarding Female Genital Surgeries*, 3 JOURNAL OF GENDER, RACE AND JUSTICE (1999–2000) 45.

80 *See* Hope Lewis and Isabelle R. Gunning, *Cleaning Our Own House: "Exotic" and Familial Human Rights Violations*, 4 BUFFALO HUMAN RIGHTS LAW REVIEW (1998) 123.

81 *See* Kerith Cohen, *Truth, Beauty and Deception: A Feminist Analysis of Breast Implant Litigation*, 1 WILLIAM AND MARY JOURNAL OF WOMEN AND LAW (1994) 149; *see also* Jenna Goudreau, *The Hidden Dangers of Cosmetic Surgery*, FORBES, June

and liberation."[82] This coercion is often cloaked in descriptions of health, deviance, or deformity. Referring to women with reduced breast size, the former president of the American Society of Plastic and Reconstructive Surgery noted:

> There is substantial and enlarging medical knowledge to the effect that these deformities [small breasts] *are really a disease* which results in the patient's feelings of inadequacies, lack of self-confidence, distortion of body image, and a total lack of well-being due to a lack of self-perceived femininity ... Enlargement is therefore . necessary to ensure the quality of life for the [female] patient.[83]

In short, women undergoing cosmetic surgery suffer from psychological afflictions and insecurities which surgery will cure, that is, the women in Western developed nations are victims. So seen, Ratna Kapur, the Indian legal feminist, has argued that the "victim subject" is located across borders and thus is in fact a "transnational phenomenon."[84] However, she notes that Western human rights feminists do not accept this duality. As she emphasizes:

> However, the Third World victim subject has come to represent the more victimized subject; that is, the real or authentic victim subject. Feminist politics in the human rights arena, as well as in parts of the Third World, have promoted this image of the authentic victim subject while advocating for women's human rights.[85]

Recognizing that violation of women's human rights through cultural norms occurs not just in the larger world "out there," but within our borders as well, the question then becomes: How do we in the human rights community, independent of the development status of the country, have a candid conversation, about the role of culture in perpetuating stereotypes of women? How can we engage in a debate that appreciates the need to eradicate all forms of cultural discrimination against women, in a manner that is thoughtful, respectful, and productive? How do we avoid the polarizing impulses that perpetuate the notion of the exotic or uncivilized "other" and the civilized or progressive "us"?

These are hackneyed, but nevertheless perennial questions that have been visited by women activists and feminists in earlier eras. Indeed, they have to be revisited constantly, particularly during this period of American global cultural

---

16, 2011 at: *http://www.forbes.com/sites/jennagoudreau/2011/06/16/hidden-dangers-of-cosmetic-surgery/*.

82   Kathryn Pauly Morgan, *Women and the Knife: Cosmetic Surgery and the Colonization of Women's Bodies*, 6 HYPATIA 3, FEMINISM AND THE BODY (1991) 25–53.

83   Laura Nader, *Tracing the Dynamic Components of Power*, 38 CURRENT ANTHROPOLOGY (December 1997) 711, 716 (emphasis added).

84   Ratna Kapur, *The Tragedy of Victimization Rhetoric: Resurrecting the "Native" Subject in International/ Post-Global Feminist Legal Politics*, *supra* Note 13.

85   *Ibid.*

dominance. If the contemporary American human rights project, in the shadow of the events of September 11, 2001, includes the liberation of women, it should incorporate not only a vigorous critique of harmful cultural practices in other societies, but also a critique that labels cultural attitudes and practices in the United States, such as many forms of cosmetic surgeries and the use of small children as sexual subjects in advertisements, as harmful and discriminatory to women.

A number of feminist activists in the U.S. have made this critique. Kathryn Pauly Morgan, a leading figure, wrote, in referring to the explosion of cosmetic surgeries in the United States:

> We need a feminist analysis to understand why actual, live women are reduced and reduce themselves to "potential women" and choose to participate in anatomizing and fetishizing their bodies as they buy "contoured bodies," "restored youth," and "permanent beauty."[86]

In many ways those of us involved in the pursuit of women's rights have benefited tremendously from the debates that surfaced during the 1980s regarding the issues of universalism and cultural relativism; in other words, whether human rights principles have applicability on a global scale or whether their applicability is limited within particular cultural contexts.[87] The dust is now settling on those debates as a result of continual reflection and widespread engagement by women from the non-Western world on the issues. They have largely eschewed a unitary evolutionary process and development stage for how women's rights are to be incorporated within the body politics and the rule of law. While not adopting cultural relativism, they have pursued cultural autonomy for women in determining how they want to advance women's rights in their societies. The Iranian feminist, Valentine Moghadam, puts it well when she says:

> It is no longer possible to speak of a feminism for the West versus a different set of priorities for the developing world.. feminist movements have proliferated in the Muslim world.... and they have taken strong objections to discourses of cultural relativism.[88]

As an illustration, South African women, when they negotiated the Constitution to govern a democratic South Africa, vehemently opposed attempts by the traditional authorities to immunize traditional law and custom from the dictates of equality,

---

86   Kathryn Pauly Morgan, *Women and the Knife: Cosmetic Surgery and the Colonization of Women's Bodies, supra* Note 82.

87   Guyora Binder, *Cultural Relativism and Cultural Imperialism in Human Rights Law*, 5 BUFFALO HUMAN RIGHTS LAW REVIEW (1999) 211.

88   Valentine M. Moghadam, *Patriarchy, the Taleban, and Politics of Public Space in Afghanistan*, 25 WOMEN'S STUDIES INTERNATIONAL FORUM (2002) 19, 27.

the primary principle of the Constitution.[89] Traditional leaders and their supporters incessantly made arguments about the uniqueness of traditional institutions, their autonomy and authenticity. In rejecting these arguments, progressive women in South Africa did not deprecate the arguments. Rather, they acknowledged the sincerity, or if you will, significance of the concerns. But they also recognized themselves as autonomous decision makers who could determine for themselves the flexibility of traditional laws and customs, and whether and how they could be made to accommodate the principle of women equality they insisted must be enshrined in the new Constitution.[90] In this way, women in many African countries have been able to get traditional leaders to come on board in support of campaigns to eradicate cultural practices which women in those countries have autonomously decided are harmful to, and discriminatory against, women. One such case occurred in Kenya when women persuaded tribal elders to join the battle for the eradication of female genital surgeries, and by pursuing alternatives for the rites of passage to "womanhood."[91]

Even though feminists from non-Western societies have largely rejected spurious claims of cultural relativism to which women's rights and equality are largely held hostage or given short shrift, there is still not a global consensus amongst women about the place of culture or religion in pursuing women's equality.[92] As Valentine Moghadam emphasizes, feminist movements exist in the Muslim world but they have largely articulated an indigenous vision of women's equality, acknowledging the role of religion and culture in their lives.[93]

The secular pursuit of human rights, as defined in most Western-style democracies, faces an uphill battle in taking a foothold in some Muslim countries.[94] This is the point made by Haleh Afshar, another Iranian feminist, who argues that Islamic women defend their faith "as a dynamic system that has offered much

---

89   PUTTING WOMEN ON THE AGENDA (Susan Bazilli ed. 1991).

90   Lisa Fishbayn, *Litigating the Right to Culture: Family Law in the New South Africa*, 13 INTERNATIONAL JOURNAL OF LAW, POLICY AND THE FAMILY (1999) 147.

91   *See* Malik Steven Reeves, *Alternative Rite to Female Circumcision Spreading in Kenya*, AFRICA NEWS SERVICE, November 1997 at: *http://www.hartford-hwp. com/archives/36/041.html*; *see also* Judie Kaberia, *Meru Elders on the Spot over FGM*, CAPITAL FM NEWS, August 13, 2011 at: *http://fgcdailynews.blogspot.com/2011/08/ meru-elders-on-spot-over-fgm.html*.

92   Radhika Coomaraswamy, *Identity Within: Cultural Relativism, Minority Rights and the Empowerment of Women*, 34 GEORGE WASHINGTON INTERNATIONAL LAW REVIEW (2002) 483.

93   VALENTINE MOGHADAM, MODERNIZING WOMEN: GENDER AND SOCIAL CHANGE IN THE MIDDLE EAST (2003).

94   *See* Karima Bennoune, *Secularism and Human Rights*, *supra* Note 35.

to women."[95] They believe that in fact their faith offers them "even more than Western-style feminism."[96] As I noted earlier, this should be viewed more as women in developing countries adopting an autonomous role as decision makers in the manner in which they express and enforce women's rights, and less as an adoption of cultural relativism per se.

CEDAW and Culture

Perhaps overshadowing these debates on cultural practices, women's equality, and women's autonomy, is the Convention on the Elimination of All Forms of Discrimination Against Women (CEDAW). This Convention provides guidelines with respect to conflicts between culture and women's rights.

CEDAW treats culture and tradition as influences shaping gender roles and relations between men and women. In Article 2, CEDAW provides that governments should:

> ... take all appropriate measures, including legislation, to modify or abolish existing laws, regulations, customs and practices which constitute discrimination against women.

In Article 5, CEDAW adds to this by urging governments to,

> ... modify the social and cultural patterns of conduct of men and women, with a view to achieving the elimination of prejudices and customary and all other practices which are based on the idea of the inferiority or the superiority of either of the sexes or stereotyped roles for men and women.

CEDAW states the universal goal and the obstacles to be overcome. It thereby generates possibilities for universalizing legal norms of gender equality in the context of enormous global disparities, and differences in culture. As highlighted in Chapter 3, CEDAW is deemed as a global benchmark for women's rights because it has been signed and ratified by a large number of nations and because it is comprehensive in its coverage. Despite widespread acknowledgement of CEDAW's reach and the possibilities of the implementation of much of its norms, it is arguable that CEDAW appears, at least at first glance, to advance a secular vision of rights and enforcement.[97] It does not address directly deeply entrenched

---

95   Haleh Afshar, *Islam and Feminism: An Analysis of Political Strategies*, in FEMINISM AND ISLAM: LEGAL AND LITERARY PERSPECTIVES (Mai Yamani ed. 1996) 197.

96   *Ibid.*

97   SALLY ENGLE MERRY, HUMAN RIGHTS AND GENDER VIOLENCE: TRANSLATING INTERNATIONAL LAW INTO LOCAL JUSTICE (2006) 89.

cultural and religious mores. But the clear implication is that whatever the cultural patterns, they are to be analyzed for the purpose of determining whether they are based upon the concept of women's inferiority and prejudice against women, and that if they are so found, then "appropriate measures" should be taken to "modify" them. What these measures are and what modifications are to be made are left unspecified with any particularity.[98]

In addition, although CEDAW recognizes collective rights, it does not adequately address the contradictions inherent in the individual rights enforcement project within communitarian imperatives. In other words, CEDAW does not provide clear guidance in balancing individual rights with community needs in societies in which the interplay of the individual's rights and the community's concerns are constantly negotiated.

Therefore any global project that sets out to advance human rights for women in line with CEDAW, particularly within non-Judeo Christian contexts, may require innovative approaches. It has been cautioned that:

> In addition to all the obvious practical problems of enforcement and implementation in many countries, the paradoxical and problematic nature of such normative universality of human rights can readily be appreciated in view of the diversity of cultural and contextual realities which conditioned people's belief and behaviors in daily life. . To assert those rights in the abstract, or to ignore their embeddedness in religiously and/or culturally conditioned notions will probably raise insuperable difficulties to their implementation.[99]

It is not hard to imagine that attempts at implementing CEDAW may occur within societies with extremely limited resources. In many, and this may be particularly pronounced in Africa, the formal institutions of the society may be ineffective or may even have broken down. For women who have to survive in these contexts, culture is largely negotiated through several considerations, particularly political and economic ones, which raise complicated and sensitive questions.

When CEDAW was promulgated in 1979, the framework of international law, politics, and economics was somewhat different from that which obtains today. Then the parameters of human rights discourse and the human rights imagination were confined to demarcated boundaries——first world and third world, East and West, capitalist and communist, developed and underdeveloped. The economic fissures of this contemporary period of globalization and particularly the structural adjustment initiatives of the 1980s and 1990s, and the recent global economic

---

98   Indira Jaising, *The Convention on the Elimination of All Forms of Discrimination Against Women (CEDAW) and Realisation of Rights: Reflections on Standard Settings and Culture*, in WITHOUT PREJUDICE: CEDAW AND THE DETERMINATION IN A LEGAL AND CULTURAL CONTEXT (Meena Shivdas and Sarah Coleman eds. 2010) 9.

99   Buthaina Ahmed Elnaiem, *Human Rights of Women and Islamic Identify in Africa*, RECHT IN AFRICA (2002) 1, 4,

crisis, had not occurred or fully appreciated.[100] Nor were the political upheavals and conflicts, a staple in Africa at the end of the twentieth century, imaginable.[101]

CEDAW is perhaps best seen as an indication of the global moment at a point in time when there was a universal consensus, albeit uneven, about the possibilities of legal processes in changing women's lives. Subsequent levels of local and global dislocation, violence, and lawlessness, could not have been predicted, and thus may have undermined that consensus. Nor perhaps was it anticipated that the implementation of rights would, thirty years later, be predicated on questions of daily survival or that competing claims of "culture and rights" would be so ferocious.

Feminist Evangelism?

Very often when we talk about a particular cultural practice that is offensive to our sensibilities, the impetus for us as human rights activists is to "liberate" the affected community or to eliminate the particular retrograde practice. This, as I said, has been the stance of many Western feminist advocates. In our ardor to advance rights, what often happens is that important questions fail to be addressed; questions such as: Which other forces are we liberating? Which other constraints are being discarded? How has this particular practice emerged and what is its historical place in the context of the overall culture? What forces are at play in the community to outlaw or alter the cultural practice? Failing to raise these questions results in a focus on the immediate cultural practice and ignorance of the entire context, cultural and otherwise, in which the practice is located.

The significance of these questions can be seem in the case of Amina Lawal, a Muslim woman in the north of Nigeria who was sentenced to death by stoning in 2002 for committing adultery.[102] The case received widespread international attention since it involved the re-introduction of Sharia law in the north of Nigeria, in particular the punishment of stoning for adultery. It rallied women activists around the world. The case highlighted the graphic inequality of treatment, status,

---

100   The impact of globalization has been documented in great detail. *See,* for example, ANTHONY GIDDENS, RUNAWAY WORLD: HOW GLOBALIZATION IS RESHAPING OUR LIVES (2000); TYLER COWEN, CREATIVE DESTRUCTION: HOW GLOBALIZATION IS CHANGING THE WORLD'S CULTURES (2002) and SURJIT S. BHALLA, IMAGINE THERE'S NO COUNTRY: POVERTY, INEQUALITY AND GROWTH IN THE ERA OF GLOBALIZATION (2002).

101   PAUL D. WILLIAMS, WAR AND CONFLICT IN AFRICA (2011).

102   *Nigerian Woman Facing Death Seeks Leniency,* NEW YORK TIMES, August 27, 2003 at: *http://www.nytimes.com/2003/08/28/world/nigerian-woman-facing-death-seeks-leniency.html?ref=aminalawal. See also* Shannon V. Barrow, *Nigerian Justice: Death-by-Stoning Sentence Reveals Empty Promises to the State and the International Community,* 17 EMORY INTERNATIONAL LAW REVIEW (2003) 1203.

and access to justice in a northern state of Nigeria where the stoning laws have been introduced.[103]

After Amina Lawal's sentence was overturned by an Islamic appeal court, Helen Habila, a Nigerian lawyer, pointed out in the *New York Times* how counterproductive the human rights campaign to "save" Ms. Lawal had been. She noted:

> There is much for human rights groups to criticize in Nigeria .... But they didn't aid the cause of human rights by taking up the case of Amina Lawal. A better solution might be to work for political and judicial stability so that all Nigerians will be persuaded to put their trust in a national system of law.[104]

I treat this as an example of the autonomous role of local women as decision makers in how to view cultural impediments to the exercise of women's rights. Returning to the issues of cultural impediments to women's equality, we should therefore ask: How do human rights activists engage in a fruitful dialogue about eradicating odious cultural norms in an environment in which legitimate fears of cultural imperialism are present? One approach is to contextualize the issues in the context of the global evolution of rights, and to engage in both inter- and intra-cultural dialogues, accepting the role of local women as legitimate autonomous decision makers in the matter.

Historically, religious, nationalist, or cultural considerations have always influenced the substance of human rights or their implementation. Indeed, the very genesis of rights owed much to religious and cultural precepts.[105] But as the preceding discussion has made clear, religious and cultural considerations have also generated substantial and contentious debates about the universality of human rights norms. In this regard, women's rights suffer the same vulnerability as human rights generally suffer.

A Constructive Dialogue

So how does one proceed with the pursuit of women's rights and equality in the face of cultural concerns? This question requires a multi-layered response, contextualized in the political, economic, social, and cultural reality of women's lives. On a theoretical level it calls for a continuing exploration of the multi-faceted

---

103   Amina Lawal's Death Sentence Quashed at Last but Questions Remain about Discriminatory Legislation, AMNESTY INTERNATIONAL, September 25, 2003 at: *http://www.amnesty.org/en/library/asset/AFR44/032/2003/en/bfab7b16-d68a-11dd-ab95-a13b602c0642/afr440322003en.html.*

104   Helen Habila, *Justice, Nigeria's Way*, NEW YORK TIMES, October 4, 2003 at A13.

105   *See*, for example, JOHN WITTE, JR., THE REFORMATION OF RIGHTS: LAW, RELIGION AND HUMAN RIGHTS IN EARLY MODERN CALVINISM (2008); *see also* TOSHIHIKO IZUTSU, ETHICO-RELIGIOUS CONCEPTS IN THE QURAN (1966).

and multi-layered global feminist project: one that seeks to eliminate patriarchal and sexist norms that insist on culture as immutable. This extrication of culture from sexism and patriarchy seeks to re-orientate an approach to culture that is historical and contextual but shorn of gender discrimination and subordination. Theoretically this approach should at the minimum embrace the consensus on women's rights as embodied in global human rights instruments like CEDAW.

At a practical level, it may be worth considering the issue of sex discrimination or gender equality on two levels. The first is that we consider the public manifestations of gender equality that appear unproblematic, such as first, women's right to be free from violence in both the public and private sphere; second, women's right to access to education, healthcare, employment, and other resources on a non-discriminatory basis; third, women's right to participate in elections and governance at both the local and national level in the same manner as me ; and fourth, women's right to the custody of their children in the same way allowed to men. Governments that are committed to the principle of gender equality generally are in agreement with these broad propositions; in any event, they are all to be found in the international human rights documents that refer to women's rights.

The second level is a more complex one which may require a nuanced approach. This level involves private choices and group imperatives which may not be easily prone to agreement and which may include, for example, the issues of veiling, dowry, polygamy, cosmetic surgery, or beauty competitions. These are broader cultural questions implicating women's choices, their options, and the interplay with cultural expectations and values.

For the purposes of legal reform, focusing on the first level, that is, the public manifestations of discrimination against women, is relatively unproblematic. The second level, involving private choices within particular cultural contexts, is more vexing. However, allowance of the autonomy of local women as decision makers may go a long way in resolving specific problems in this area as they occur.

It is at this level that the dialogue among women must negotiate competing perspectives, one that demands a certain candor about us (in the West) and them (the rest). The dialogue also has to appreciate that for the majority of women in the world, particularly in developing countries, life is not a series of choices, but rather a predestined set of arrangements based on, for example, geographical location, family status, ethnic community, family expectations, and access to economic resources.[106] Woman's rights proponents may insist on a series of seemingly rational choices to advance women's rights, but these choices cannot be viewed in isolation. They have to be contextualized in the life mosaic in which all choices are inter-related. And in this cauldron of considerations, cultural constraints loom large. When we consider the project of gender equality in the West, we should note:

---

106   For a comprehensive analysis of these issues, *see* THEORETICAL PERSPECTIVES ON GENDER AND DEVELOPMENT (Jane L. Parpart *et al.* eds. 2000).

While "Western" feminist discourse did not hold abandonment of "Western" culture as an essential prerequisite for liberation and equal rights at any stage of their struggle, it has been argued that progress of women in non-western cultures can only be achieved by giving up their native cultures.[107]

"Giving up culture" is not an option, but clearly those aspects of culture that continue to subordinate women can no longer be defended. Cultural practices once held dear and with apparent rational underpinnings have gone the way of the cotton loom, unable to withstand universal human rights norms. Note, for example, that early periods of Western civilization embraced racism in slavery, colonialism, and segregation.[108] These practices were rooted in values sustained by widely respected philosophies of racial superiority and racial inferiority. Now discredited and their sustaining practices eliminated, these "cultural norms" were taken as "normal" for centuries. The elimination of these practices required considerable local and global movements for human rights and a universal consensus involving many constituencies. For example, the decades-long struggle against apartheid in South Africa and the development of international legal principles proscribing racism, were outgrowths of this global movement.[109] Surely it is not hard to imagine that the cultural underpinnings of sexism and their outward manifestations will suffer the same fate?

Cultural proponents insist on arguing for an intransigent version that belies the dynamism of culture—which is constantly evolving and changing to accommodate all kinds of modern demands. Racism was very much a part of Western culture — but racism, at least at the formal level, had to be eradicated in a world of changing cultural norms congruent with human rights.

In the final analysis, however, an assault on specific cultural practices is predicated on changing the social, political, and economic conditions of the communities within which women reside. Women who are trapped in dire economic circumstances are unable to challenge much about their lives, including the eradication of practices that continue to disadvantage and subordinate them in the most burdensome ways.[110] The cultural context can therefore not be removed from the political and economic one. Moreover, insisting on universal standards to ensure equal justice for women does not mean that the entire global community

---

107   SHAHEEN SARDAR ALI, GENDER AND HUMAN RIGHTS IN ISLAM AND INTERNATIONAL LAW: EQUAL BEFORE ALLAH, UNEQUAL BEFORE MAN (2000) at 6.

108   SLAVERY (Stanley Engeran *et al.* eds. 2001); NORRIE MCQUEEN, COLONIALISM (2007); SEGREGATION (James H. Carr *et al.* eds. 2008).

109   NORMS IN INTERNATIONAL RELATIONS: THE STRUGGLE AGAINST APARTHEID (Audie Klotz and Peter J. Katzenstein eds. 1999).

110   These issues are thoughtfully explored in SPIRITUAL PRACTICES AND ECONOMIC REALITIES: FEMINIST CHALLENGES (Renata Jambrešic Kirin and Sandra Prlenda eds. 2011).

has to subject itself to the Western cultural model. It merely requires that a baseline of rights be established. As the Polish legal scholar, Wiktor Osiatynski, has suggested:

> The selection and definition of this minimum catalogue of human rights should be the subject of debate, though the debate in and of itself cannot justify mass violations of human rights by rulers in the name of cultural differences.[111]

Richard Falk has eloquently suggested that human rights should be mediated "through the web of cultural circumstances" if they are to take root in non-Western societies. He however warns that:

> ... without cultural practices and traditions being tested against the norms of international human rights, there will be a regressive disposition toward the retention of cruel, brutal, and exploitative aspects of religious and cultural tradition.[112]

Women's rights and women's equality underpin this conundrum. But this conundrum also may provide the opportunity to explore a comprehensive approach to rights, mindful of cultural and religious considerations.

---

111 Wiktor Osiatynski, *Human Rights for the 21st Century*, SAINT LOUIS-WARSAW TRANSATLANTIC LAW JOURNAL (2000) 29, 40.

112 Richard Falk, *Cultural Foundations for the International Protection of Human Rights*, in HUMAN RIGHTS IN CROSS-CULTURAL PERSPECTIVES: A QUEST FOR CONSENSUS (Abdullah Ahmed An-Na'im ed. 1992), 44, 45–6.

Chapter 5

South Africa's Constitutional Project: Constitutional Text and Constitutional Jurisprudence

Wathint' abafazi, wathint' imbokodo, uzokufa'—now you have touched the women you have struck a rock.[1]

In a country where the Constitution clearly stipulates that no person may unfairly discriminate directly or indirectly against anyone because of their sexual orientation, reports about lesbians being victims of corrective rape and murder have become a worrying trend ....[2]

Transition from Apartheid to Democracy

Nelson Mandela's release from prison and subsequent appointment as the first President of a democratic South Africa marked the beginning of a momentous turn

---

1   HILDA BERNSTEIN, FOR THEIR TRIUMPH AND THEIR TEARS (1985) 90. The phrase "striking the rock" first made its way into South African political parlance in the 1950s, when a large number of women marched on Pretoria to protest the application of "pass laws" to African women. "Pass laws" required all Africans to carry passes (identity documents) which described both their status and the geographical areas in which they were permitted. The central piece of legislation was the Black (Urban Areas) Consolidation Act of 1945 and its subsidiary regulations. Section 10 of the Act contained the key provisions and, with certain exceptions, stated that it was illegal for a Black person to remain in a prescribed (White) area for longer than seventy-two hours. Penelope Andrews, *The Legal Underpinnings of Gender Oppression in Apartheid South Africa*, 3 AUSTRALIAN JOURNAL OF LAW AND SOCIETY (1986) 92, 97. Until that period the pass laws had not applied to women, and the official shift in policy pushed women to protest. The women said to the Prime Minister: *Wathint' abafazi, wathint' imbokodo, uzokufa'*—"now you have touched the women you have struck a rock, you have dislodged a boulder, you will be crushed."

2   *All South Africans Must Act against Corrective Rape*, WEEKLY MAIL AND GUARDIAN, May 11, 2011 at: *http://mg.co.za/article/2011-05-11-all-south-africans-must-act-against-corrective-rape*. The term "corrective rape" is used to describe the rape of lesbians, who are raped in order to "cure their sexuality."

in South African history.[3] This development resulted in and overlapped an event also of far reaching consequence in the nation's history, and critical for progress the country achieved later in women rights. I am referring to the inauguration in South Africa of a transitional phase, between the old order and the establishment of a new order, where selective South African representatives would make key decisions on what kind of government and constitution would be proposed to voters for adoption in an election. The expiration of the transitional phase was to be followed with a permanent one beginning with the adoption of a new constitution and installation of a new government.

There was, of course, nothing unique about South Africa in having a transitional phase of governance followed by a permanent political and constitutional arrangement. Other nations have done likewise.[4] What is different in the modern era is the potential for a transitional phase to become an inflection point for determining women's rights and the roles of women in government and society.[5] Thus, the manner in which South Africa handled its own transitional phase can be instructive for women in other developing nations when their countries undergo similar transitional periods.

The transitional phase in South Africa served the nation well because it was an important factor in helping to secure women's rights and gender equality as an integral part of the new constitution and in helping to guarantee that women, in the future South Africa, would have opportunities of participating in governance and society comparable to those of men.[6] Transitional phases in other countries, such as Libya, Afghanistan, Egypt, and Myanmar, have a similar potential.

On the other hand, South Africa had something unique to it which contributed mightily to such a fruitful outcome. The advantage was Nelson Mandela. His presence, stature, and involvement generated high expectations, both inside and

---

3   WILLARD CROMPTON SAMUEL, NELSON MANDELA: ENDING APARTHEID IN SOUTH AFRICA (2007). For a perspective on the challenges facing post-apartheid South Africa, *see* Bernard Makhosezwe Magubane, *Reflections on the Challenges Confronting Post-Apartheid South Africa*, UNESCO (1994) at: *http://www.unesco.org/most/magu.htm*.

4   *See*, for example, Jeremy J. Sarkin and Erin Daly, *Too Many Questions, Too Few Answers: Reconciliation in Transitional Societies*, 35 COLUMBIA HUMAN RIGHTS LAW REVIEW (2004) 101; *see also* Jaya Ramji-Nogales, *Designing Bespoke Transitional Justice: A Pluralist Process Approach*, 32 MICHIGAN JOURNAL OF INTERNATIONAL LAW (2010) 1.

5   GEORGINA WAYLEN, ENGENDERING TRANSITIONS: WOMEN'S MOBILIZATION, INSTITUTIONS, AND GENDER OUTCOMES (2007).

6   *See* Christina Murray and Felicity Kaganis, *The Contest between Culture and Gender Equality under South Africa's Interim Constitution*, 5 OXFORD INTERNATIONAL LAW REVIEW (1994) 17; *see also* Celina Romany, *Black Women and Gender Equality in a New South Africa: Human Rights Law and the Intersection of Race and Gender*, 21 BROOKLYN JOURNAL OF INTERNATIONAL LAW (1996) 857, 895.

outside of South Africa, for the future of democracy, the rule of law, liberty, equality generally, and women's rights in particular.[7]

President Mandela held South Africans to high standards and they expected, and welcomed, high standards from their President. Because of President Mandela's leading role, I think it is fair to assume that a large majority of people inside South Africa expected that the end of the transitional phase would usher in a new role for their country. This included the status of being one of the freest and most expansive democracies in the world and having a constitution that contained the world's most liberal Bill of Rights.[8]

In part, because of the symbolism of President Mandela, women in South Africa expected women's rights to be a major focus of planning for the new constitution. With President Mandela's leadership and involvement, they were confident that, for the first time in their history, women in South Africa would have equal status with men and would enjoy all the rights and privileges that had previously been open only to (white) men. This is what they ultimately obtained. However, the road to these opportunities was mined with obstacles.[9]

To realize the opportunities, two important questions had to be answered. First, what role, if any, would women play during the transitional stage in making decisions on the form of government and constitution which would be proposed to the nation for adoption? Second, what rights would the new constitution accord to women and what would be the actual level of participation of women in the new government?

If women were excluded from the decision making process during the transitional phase, then there would be less likelihood the new constitution would be fully protective of their rights, or that their interests would be secure against the vagaries of politics and the whims of chance and personal influence. Such a result would, of course, make a charade of any pretensions of South Africa as a nation that accorded equal treatment and respect to all its residents. Thus, the potential for advancing women's rights in South Africa was intimately tied up with the resolution of these two questions. By answering these questions in the most positive manner imaginable, South Africa avoided a bullet that would have been debilitating to the evolving democratic society. However, avoiding the bullet

---

7 ALLISTER SPARKS, TOMORROW IS ANOTHER COUNTRY: THE INSIDE STORY OF SOUTH AFRICA'S ROAD TO CHANGE (1996).

8 Audrey E. Haroz, *South Africa's 1996 Choice on Termination of Pregnancy Act: Expanding Choice and International Human Rights to Black South African Women*, 30 VANDERBILT JOURNAL OF TRANSNATIONAL LAW (1997) 863, 903 [South Africa's Bill of Rights is one of the most liberal and elaborate in the world]; THE CONSTITUTION OF SOUTH AFRICA FROM A GENDER PERSPECTIVE (Sandra Liebenberg ed. 1994).

9 GENDER AND THE NEW SOUTH AFRICAN LEGAL ORDER (Christina Murray ed. 1994).

was no easy task, for the country had to overcome formidable obstacles that had defeated many other countries, particularly African countries.[10]

When colonialism came to an end in Africa during the 1960s and 1970s, African countries declared independence and established new governments but did not promulgate constitutions providing for gender equality or otherwise promoting women's rights.[11] To be sure, the founders of many of these nations also did not believe in women's rights. Opposition to such actions was strong at that time and the effective action to provide for and protect women's rights would have generated enormous resistance.[12]

For many of the leaders of these countries, first, and foremost, was the task of establishing a sovereign independent nation capable of preventing the return to power of former oppressors and of ensuring control of the government by a major indigenous population group.[13] This, they saw, as the principal urgency. Since these leaders were instrumental in forging the new governments and constitutions of their country, this meant that women's rights took a back seat to what they deemed the primary and immediate focus on securing national liberation. As seen from this perspective, women's rights were subordinate to the larger nationalistic purpose, and thus were considered something that could wait until a "proper time," a time period that could not be further defined beyond stating that it would occur after the new government had proven its ability to maintain itself internally and to protect itself against external enemies.[14]

A second obstacle arose from a different set of beliefs and claims of some of these leaders. Typically, this centered around the notion that civil war, or strife, would result if women's rights were recognized and then operated to displace, or invalidate, traditional indigenous practices and values.[15] The fear imagined was that resistance to such rights and attempts to shield traditional practices threatened by them would engulf the country in civil war and dissension, thereby dooming the prospects of a unitary nation and making the nation vulnerable to oppressors

---

10   FAREDA BANDA, WOMEN, LAW AND HUMAN RIGHTS: AN AFRICAN PERSPECTIVE (2005).

11   *Ibid.*

12   AFRICAN WOMEN: A POLITICAL ECONOMY (Meredeth Turshen ed. 2010).

13   *See*, for example, JEFFREY HERBST, STATES AND POWER IN AFRICA: COMPARATIVE LESSONS IN AUTHORITY AND CONTROL (2000) and RUTH IYOB, THE ERITREAN STRUGGLE FOR INDEPENDENCE DOMINATION, RESISTANCE, NATIONALISM 1941–1993 (1997).

14   These issues are explored extensively in African literature. *See*, for example, BUCHI EMECHETA, SECOND-CLASS CITIZEN (1983); *see also* MIRIAMA MBA, SO LONG A LETTER (2008) and NGUGI WA THIONG'O, THE RIVER BETWEEN (2008) .

15   AILI MARI TRIPP, ISABEL CASIMIRO, JOY KWESIGA AND ALICE MUNGWA, AFRICAN WOMEN'S MOVEMENTS: TRANSFORMING POLITICAL LANDSCAPES (2008); VOICES OF AFRICAN WOMEN: WOMEN'S RIGHTS IN GHANA, UGANDA AND TANZANIA (Iohanna Bond ed. 2005).

recently overthrown. The extent to which these concerns were real, exaggerated, or a pretext for continued masculine domination, was not easily ascertainable.[16]

But even if the fears were credible, what was generally overlooked was potential for women's rights to bring healing and unifying power to the nation, not to mention the enhanced economic power it could bring by unleashing, as was done in many Western nations and some communist nations, the productive power of women.[17] In any event, it is now widely known that yielding to such fears and delaying the recognition of women's rights resulted in many lost decades for African countries, and left far too many women unprotected, with their dignity destroyed, and who ended up being treated as objects for the use of men. It has taken several decades for many of these African countries to get around finally to protecting the rights of women.[18]

Each nation has to make its own determination when setting into motion a transitional phase to draft a constitution and plan a government. And it must make its own calculations and determinations on how to deal with the aforementioned opportunities and obstacles. Although few countries have a leader like Nelson Mandela, they have the aspirations of their own people. In addition, international covenants are applicable to the circumstances of most countries, covenants that guarantee the exercise of basic human rights, particularly women's rights.[19] During the anti-apartheid struggle, women in South Africa looked to international human rights instruments for guidance and support. Thus, other nations, apart from appealing to the values and hopes of their own people, can appeal to these international documents, citing the achievements of countries which have recognized them, and citing the examples, such as South Africa, where the rights in these documents have been both recognized and enshrined in laws and the constitution.

The Path to Gender Equality: The Transitional Executive Council

Returning to events in South Africa during this transitional phase, I want to emphasize its significance because I believe the path chosen by South Africa is a model for many other nations. During the transitional phase, South Africa largely

---

16   AILI MARI TRIPP, ISABEL CASIMIRO, JOY KWESIGA AND ALICE MUNGWA, AFRICAN WOMEN'S MOVEMENTS *Ibid.*

17   THEORETICAL PERSPECTIVES ON GENDER AND DEVELOPMENT (Jane L. Parpart *et al.* eds. 2000).

18   *See* Adrien Katherine Wing and Tyler Murray Smith, *The New African Union and Women's Rights*, 13 TRANSNATIONAL LAW AND CONTEMPORARY PROBLEMS (2003) 33.

19   ENGENDERING HUMAN RIGHTS: CULTURAL AND SOCIO-ECONOMIC REALITIES IN AFRICA (Obioma Nnaemeka and Joy Ezello eds. 2005).

seized the opportunities as they arose, and also avoided many obstacles, though not entirely.

The path taken by South Africa in 1993 is a path open to any nation today that seeks to draft a new constitution and create a government, namely, South Africa enacted a statute which established a transitional structure empowered with authority to plan and propose for adoption a new national constitution.[20] This statute created a Transitional Executive Council (TEC) that was authorized to superintend preparations for a new government and constitution. I do not intend here to go into the myriad details of the Act or of the TEC. They are amply described elsewhere.[21] My intent here is to emphasize a single provision which was instrumental in getting a version of women's rights incorporated into the Constitution that had widespread support amongst women, and that can serve as a model for other countries when faced with the need South Africa faced in 1993. The provision of the Act relevant to the specifics of this discussion was the mandate to the TEC to "ensure the full participation of women in the transitional and electoral structures and processes."[22]

This Act, and the concomitant mandate to the Transitional Executive Council, was of supreme importance. In one step, it created the conditions prerequisite for bringing to fruition the set of important women's rights incorporated in the current South African Constitution. By this mandate, women were assured at the outset that their voices would be heard in all aspects of constitutional planning and decision making on the composition and function of the new government. In short, the TEC Act served both as a confidence builder for women and as a mechanism for making women's rights an integral part of South Africa's Constitution. This is the type of mandate that is, in my opinion, needed in any country embarking upon drafting a new constitution or creating a new government.

Neither the passage of the TEC Act nor the adoption of the new constitution (or for that matter the installation of a democratic government in which women were full participants) solved the problem of women's rights. For example, issues pertaining to traditional indigenous practices did not go away. Instead, as will be seen later, the conundrum the issues presented became embedded in the new Constitution with expectation that the courts, with guidance from the Constitution on the primacy of women's rights, would resolve whatever questions they presented in the course of time.[23] Although the delay in resolving matters was something of a setback, the transference of the issues to the courts nonetheless was potentially a great advance for women's rights. Ideally, the courts would be duty bound to defend women's rights, women would be able to influence judicial appointments

---

20   TRANSITIONAL EXECUTIVE COUNCIL ACT No. 151 of 1993.

21   For a thoughtful examination of the working of the Transitional Executive Council, *see* HEINZ KLUG, THE CONSTITUTION OF SOUTH AFRICA (2010).

22   TRANSITIONAL EXECUTIVE COUNCIL ACT, *Supra* Note 20, Section 3 (a) (iv).

23   Albie Sachs, *Judges and Gender: The Constitutional Rights of Women in a Post-Apartheid South Africa*, 7 AGENDA (1990) 1.

in the new government, judicial appointments would include women, and the new Parliament with women as members would be empowered to enact statutes to help delimit or defuse conflicts between women's rights and traditional indigenous practices.[24]

Another set of issues that did not disappear with the TEC Act and the new Constitution involved problems that afflict a large plurality, if not a majority, of women, such as matters of violence, the HIV/AIDS epidemic, poverty, and expectations by many in society that women will fulfill certain roles.[25] These issues had a material impact on the ability of women to exercise, as a practical matter, rights granted by the Constitution.[26] But how the Constitution would deal with issues of adverse impact was not spelled out in detail and would be determined by the constitutional jurisprudence that would emerge under the new Constitution.

A third set of issues bearing upon the practical realization of equality for women involved traditional indigenous practices. The new Constitution and form of government would also have to address these two sets of issues. It was apparent to women in South Africa that ensuring true equality for women would be a complex and daunting process, one that was susceptible to simple formulations and generalizations.[27]

This quest for women's rights and gender equality in South Africa is one that may be interpreted in two distinct but complementary narratives. One is a hopeful and inspirational story derived in part from the egalitarian and freedom impulses with which President Mandela, as South Africa's first President, imbued the nation. In its essence, this is the story of South Africa's Constitution and expansive Bill of Rights and a society that transitioned from authoritarianism and racism to one that embraced both democracy and human rights for all. It is the story of a societal transition where gender equality has been placed on the same constitutional

---

24   MAVIVI MYAKAYAKA-MANZINI, *Women Empowered: Women in Parliament South Africa*, WOMEN IN PARLIAMENT: BEYOND NUMBERS (International IDEA, 1998) at: *http://archive.idea.int/women/parl/studies5a.htm*. However, the record on the appointment of women judges in South Africa has been rather disappointing. *See Lack of Female Judges Worries JSC*, WEEKLY MAIL AND GUARDIAN, October 25, 2011 at: *http://mg.co.za/article/2011-10-25-lack-of-female-judges-worries-jsc/*.

25   *See* Chineze J. Onyejekwe, *The Interrelationship between Gender Based Violence and HIV/AIDS in South Africa*, 6 JOURNAL OF INTERNATIONAL WOMEN'S STUDIES (2004) 34; *see also* MARK HUNTER, LOVE IN THE TIME OF AIDS: INEQUALITY, GENDER, AND RIGHTS IN SOUTH AFRICA (2010) and Johanna Kehler, *Women and Poverty in South Africa*, JOURNAL OF INTERNATIONAL WOMEN'S STUDIES (2001) at: *http://www.bridgew.edu/soas/jiws/fall01/index.htm*.

26   Johanna Kehler, *Women and Poverty in South Africa, Ibid.*

27   Penelope E. Andrews, *Striking the Rock: Confronting Gender Equality in South Africa*, 3 MICHIGAN JOURNAL OF RACE AND LAW (1998) 307.

footing as racial equality. Moreover, such transition occurred without the civil war and widespread violence that were widely predicted.[28]

The widespread acclaim which South Africa's Constitution has achieved has been inseparable from the high regard in which its Constitutional Court is held for its decisions. The judgments of the Constitutional Court have given effect to the transformative possibilities immanent in the Constitution and Bill of Rights.[29] Sandra Liebenberg notes the transformative potential of the South African Constitution, that "unlike many classic liberal constitutions," the South African constitutional "concern is not to restrain state power, but to facilitate a fundamental change in unjust political, economic and social relations."[30] Karl Klare elaborates on this notion of transformative constitutionalism as,

> ... a long-term project of constitutional enactment, interpretation, and enforcement committed (not in isolation, of course, but in a historical context of conducive political developments) to transforming a country's political and social institutions and power relationships in a democratic, participatory, and egalitarian direction.[31]

Most significantly, the South African Constitution has adopted equality and dignity as its centerpiece, within a pluralist framework that endeavors to accommodate the aspirations and concerns of religious and linguistic minorities.[32] Gender equality is placed on the same constitutional footing as racial equality and invites the same level of scrutiny. This is unlike the situation in the U.S.A., for example, where

---

28   SOUTH AFRICA: TWELVE PERSPECTIVES ON THE TRANSITION (Helen Kitchen and J. Coleman Kitchen eds. 1994).

29   *See* Karl Klare, *Legal Culture and Transformative Constitutionalism*, SOUTH AFRICAN JOURNAL OF HUMAN RIGHTS (1998) 146; *see also* D. Moseneke, *Transformative Adjudication*, SOUTH AFRICAN JOURNAL OF HUMAN RIGHTS (2002) 309.

30   Sandra Liebenberg, *Needs, Rights and Social Transformation: Adjudicating Social Rights*, CENTER FOR HUMAN RIGHTS AND GLOBAL JUSTICE WORKING PAPER, No. 8 (2005).

31   *See* Karl Klare, *Legal Culture and Transformative Constitutionalism*, *supra* Note 29 at 150.

32   CONSTITUTION OF SOUTH AFRICA [Hereinafter "THE CONSTITUTION"]. Section 9 provides an expansive definition of equality and Section 10 provides that: "Everyone has inherent dignity and the right to have their dignity respected and protected." Section 15 provides that: "Everyone has the right to freedom of conscience, religion, thought, belief and opinion." Section 31 also reiterates these rights, providing that: "persons belonging to a cultural, religious or linguistic community may not be denied the right, with other members of that community."

racial equality is subjected to strict scrutiny and gender equality to intermediate scrutiny.[33] This, in essence, is the hopeful and inspirational story.

The second story is perhaps a less hopeful one since it concerns poverty and economic inequality, the HIV/AIDS epidemic, and violence against women, issues which affect women disproportionately in South Africa and which do not automatically disappear with a Constitution's promulgation of formal equality.[34]

There are many reasons why the second story has been less hopeful. One reason involves a critical distinction between the struggle against racism and the struggle against gender discrimination. Throughout postcolonial Africa, eradicating racism was always paramount in the liberation struggles, and there was a substantial consensus about the means for eradicating racism and what type of society would exist in the absence of racism and its effects. The consensus was also strong about the nature and form of a democratic society although historically the desirability of a democratic society was at times open to question.[35]

When one observes the experiences of women, whether in Africa or elsewhere, we see only a limited consensus regarding the eradication of sexism. This is evident in the history of the anti-apartheid movement in South Africa as shown by the events that led to the adoption of the interim Constitution.[36] Indeed, as stated previously, it was the purpose in enacting section 3 of the Transitional Executive Council Act to ensure that women would not be left out of the decision making processes. This would thus prevent the lack of a consensus on women's rights from precluding a full airing of the protections women's rights warranted in the new Constitution. By fighting to guarantee that the rights of women, other than

---

33   ERWIN CHEMERINSKY, CONSTITUTIONAL LAW: PRINCIPLES AND POLICIES 4th ed. (2011).

34   A study for the period of 1998–2000, conducted by the Community of Information, Empowerment, and Transparency found that one in three South African women had been raped in the past year. REPRODUCTIVE HEALTH RESEARCH UNIT, HIV AND SEXUAL BEHAVIOR AMONG YOUNG SOUTH AFRICANS: A NATIONAL SURVEY OF 15–24 YEAR OLDS (April 6, 2004), at: *http://ww.health08.org/southafrica/upload/ HIV-and-Sexual-Behaviour-Among-Young-South-Africans-A-National-Survey-of-15-24- Year-Olds.pdf*. One out of every six women is assaulted regularly by her partner. HUMAN RIGHTS WATCH, VIOLENCE AGAINST WOMEN IN SOUTH AFRICA: STATE RESPONSE TO DOMESTIC VIOLENCE AND RAPE (1 November 1995), at: *http:// www.unhcr.org/refworld/docid/3ae6a8294.html*; see also Lorenzo Di Silvio, *Correcting Corrective Rape: Carmichele and Developing South Africa's Affirmative Obligations to Prevent Violence against Women*, 99 GEORGIA LAW JOURNAL (2011) 1469.

35   C.R.D. HALISI, BLACK POLITICAL THOUGHT IN THE MAKING OF SOUTH AFRICAN DEMOCRACY (2000); NIGEL WORDEN, THE MAKING OF MODERN SOUTH AFRICA: CONQUEST, APARTHEID, DEMOCRACY 4th ed. (2012).

36   Suzanne A. Kim, *Betraying Women in the Name of Revolution: Violence against Women as an Obstacle to Nation-Building in South Africa*, 8 CARDOZO WOMEN'S LAW JOURNAL (2001) 1.

as mothers, sisters, and daughters, these concerns were not given short-shrift and were fully included in the interim Constitution.[37]

Conflicting "Liberatory" Discourses?

Broadly speaking, South Africa remains an amalgam of two "liberatory' discourses. One is African nationalism and the related nationalism of indigenous communities. The other is, of course, feminism. In South Africa, the eradication of apartheid and racism, while immensely challenging and still ongoing, has been popular and not as onerous as eradicating the numerous forms of discrimination against women.[38] Dislodging the legacy of patriarchy and masculinity, the foundations of sexism, simply goes against the grain of the existing power brokers and thus is considerably more challenging.

In previous articles I have examined the tripartite contours of the cultures of masculinity in South Africa.[39] I have argued that the peculiar flavor of South African patriarchy emanates from three interlinked political and cultural origins, and that these origins overlap and combine to create particularly vexing political, social, and cultural conditions in which to pursue gender equality.[40] The three sources I identify are first, a masculinist culture emanating from an authoritarian and militaristic apartheid state; second, the masculinist cultural remnants of a

---

37   *See* THE CONSTITUTION, *supra* Note 32; *see also* Penelope Andrews, *The Step-Child of National Liberation: Women and Rights in the New South Africa*, in THE POST-APARTHEID CONSTITUTIONS: REFLECTIONS ON SOUTH AFRICA'S BASIC LAW (Penelope E. Andrews and Stephen Ellmann eds. 2001) 326; and Amanda Kemp *et al.*, *The Dawn of a New Day: Redefining South African Feminism*, in THE CHALLENGE OF LOCAL FEMINISMS: WOMEN'S MOVEMENTS IN GLOBAL PERSPECTIVE (Amrita Basu ed. 1995) 131.

38   From 1983 to 1994 rape more than doubled from 15,342 to 32,107. HUMAN RIGHTS WATCH/AFR., HUMAN RIGHTS WATCH WOMEN'S RIGHTS PROJECT, VIOLENCE AGAINST WOMEN IN SOUTH AFRICA: THE STATE RESPONSE TO DOMESTIC VIOLENCE AND RAPE (Bronwen Manby and Dorothy Q. Thomas eds. 1995), 50 n. 94, citing the South Africa Institute of Race Relations, *Race Relations Survey 1993/94* at p. 299. *See* Suzanne A. Kim, *Betraying Women in the Name of Revolution: Violence against Women as an Obstacle to Nation-Building in South Africa*, *supra* Note 36.

39   *See* Penelope E. Andrews, *Democracy Stops at My Front Door: Obstacles to Gender Equality in South Africa*, 5 LOYOLA UNIVERSITY OF CHICAGO INTERNATIONAL LAW REVIEW (2007) 15; *see also* Penelope Andrews, *Learning to Love after Learning to Harm: Post-Conflict Reconstruction, Gender Equality and Cultural Values*, 15 MICHIGAN STATE JOURNAL OF INTERNATIONAL LAW (2007) 41.

40   Penelope E. Andrews, *Violence against Women in South Africa: The Role of Culture and the Limitations of the Law*, 8 TEMPLE POLITICAL AND CIVIL RIGHTS LAW REVIEW (1999) 425; *see also* Penelope E. Andrews, *Learning to Love after Learning to Harm*, *Ibid.*

violent anti-apartheid struggle; and third, aspects of indigenous customary law that continue to subordinate women.

Regarding the first, the Final Report of the Truth and Reconciliation Commission has delineated in graphic detail the depths to which the South African military and security establishment went to retain white supremacy in the face of overwhelming opposition to apartheid.[41] Such violence became an integral part of white South Africa's maintenance of rigid racial hierarchies, and it also reinforced a militaristic masculinity predicated on the subordination of white women and the suppression of black women. The architecture of the migrant labor system and other apartheid policies adopted to enforce white supremacy was predicated on the assumption of the male as head of household.[42]

The liberation movements were scrutinized as well by the Truth and Reconciliation Commission, and their methods also raised questions about male violence and female subordination.[43] Despite popular rhetoric, the very nature of this clandestine military struggle and the inevitable absence of transparency and accountability reinforced patterns of masculinity that disadvantaged women disproportionately. The mythologized and lionized "comrade" became the penultimate symbol of black political opposition, epitomizing male strength and male defiance.[44]

The third component of this masculinist culture in South Africa was a patriarchy rooted in some indigenous and religious institutions, and in indigenous and religious practices that subordinate and disadvantage women in a host of areas, including the custody of children, access to property, and rights to inheritance.[45] These systems have also come under scrutiny as more women exert their autonomy in the face of new opportunities generated by the equality framework in the Constitution.[46]

---

41 *See* FINAL REPORT OF THE TRUTH & RECONCILIATION COMMISSION (2004).

42 Penelope E. Andrews, *Striking the Rock, supra* Note 27.

43 A. Krog, *Locked into Loss and Silence: Testimonies of Gender and Violence at the South African Truth Commission,* in VICTIMS, PERPETRATORS, OR ACTORS?: GENDER, ARMED CONFLICT AND POLITICAL VIOLENCE (C. Moser and F. Clark eds. 2001) 203.

44 Catherine Campbell, *Learning to Kill? Masculinity, the Family and Violence in Natal,* 18 JOURNAL OF SOUTHERN AFRICAN STUDIES (1992) 614.

45 Martin Chanock, *Neither Customary nor Legal: African Customary Law in an Era of Family Law Reform,* 3 INTERNATIONAL JOURNAL OF LAW, POLICY AND THE FAMILY (1989) 72.

46 *See* Christina Murray and Felicity Kaganis, *The Contest between Culture and Gender Equality under South Africa's Interim Constitution, supra* Note 6; and Ronald Thandabantu Nhlapo, *International Protection of Human Rights and the Family: African Variations on a Common Theme,* 3 INTERNATIONAL JOURNAL OF LAW AND FAMILY (1989) 1.

These interlocking and overlapping patriarchal norms have provided tremendous challenges for South Africa in its quest towards gender equality.

As a result of this analysis, I have concluded that these paradoxes or contradictions are embedded in the constitutional framework, and are mediated by a liberal constitutional framework that is a ticking time bomb with respect to constitutional analysis and the formation of governmental policy. An example of one of the contradictions is found in two prominent weddings that occurred a few years ago. One was the wedding of President Jacob Zuma to his fourth wife.[47] Here we see the survival of a patriarchal norm and an indigenous practice. The other was the wedding of Zachie Achmat to his male partner.[48] Here we see a South Africa committed to contemporary human rights norms of equality and dignity. The juxtaposition of these two sets of nuptials reveals much about the confluence of the tradition and the contemporary in South Africa. What we are left to ponder are the consequences of such confluence for women's right to equality.

The Constitutional Framework

Against this backdrop, I want to explore, in the context of the two narratives mentioned earlier about women's rights and gender equality, the meaning of democratic and equal citizenship for women in a postcolonial setting like South Africa. The exploration will underscore that democratic and equal citizenship involves more than political representation and voting. What is required involves three dimensions of citizenship that are interconnected. They are access to economic resources without discrimination, freedom from violence, and freedom from cultural practices that subordinate women's interests and degrade their dignity.

Critical to this analysis are provisions of South Africa's Constitution and the jurisprudence of the Constitutional Court pertaining to women's rights. My reference to women's rights is a loose way of referring to what might better be

---

47 *See* Monica Laganparsad and Yasantha Naidoo, *Four Better or for Worse*, SUNDAY TIMES (Johannesburg), January 6, 2008 at: *http://www.thetimes.co.za/PrintEdition /Article.aspx?id=673124.*

"ANC president Jacob Zuma married his fourth wife, Nompumelelo Ntuli, in a closely guarded, traditional Zulu ceremony in the rural village of Nkandla, in northern KwaZulu-Natal, yesterday. At his KwaNxamala homestead behind green security gates local police barred the media and daring wedding crashers while bodyguards monitored the premises as Zuma, 65, an unashamed traditionalist, appeased his ancestors. Inside, a handful of Zuma well-wishers, including SA Road link's chief executive Alan Reddy and businessman Abdul Rahim Malek, witnessed the traditional ceremony." *Ibid.*

48 Diana-Marie Strydom, *Zackie Achmat to Tie the Knot*, DIE BURGER, March 12, 2007 at: *http://www.news24.com/News24/Entertainment/Celebrities/0,2-1225-2108_223218000. html.*

termed as democratic and equal citizenship rights of women.[49] This is a succinct and more accurate way of describing the plethora of rights under analysis. It reinforces the idea that what is under discussion are citizenship rights such that, in a democracy, women, as citizens, should have the same citizenship rights as men. Moreover, it reinforces the idea that the purpose of a democracy is to transform the rights of previously marginalized individuals or groups so that they cease to be marginalized, whether in law, in government, or in society.[50]

This analysis makes it possible to track, in South Africa, the progress of women's rights as an element of democratic citizenship and in terms of women being a group no longer marginalized, as well as to measure the progress in terms of the application of the CEDAW, as determined by the Constitutional Court of South Africa. To this end, the South African constitutional project generates profound possibilities. The constitutional text is truly expansive, incorporating a range of the standard civil and political rights found in many constitutions. But the Constitution also incorporates a range of social, economic, and cultural rights.

To recapitulate, the TEC Act, by guaranteeing the full participation of women in the transitional and electoral structures and processes, laid the groundwork of the new constitution and government and accomplished three important tasks. First, women were able early on to debate and resist objections to having a constitution with strong protections for women's rights. Second, women were able to ensure that those rights would embrace the ordinary rights of citizens. And, third, women were able to help determine exactly what those rights would be. It is to the last of these, namely, the identity of the rights that were created as a result of this process, that I now want to turn. This will be a two part discussion. The first will be about the rights of women that were finally incorporated into the Constitution. The second will be about how those rights have fared in the courts when women have sought to invoke them.

The present day South African Constitution is the ultimate outcome of the TEC Act and of the full participation of women in preparing the Constitution. It will be evident from examining the various provisions in the Constitution on women's rights why it is important at the outset to ensure that women will be able to participate fully in drafting their nation's constitution.

South Africa's Constitution is unequivocally committed to the principles of non-sexism and to gender equality. These commitments are reflected in Chapter 1 of the Constitution, namely, the "Founding Provisions." Chapter 1 identifies the fundamental values upon which the South African state is founded.[51]

Chapter 1 contains 6 sections. For the purposes here, the key ones are Sections 1, 2, and 3. Section 2 mandates the supremacy of the Constitution and is not unusual in nations ruled by a written constitution. Section 1 states explicitly that

---

49   GENDER EQUALITY: DIMENSIONS OF WOMEN'S EQUAL CITIZENSHIP (Linda C. McClain and Joanna L. Grossman eds. 2009).

50   *Ibid.*

51   THE CONSTITUTION, *supra* Note 32, Chapter 1.

the Republic of South Africa is a "sovereign democratic state" founded upon "(a) Human dignity, the achievement of equality and the advancement of human rights and freedoms, (b) Non-racialism, and non-sexism, (d) Universal adult suffrage."[52] Thus, at the outset, the Constitution highlights the importance it places upon equality and non-sexism. Indeed, Section 1 (b) goes so far as to group "Non-racialism and non-sexism" together, thereby providing an early forecast that, under the Constitution, rights against sexism will be as strong and as broad as those against racism. Putting freedom against sexism, or gender discrimination, on a par with freedom against racism constitutes a major advancement for the South African Constitution. The remaining subsections of section 1, namely, subsections (c) and (d), list the supremacy of the Constitution, the rule of law, right of universal adult suffrage, right to a democratic government, and rights to open, accountable, and responsive government, as other values upon which the new nation is founded.[53]

Before attending to the substantive provisions of the Bill of Rights providing for gender equality, I want to dwell a moment on Section 3. It is entitled "Citizenship." It stipulates that there is a "common South African citizenship,"[54] and that "[A]ll citizens are equally entitled to the rights, privileges and benefits of citizenship."[55] I mention this because this provision of equal citizenship rights is another avenue that can be invoked under the South African Constitution for protecting gender equality. This, however, is less explicit than the provisions under Chapter 2, the Bill of Rights, to which I now turn.

The most important provisions of the Constitution providing for gender equality are found in Chapter 2, the Bill of Rights. Because of its extreme specificity, directness, and marked applicability under most circumstances, Section 9, entitled "Equality," must be deemed the provision most influential and protective of women's rights. It is here, in Section 9, that we ascertain the nature of the protections that the values in Section 1 express.

Section 9 has five subsections. The first two do not single out gender or women's issues but rather affirm general equality principles.[56] Subsection (3), however, is different in that sex, gender, pregnancy, and sexual orientation are specifically mentioned. Section 9 (3) states affirmatively, in ringing tones:

> The state may not unfairly discriminate directly or indirectly against anyone on one or more grounds, including race, gender, sex, pregnancy, marital status, ethnic or social origin, color, sexual orientation, age, disability, religion, conscience, belief, culture, language and birth.[57]

---

52   *Ibid.* Chapter 1, Section 1.
53   *Ibid.*
54   *Ibid.* Section 3 (1).
55   *Ibid.* Section 3 (2).
56   *Ibid.* Section 9.
57   *Ibid.* Chapter 2, Section 9 (3).

The prohibition is, however, limited to the state. The next subsection, (4) removes the limitation and states directly: "No person may unfairly discriminate directly or indirectly against anyone on one or more grounds in terms of subsection (3)."[58] Thus, between them, subsections (3) and (4) of Section 9 outlaw altogether discrimination, whether by the "state" or by any "person," on the grounds of gender, sex, pregnancy, marital status, or sexual orientation. These are important protections for women inasmuch as much of the discrimination they face is based on one or more of these grounds.

Another innovation in the South African Constitution that aids the pursuit of women's rights is the way in which the Constitution handles a litigant's burden to demonstrate discrimination. The provision for taking care of this is in subsection (5) of Section 9. It provides that "discrimination on one or more of the grounds listed in subsection (3) is unfair unless it is established that the discrimination is fair."[59] Thus, a showing of discrimination under subsection (3) can be deemed presumptively unfair unless the defender of the discrimination shows affirmatively that it is fair. In lay terms, the person discriminating must justify the discrimination if it is to be upheld. Proponents of discriminatory practices against women will thus be compelled to uncover evidence sufficient to prove the discriminatory practices are in fact fair. This is a heavy burden to sustain, and many discriminatory practices may not survive constitutional muster in this regard.[60]

As is apparent from the range of prohibitions listed in subsection (3) above, the grounds for constitutional protection under section 9 of Chapter 2 are far reaching, including not just race and gender, but also sexual orientation, ethnic or social origin, marital status, color, religion, belief, culture, pregnancy, age, disability, conscience, language, and birth. Also, subsection (4) makes clear that the prohibition against discrimination delineated in subsection (3) extends to both direct and indirect discrimination.

The manner in which Section 9 sets out to protect gender equality and other interests of women exemplifies the strategic importance South Africa places upon women's rights. This can be understood from five perspectives. First, by providing that discrimination against women is just as constitutionally suspect as discrimination on the basis of race, the South African Constitution provides broader protections for women's rights than those found in American constitutional jurisprudence.[61] Parallel treatment is thus required for both cases and the stringency

---

58   *Ibid.* Chapter 2, Section 9 (4).

59   *Ibid.* Chapter 2, Section 9 (5).

60   Rebutting the presumption of unfairness regarding gender has been successful in a few high-profile cases. *See,* for example, *President of the Republic of South Africa and Another v Hugo* 1997 (6) BCLR 708.

61   For a thoughtful comparative analysis of the two systems, *see* MARK KENDE, CONSTITUTIONAL RIGHTS IN TWO WORLDS: SOUTH AFRICA AND THE UNITED STATES (2010).

of scrutiny of the offending discrimination is to be no less in the one case than in the other.

Second, the "prohibition on direct and indirect discrimination implicitly acknowledges the invidiousness and tenacity of institutionalized discrimination."[62] This acknowledgment reflects views expressed by feminist and other critical scholars about the need to include a clear prohibition on indirect discrimination.[63] Section 9 satisfies this need by treating indirect gender discrimination on a par with indirect racial discrimination, and by presuming that indirect gender discrimination is unfair unless the proponent of the discrimination proves it to be fair.

Third, the inclusion of both sex and gender as grounds for proscribing discrimination has the potential of protecting women from invidious discrimination based not only on biological or physical attributes, but also on social or cultural stereotypes about the perceived role and status of women.[64] There is, however, a limitation. Section 37 of the Constitution permits certain emergency derogation from Section 9's protections of equality. However, the derogation does not extend to grounds of discriminations provided on a list in that section.[65] The list includes sex but not gender. It can only be concluded that the distinction thus drawn between sex and gender as grounds for discrimination reflects a certain reticence on the part of the constitutional drafters to upset prevailing stereotypes about the role and status of women.

Fourth, Section 9, which prohibits discrimination by private individuals, also obliges the government to act affirmatively to enact legislation "to prevent or prohibit unfair discrimination."[66] Lastly, all of the obligations under Section 9, whether for everyone to refrain from proscribed acts of discrimination or for the government to enact legislation to prohibit unfair discrimination, must be carried out in conformity with Section 9 (5)'s directive to deem discrimination proscribed under Section 9 (3) as "unfair unless it is established that the discrimination is fair."[67]

One subsection of Section 9 not yet mentioned is subsection (2). It is an important and fundamental provision without parallel in the Constitution of the United States. It has two parts; one, a general statement about equality which provides that: "Equality includes the full and equal enjoyment of all rights and

---

62   Penelope Andrews, *From Gender Apartheid to Non-Sexism: The Pursuit of Women's Rights in South Africa*, 26 NORTH CAROLINA JOURNAL OF INTERNATIONAL LAW AND COMMERCIAL REGULATION (2001) 693, 699.

63   *See* Reg Graycar and Jenny Jane Morgan, *Examining Understandings of Equality: One Step Forward, Two Steps Back?*, 20 AUSTRALIAN FEMINIST LAW JOURNAL (2004) 23.

64   Margaret Thornton analyses these issues in relation to anti-discrimination laws in Australia. *See* MARGARET THORNTON, THE LIBERAL PROMISE (1990).

65   THE CONSTITUTION, *supra* Note 32, Section 37 (5).

66   *Ibid.* Section 9 (4).

67   *Ibid.* Section 9 (5).

freedoms."[68] It captures the importance of equality in South African life under the new Constitution.

The second part of Section 9 (2) is what is unique because of the expansive approach it takes towards dealing with an issue that has been problematical in the United States, namely, affirmative action. This part provides that:

> To promote the achievement of equality, legislative and other measures designed
> to protect or advance persons or categories of persons disadvantaged by unfair
> discrimination, may be taken.[69]

It is in fact the constitutional underpinning for affirmative action. I have argued elsewhere that it is patently,

> ... clear that a constitutional mandate for affirmative action is an important
> weapon for tackling structural discrimination in a comprehensive manner, as
> well as shielding affirmative action programs from constitutional challenges.[70]

This incorporation of affirmative action in the Constitution showcases South Africa's commitment to gender equality, a commitment buttressed by the governments ratification of the CEDAW. CEDAW authorizes affirmative action and provides that,

> ... adoption by States Parties of temporary special measures aimed at
> accelerating de facto equality between men and women shall not be considered
> discrimination. These measures shall be discontinued when the objectives of
> equality of opportunity and treatment have been achieved.[71]

Section 10 of Chapter 2 of the South African Constitution is another provision with enormous potential and importance for women. It provides that: "Everyone has inherent dignity and the right to have their dignity respected and protected."[72] It is not a stretch of ordinary language or a failure to abide by proper legal rules of interpretation to regard many common forms of violence by men against women as violations, under the Constitution, of a woman's dignity, and failures of the state to prevent, deter, or provide redress for the violence. But regardless of whether one accepts Section 10 as a proper vehicle for according women with a constitutionally sanctioned right against violence, another provision of the Constitution, namely, Section 12 of Chapter 2, entitled "Freedom and security of the person" is explicit

---

68   *Ibid.* Section 9 (2).

69   *Ibid.* Section 9 (2).

70   Penelope Andrews, *From Gender Apartheid to Non-Sexism: The Pursuit of Women's Rights in South Africa, supra* Note 62 at 700.

71   CEDAW, *supra* Chapter 2, Note 9, Article 4.

72   THE CONSTITUTION, *supra* Note 32, Chapter 2, Section 10.

on the point. Section 12 (1), the operative provision, states: "Everyone has the right to freedom and security of the person which includes the right ... (c) to be free from all forms of violence from either public or private sources."[73]

Feminist scholars have long argued that the public/private distinction discriminates against women and perpetuates violence against them.[74] Clearly, this is based upon the commonly known fact that women are more likely to be subjected to violence from loved ones within the family than from strangers.[75] To be sure, this is part of a broader argument feminists have presented in documenting the dichotomy of the public/private divide in law, depicting its deleterious impact on women.[76] Section 12 (1) was drafted to pierce the public/private distinction and to the extent it does so, this section has enormous potential to protect women from violence both within the home as well as outside of it.

This constitutional solicitude for protecting human dignity and freedom from violence clearly had the protection of women and the ending of sexism as intended goals. Indeed, in the second subsection of Section 12, namely Section 12 (2), the Constitution states:

> Everyone has the right to bodily and psychological integrity, which includes the right (a) to make decisions concerning reproduction; (b) to security in and control over their body; and (c) not to be subjected to medical or scientific experiment without their informed consent.[77]

Clearly, Section 12 (2) was designed to put beyond doubt the legal right of women to be protected with regard to personal choices about birth control and reproduction. Few things restrict women's freedom and the ability to improve their lives as much as deprivation of the right to control their own bodies and when to take pregnancy to term.[78] By providing this right explicitly, the Constitution augments immeasurably the potential for each woman to shape her own individual destiny, preserve her independence and autonomy, and to help other women to do

---

73   *Ibid*, Chapter 2, Section 10.

74   *See* Celina Romany, *State Responsibility Goes Private: A Feminist Critique of the Public/Private Distinction in International Human Rights Law*, in HUMAN RIGHTS OF WOMEN: NATIONAL AND INTERNATIONAL PERSPECTIVE (Rebecca Cook ed. 1994) at 85; *see also* Judith Resnick, *Reconstructing Equality: Of Justice, Justicia, and the Gender of Jurisdiction*, 14 YALE JOURNAL OF LAW AND FEMINISM (2002) 393.

75   Patricia Tjaden and Nancy Thoennes, *Extent, Nature, and Consequence of Intimate Partner Violence*, FINDINGS FROM THE NATIONAL VIOLENCE AGAINST WOMEN SURVEY (2000) at: *https://www.ncjrs.gov/pdffiles1/nij/181867.pdf.*

76   *See* Celina Romany, *State Responsibility Goes Private*, *supra* Note 74.

77   THE CONSTITUTION, *supra* Note 32, Chapter 2, Section 12.

78   Rebecca J. Cook and Charles Ngwena, *Women's Access to Health Care: The Legal Framework*, 94 INTERNATIONAL JOURNAL OF GYNECOLOGY AND OBSTETRICS (2006) 216.

the same. The restriction that Section 16 (c) imposes on freedom of expression with respect to "advocacy of hatred that is based on race, ethnicity, gender or religion, and that constitutes incitement to cause harm,"[79] is not likely to be germane to the rights recognized by Sections 12 (1) and 12 (2).

Of course, the provision of rights such as those that we have been considering are insufficient, especially in many developing nations, to eliminate the subordination and disadvantages which disproportionately burden women. In particular, rights recognized in these sections of the Constitution will not ensure that women's need for access to education, housing, health care, food, water, and social security are met. These needs are compounded when women's roles as mothers are taken into account. The South African Constitution tries to meet this problem, at least in part, by including a set of social and economic rights.

An important example is provided by Section 28 of Chapter 2. Although the Section is entitled "Children," women as mothers will especially benefit from it because so often they are the principal caretaker, or the caretaker of last resort. The rights of children are comprehensively embraced in this Section, and especially as they relate to their social and economic well-being. For example, Section 28 (c) provides that every child has the right to "basic nutrition, shelter, basic health care services, and social services."[80] Section 28 (d) provides that every child has the right to be protected from "maltreatment, neglect, abuse or degradation" while Section 28 (c) provides that every child has the right to be protected from "exploitative labor practices."[81]

This recognition of economic and social rights of children is key to protecting and preserving women's rights, particularly in poor societies. Other socio-economic sections of the Constitution, such as Sections 26 and 27, which deal with housing, health care, food, water, and social security, limit the state's duty to provide access to a particular socio-economic right by requiring the state only to take reasonable measures to assure access "within its available resources, to achieve the progressive realization" of the right.[82] No such restriction, however, is incorporated in Section 28 for children.

Just as the Constitution protects women against disabilities arising from certain social and economic inequities, it also protects their rights against infringement from religious, cultural, and linguistic communities. This work is done by Section 31 (2) insofar as it places a limitation upon rights otherwise granted under Section 31 (1) to people in a "cultural, religious or linguistic community" to "enjoy their culture, practice their religion and use their language."[83] Section 31 (2) states unambiguously: "The rights in subsection (1) may not be exercised in a manner

---

79   THE CONSTITUTION, *supra* Note 32, Section 16 (2) (c).

80   *Ibid.* Section 28 (1) (c).

81   *Ibid.* Section 28 (1) (d).

82   *Ibid.* Section 26 (2) [housing]; Section 27 (2) [health care, food, water, and social security].

83   *Ibid.* Section 31.

inconsistent with any provision of the Bill of Rights." This includes, of course, the equality provisions in the Bill of Rights. As a result of Section 31 (2), people in such communities cannot deprive the women of those communities of rights granted by the Constitution and thereby relegate them to second-class status.[84]

Those who participated in drafting the Constitution were concerned that the rights they had so laboriously worked to create would not turn out to be illusory. To that end, they placed in the Constitution measures to ensure enforcement, compliance, and monitoring. One method used was the insertion of provisions to ensure that litigants in courts would have standing to sue to enforce the rights. This was done in a very comprehensive way. Section 38 states that anyone listed in subsections (a)–(e) who alleges "a right in the Bill of Rights has been infringed or threatened" possesses "the right to approach a competent court" for relief.[85] The persons listed are:

  a. anyone acting in their own interest;
  b. anyone acting on behalf of another person who cannot act in their own name;
  c. anyone acting as a member of, or in the interest of, a group or class of persons;
  d. anyone acting in the public interest; and
  e. an association acting in the interest of its members.[86]

A second way in which drafters of the Constitution sought protection for rights enshrined in the Constitution was, as previously stated, to make the Constitution, under Section 2, the "supreme law of the Republic" and to mandate courts, tribunals, and forums to interpret the rights in the Constitution in a way that comports with the Constitution's underlying ideals.[87] The latter requirement is set forth in Section 39 which states:

> When interpreting any legislation and when developing the common law or customary law, every court, tribunal or forum must promote the spirit, purport and objects of the Bill of Rights.[88]

Where some aspect of women's rights, or other rights, is found instead in international law or foreign law, Section 39 authorizes courts, tribunals, and

---

  84 *See* NAJMA MOOSA, UNVEILING THE MIND: A HERSTORY OF THE HISTORICAL EVOLUTION OF THE LEGAL POSITION OF WOMEN IN ISLAM (2004). *See also* Aninka Claasens, *Who Told Them We Want This Bill? The Traditional Courts Bill and Rural Women*, 82 AGENDA (2009) 9 and Aninka Claasens and Sindiso Mnisi, *Rural Women Redefining Land Rights in the Context of Living Customary Law*, 25 SOUTH AFRICAN JOURNAL ON HUMAN RIGHTS (2009) 491.
  85 THE CONSTITUTION, *supra* Note 32, Section 38.
  86 *Ibid.* Section 31.
  87 *Ibid.* Section 39.
  88 *Ibid.* Section 39 (1) (h).

forums "to consider international law and may consider foreign law" when interpreting the Bill of Rights.[89] As is the case with legislation, common law and customary law, rights under international law and foreign law cannot be used, as Section 39 (3) makes clear, and cannot be invoked in ways that are inconsistent with the Constitution's Bill of Rights.[90]

Finally, a third way the Constitution provided for ensuring observance of rights was the establishment of two special commissions, one for gender equality, namely, the Commission for Gender Equality, and one for human rights generally, namely the Human Rights Commission. The establishment of these commissions is another innovation made by the South African Constitution in protecting women's rights. The outlines of the powers and responsibilities of the Commission for Gender Equality are set out in Section 187 of the Constitution. It provides that:

1. The Commission for Gender Equality must promote respect for gender equality and the protection, development and attainment of gender equality.
2. The Commission for Gender Equality has the power, as regulated by national legislation, necessary to perform its functions, including the power to monitor, investigate, research, educate, lobby, advise, and report on issues concerning gender equality.
3. The Commission for Gender Equality has the additional powers and functions prescribed by national legislation.[91]

The enabling provisions in the Constitution for the Human Rights Commission are set forth in Section 184. Subsection (1) (c) specifically provides that the Commission must "monitor and assess the observance of human rights in the Republic" and subsection (2) states the Commission is empowered to carry out this function as well as "to take steps to secure appropriate redress where human rights have been violated."[92] This Commission is invaluable for women since many women in South Africa, like in other developing nations, will often lack financial means for suing in court to enforce their rights.

Other agencies established by the Constitution will also be able to enforce the rights of women. One such agency is the Public Protector which, under Section 182, is authorized,

---

89   *Ibid.* Section 187.

90   "The Bill of Rights does not deny the existence of any other rights or freedoms that are recognised or conferred by common law, customary law or legislation, to the extent that they are consistent with the Bill." *Ibid.* Section 39 (3).

91   *Ibid.*

92   *Ibid.* Section 184 (2) (b).

... to investigate any conduct in state affairs, or in the public ... [sector that is] suspected to be improper or to result in any impropriety or prejudice [and] to take appropriate remedial action.[93]

All together, the constitutional provisions for standing, the commissions, and the courts are potent weapons women can employ in protecting and preserving their rights. A qualification, however, must be made since the effective functioning of the commissions and the courts is predicated on the availability of state resources, that is, upon the state's commitment to continued vigilance in ensuring compliance with women's rights.

It is worth pausing for a moment to reflect on the moment of South Africa's political transition, since the historical context is often one of the best guides to explaining the particular constitutional path a country adopts. South Africa was always an issue of international concern and the movement to end apartheid was a global one. The United Nations declared apartheid a crime against humanity in 1973.[94] In time the release of Nelson Mandela, as the world's most prominent prisoner, was to become one of the foremost political movements in the world. After his inauguration as South Africa's first democratically elected President, Nelson Mandela became the world's most beloved President.[95]

The text of the Constitution, and particularly the Bill of Rights, reflects the global consensus, formally at least, around human rights and especially women's human rights. As Dean Makau wa Matua has noted:

> The construction of the post-apartheid state represents the first deliberate and calculated effort in history to craft a human rights state—a polity that is primarily animated by human rights norms. South Africa was the first state to be reborn after the universal acceptance, at least rhetorically, of human rights ideals by states of all the major cultural and political traditions.[96]

There were major global political events unfolding as South Africa emerged from apartheid to a constitutional democracy, such as the 1989 destruction of the Berlin Wall and the collapse of communist states.[97] Perhaps, one can characterize

---

93   *Ibid.* Chapter 9, Section 182 (1).

94   INTERNATIONAL CONVENTION ON THE SUPPRESSION AND PUNISHMENT OF THE CRIME OF APARTHEID (1973). G.A. res. 3068 (XXVIII)), 28 U.N. GAOR Supp. (No. 30) at 75, U.N. Doc. A/9030 (1974), 1015 U.N.T.S. 243, *entered into force* July 18, 1976.

95   *See* Euserbius McKaiser, *When Mandela Goes*, NEW YORK TIMES, January 4, 2012 at: *http://latitude.blogs.nytimes.com/2012/01/04/when-mandela-goes/?ref=nelsonmandela.*

96   Makau wa Mutua, *Hope and Despair for a New South Africa: The Limits of Rights Discourse*, 10 HARVARD HUMAN RIGHTS LAW JOURNAL (1997) 63, 65.

97   CHARLES S. MAIER, DISSOLUTION: THE CRISIS OF COMMUNISM AND THE END OF EAST GERMANY (1999).

this change as one in which the language of rights replaced the language of redistribution. As Upendra Baxi has commented, with the end of communism the language of rights becomes a hegemonic political language, the lingua franca of progressive politics, "usurping all other ethical discourse."[98]

The drafters of the South African Constitution extracted the values and principles underpinning the rights found in international human rights instruments and transformed those rights to conform to local South African conditions. In fact, a notable constitutional scholar and judge has commented that between 1990 and 1994, South Africa seemed to be hosting one continuous constitutional workshop.[99]

An Evolving Constitutional Jurisprudence

Before examining cases of the Constitutional Court of South Africa to see how some of the rights we have discussed have fared in litigation, I want to highlight a few important features of South Africa's constitutionalism in order to show why it has such transformative potential, a circumstance that Karl Klare and others have noted.[100] The first is the horizontal and vertical nature of the Constitution, applying to relationships between the state and citizens, as well as to relationships between citizen and citizen. This approach is a recognition on the part of the constitutional drafters that discrimination is often shielded by and embedded in private as well as public relationships.[101]

Second, the Constitution creates an imperative to derogate from the status quo. Constitutional interpretation in South Africa occurs in a context in which judges and others recognize that disadvantage, subordination, and discrimination are deeply embedded in the nation's political, economic, and legal system.[102] This

---

98   Upendra Baxi, *Voices of Suffering and the Future of Human Rights*, 8 TRANSNATIONAL LAW AND CONTEMPORARY PROBLEMS (1998) 125, 147. Others have commented on the primacy of human rights as the hegemonic language of progressive politics. *See*, for example, BOAVENTURA DE SOUSA SANTOS, TOWARD A NEW COMMON SENSE: LAW SCIENCE AND POLITICS IN THE PARADIGMATIC TRANSITION (1995) 266–7.

99   My friend and colleague, Judge Dennis Davis, of the Cape High Court, made this comment at a conference that we both attended at Valparaiso University in 2008.

100   *See* Karl Klare, *Legal Culture and Transformative Constitutionalism, supra* Note 29; *see also* D. Moseneke, *Transformative Adjudication, supra* Note 29.

101   *See* Justice Dikgang Moseneke, *Transformative Constitutionalism: Its Implications for the Law of Contract*, ANNUAL PUBLIC LECTURE, UNIVERSITY OF STELLENBOSCH, October 22, 2008.

102   The centrality and nature of this economic and political inequality is typified by the question of land in South Africa. It is thoughtfully explored in ANINKA CLAASSENS AND BEN COUSINS, LAND, POWER AND CUSTOM (2008), especially Chapter 1, *Contextualizing the Controversies: Dilemmas of Communal Tenure Reform in Post-Apartheid South Africa*, at 3.

is unlike the situation, for example, in the United States, where derogation from the status quo is hotly contested amongst judges and legal scholars.[103] Third, the Constitution mandates that the courts must consider international law and may consider foreign law in its deliberations.[104]

I now turn to cases in which the courts, primarily the Constitutional Court, have interpreted some of the constitutional provisions previously discussed.

The evolving constitutional jurisprudence of the Constitutional Court suggests a clear break from South Africa's ignominious apartheid legal past to one forged on principles of dignity, equality and non-discrimination. The cases discussed below indicate how the Court has thoughtfully articulated the need to eradicate vestiges of subordination and discrimination against women. These cases demonstrate the Constitutional Court's role as one of the major institutions responsible for realizing the full scope of the rights and values embodied in the Constitution. In carrying out its functions, the Court has adopted an approach that is mindful of this role while simultaneously cognizant of the imperatives of the doctrine of separation of powers.[105]

To fulfill its responsibility, the Court has had to strike a sound balance between its mandate to interpret and enforce the rights, on the one hand, and its awareness of limited government resources, on the other. The Court has also been mindful of its institutional limitations with respect to its ability to assess competing claims from diverse sectors of disadvantaged and marginalized South Africans against its ability to determine how the government should allocate and spend resources amongst the neediest South Africans.[106]

Pursuing Substantive Equality

On the issue of gender equality, the Court has for the most part articulated a comprehensive approach to equality, eschewing narrow formalistic approaches to equality in favor of approaches that adopt substantive equality.[107] This attitude was demonstrated very early on. In a series of cases since the inauguration of the Court in 1994, the Court has underscored the primacy of equality. These cases include those involving the right of HIV-positive persons not to be discriminated against

---

103   *See,* for example, JUSTICE STEPHEN BREYER, ACTIVE LIBERTY: INTERPRETING OUR DEMOCRATIC CONSTITUTION (2005); *see also* Jamal Greene, *Selling Originalism,* 97 THE GEORGETOWN LAW JOURNAL (2009) 657.

104   THE CONSTITUTION, *supra* Note 32, Section 39 (1) (b) and (c).

105   JUSTICE KATHERINE O'REGAN, HELEN SUZMAN MEMORIAL LECTURE, November 22, 2011 at: *http://writingrights.nu.org.za/2011/11/24/justice-kate oregans-helen-suzman-memorial-lecture/.*

106   *Ibid.*

107   Penelope Andrews, *From Gender Apartheid to Non-Sexism: The Pursuit of Women's Rights in South Africa, supra* Note 62.

in their employment;[108] the right of prisoners to vote;[109] the rights of unmarried fathers in relation to adoption of their children;[110] the rights of permanent residents not to be treated unfairly in comparison to citizens in the workplace;[111] the rights of homosexuals to engage in consensual sexual conduct;[112] and the rights of African girls and women not to be discriminated against under indigenous customary law.[113]

In a 1996 case, the Constitutional Court considered the constitutionality of an executive order signed by President Nelson Mandela, that sought to pardon "all mothers in prison on 10 May 1994, with minor children under the age of 12 years."[114] This section of the Presidential Act was challenged by a male prisoner who argued that the remission of sentences applicable only to mothers violated the constitutional rights of fathers. The basis of his challenge was that the provision in question unfairly discriminated against him on the grounds of sex or gender, and indirectly against his son because his son's incarcerated parent was not female, and therefore deprived him of a possible presidential pardon based upon his gender.[115]

This case can be viewed through several lenses. It can be seen as a case challenging affirmative action on behalf of women, as a gender discrimination case, and as a case in which the father sought standing to raise a claim on behalf of his child. The lower court agreed with the complainant and found that the Presidential Act discriminated against him on the grounds of sex and gender. The court also found that the presumption of unfairness had not been rebutted by the President.[116]

However, after hearing the case on appeal, the Constitutional Court reversed the lower court's decision. In a lengthy opinion, the Court first considered the nature of the power granted to the President under the Interim Constitution to pardon individuals or groups.[117] It then concluded that the presidential power to

---

108   *Hoffmann v South African Airways* 2001 (1) SA 1.

109   *Minister of Home Affairs v National Institute for Crime Prevention* (2004) 5 BCLR 445 (CC).

110   *Fraser v The Children's Court, Pretoria North and Others* 1997 (2) BCLR 153 (CC).

111   *Larbi-Odam and Others v MEC for Education (Northwest Province) and Another* (1998) 1 SA 745 (CC).

112   *The National Coalition for Gay and Lesbian Equality and Another v The Minister of Justice and Others*, 1999 (1) SA 6 (CC).

113   *Bhe & Others v The Magistrate, Khayelitsha*, 2005 (1) SA 581 (CC).

114   *President of the Republic of South Africa v. Hugo*, *supra* Note 60.

115   *Ibid.*

116   THE CONSTITUTION, *supra* Note 32, Section 9 (5). ["Discrimination on one or more of the grounds … is unfair unless it is established that the discrimination is fair.] *See* Adrien Katherine Wing's explanation of the multi-pronged test for unfairness in the South African Constitution. *The South African Constitution as a Role Model for the United States*, 74 HARVARD BLACK LETTER LAW JOURNAL (2008) 24.

117   This case was brought under South Africa's Interim Constitution of 1993, which was replaced by the 1996 Constitution, *Supra* Note 32.

pardon is guided by the principle of equality as articulated in the Constitution notwithstanding its origins in the royal prerogative. In reaching its decision, the Court undertook a comprehensive journey of the laws of a number of nations that had addressed the question of judicial review of presidential pardons.[118] The Court ultimately concluded that the President's decision to grant the pardon to women and not men was done in the best interests of the child.

Justice Goldstone, writing for the majority, first found that the presidential pardon discriminated against the complainant.[119] Next, the Court addressed the presumption of unfairness triggered by a showing of discrimination on the basis of gender. Note that, as articulated in the Constitution, the burden is to establish that the discrimination is fair. On this issue, the Court turned to an examination of the rationale underlying the Presidential Act in allowing special remission for mothers of minor children.[120] The Court referenced the special testimony of the Director of the South African National Council for Child and Family Welfare on the peculiar role that mothers play in the rearing of their children. The Court noted the apparent contradiction between the reality that mothers bear the greatest burden of childrearing and the constitutional imperative that everyone be treated equally.[121] The Court decided it could not be blind to the contemporary reality in South Africa in which mothers have the greater share of childrearing. Distinguishing between the idealized situation in which fathers and mothers equally share childrearing functions, and the generalized situation of unequal childrearing, the Court determined that children would substantially benefit from the Presidential Act.[122]

The Court acknowledged, however, that the generalization about women bearing the greater proportion of the burden of childrearing had historically been used to justify the unequal treatment of women. In this respect, the Court made reference to an earlier court decision in South Africa in which women were denied entry to the legal profession in part because of their childrearing responsibilities.[123] The Court, however, distinguished this case from the one before it because it was about an undue burden flowing from generalizations about women and childbearing whereas the Court saw the case before it as providing an opportunity, through the presidential pardon for women, to lift an undue burden from women.[124]

The Constitutional Court also considered what the likely outcome would be if equal treatment were applied, namely, the release of all prisoners, male and female, with children under the age of twelve. It concluded that no public benefit would be gained by releasing fathers because they were not the primary caretakers of children. Pointing out that the Presidential Act provides for the

---

118   *President of the Republic of South Africa v. Hugo, supra* Note 60 at 7–27.
119   *Ibid.* at 40.
120   *Ibid.* at 42–51.
121   *Ibid.* at 46.
122   *Ibid.* at 47.
123   *Ibid.* at 46.
124   *Ibid.* at 41.

individual application for remission of sentences by male prisoners where special circumstances can be shown, the Court therefore found the discrimination to be fair.[125]

Justice Kriegler dissented. His dissent is worth noting because it appears to comport with current American equal opportunity jurisprudence, namely, a focus on intent as opposed to outcomes or impact. He agreed with the Court's conclusion that the power of presidential pardon granted under the clemency powers of the South African Constitution is subject to judicial review for consistency with the equality section of the Constitution. He also agreed that the court below made an error in holding otherwise.

He disagreed, however, with the Court's conclusion that the clemency granted for mothers of young children was fair. In his opinion, the presidential pardon did not pass constitutional muster. Like the majority, he found that the President committed gender discrimination under the Constitution by distinguishing between classes of parents on the basis of their gender. But, unlike the majority, he concluded that the presumption of unfairness in "attaching that distinction has not been rebutted."[126] Justice Kriegler raised an issue concerning a matter that had not been fully explored by the majority but which was an underlying assumption of the presidential decree on pardons. This was the concern that large numbers of men being released from prison would shake public confidence. He questioned the absence of empirical data to support this proposition, noting that the majority had instead relied on public perceptions about crime.[127]

Justice Kriegler insisted that where some rebuttal is provided for the presumption of unfairness, such rebuttal must be scrutinized thoroughly and must not be "discharged with relative ease."[128] He took issue with the rationale that women were the primary caregivers of young children, stating this generalization to be,

> ... a root cause of women's inequality in our society. It is both a result and a cause of prejudice: a societal attitude which relegates women to a subservient, occupationally inferior yet unceasingly onerous role. It is a relic and feature of the patriarchy which the Constitution so vehemently condemns.[129]

Justice Kriegler concluded that a small number of women would benefit from this pardon, but the rebuttal and the rationale for the rebuttal used by the majority would operate as a "detriment to all South African women who must continue to labor under the social view that their place is in the home."[130] He argued that

---

125 *Ibid.* at 52.
126 KRIEGLER, J. DISSENT *Ibid.* at 66.
127 *Ibid.* at 72.
128 *Ibid.* at 75.
129 *Ibid.* at 80.
130 *Ibid.* at 83.

the benefit to a few hundred women cannot justify the continued stereotyping of women as the primary caregivers.

Justice O'Regan's concurring opinion is also particularly noteworthy. She agreed with the statements made by the majority about the reviewability of the presidential pardon and focused her comments entirely on the question of whether the discrimination inherent in the presidential order was unfair. She found Justice Kriegler's approach too restrictive, instead noting that the determination of whether the discrimination was unfair required a recognition that,

> ... although the long-term goal of our constitutional order is equal treatment, insisting upon Equal treatment in circumstances of established inequality may well result in the entrenchment of that inequality.[131]

Justice O'Regan noted that there were two factors relevant to the determination of unfairness: an analysis of the group that has suffered discrimination, and the "effect of the discrimination on the interests of those concerned."[132] She evaluated the vulnerability of the group affected by the discrimination and the particularly invasive nature of the discrimination.

Justice O'Regan noted that even though the goal of equality in the Constitution is very clear, the factual reality in South Africa was that women did carry, and would continue to carry in the foreseeable future, the greater burden of childrearing. She considered this a crucial fact in looking at discrimination and determining the unfairness of the distinction made. Referring to Justice Kriegler's proposition that there would be a profound disadvantage for women in perpetuating the stereotype through the distinction, Justice O'Regan pointed out that the profound disadvantage did not result from the presidential decree but from the inequality which was part of the social fabric of South African society.[133] She disagreed with Justice Kriegler that this presidential pardon harmed women. She also pointed out that any discrimination that men may suffer as a result of the presidential pardon was not severe. Justice O'Regan argued further that even though fathers were denied the special remission of sentence by the general decree, they did have the opportunity to make individual applications.[134]

The majority and concurring opinions in this judgment indicate the broad contours of equality that the Constitutional Court is prepared to embrace. The Court is concerned not just with formal equality (equal treatment), which can at times lead to inequality, but also with substantive equality, which contextualizes the actual experiences and reality of women within the formal impediments to equality.[135]

---

131   O'REGAN, J CONCURRENCE, *Ibid.* at 112.

132   *Ibid.*

133   *Ibid.* at 113–14.

134   *Ibid.* at 114.

135   Karthy Govender, *The Developing Equality Jurisprudence in South Africa*, 107 MICHIGAN LAW REVIEW FIRST IMPRESSIONS (2009) 120.

The case also demonstrates the absence of a bright line in determining whether the presumption of unfairness that attends a finding of gender discrimination has been rebutted. Thus, promulgation of a constitutional provision protecting women is just the beginning of a long process, a process that can be dragged out in the courts for an interminable number of years.

Another early case on gender equality but raising a different issue involved an unmarried father who challenged the provisions of the Child Care Act permitting the adoption of children born out of wedlock without the consent of the father.[136] For children born in wedlock, the consent of both parents was required. The father successfully challenged the law and it was declared unconstitutional. In evaluating the Child Care Act, and particularly the gender equality issues raised in this case, the late Justice Mahomed noted:

> In considering appropriate legislative alternatives, parliament should be acutely sensitive to the deep disadvantage experienced by single mothers in our society. Any legislative initiative should not exacerbate that disadvantage.[137]

Adopting a contextual approach reflecting social reality, the Court stated that a mother's "biological relationship with the child," nurtured during pregnancy and breastfeeding, is a special one.[138] The Court also noted that a mother gives "succor and support" to a child that is "very direct and not comparable to that of a father."[139]

In its analysis, the Court surveyed several systems of marriage in South Africa, including some that were not formal. Children who were products of such informal unions were rendered illegitimate, therefore disposing of the father's permission for adoption. Such situations of non-recognition placed fathers at an enormous disadvantage vis-à-vis their children with respect to adoption, and were therefore discriminatory.[140] In addition, the Court also considered that the core issue was really the relationship between a father and a child, and that the statute was too broad in its blanket exclusion of the need for an unmarried father's permission for adoption of his child.[141] The Constitutional Court, however, citing the best interest of the child, declined to allow further judicial action to set aside the adoption and instead instructed Parliament to remedy the situation in a revised statute.

Confronting Violence against Women

The Court has pursued a similar approach to equality in cases that have dealt with violence against women, seemingly one of the most intractable social issues

---

136 *Fraser v The Children's Court, Pretoria North, supra* Note 110.
137 *Ibid.* at 44.
138 *Ibid.* at 25.
139 *Ibid.*
140 *Ibid.*
141 *Ibid.* at 28.

confronting South African society.[142] In the case of *S. v. Baloyi*, the Constitutional Court considered the constitutionality of a section of the Prevention of Family Violence Act.[143] The subsection had been declared invalid by the Transvaal High Court, which had referred its finding to the Constitutional Court for confirmation.[144] The High Court's declaration of invalidity was based on its finding that the section of the statute under review "placed a reverse onus of proving absence of guilt on a person charged with breach of a family violence interdict,"[145] thus conflicting with the constitutionally protected presumption of innocence without compelling constitutional justification. The case presented the opportunity for the Constitutional Court to confront the vexing issue of domestic violence and to balance the need to eradicate domestic violence against the constitutional rights of accused persons to a fair trial.

The complainant, the wife of an army officer, had been granted an interdict against her husband by a magistrate in Pretoria. The husband appellant was ordered not to assault either the complainant or their child and not to prevent them from entering or leaving the marital home. The husband, appellant in the case, ignored the interdict and subsequently assaulted and threatened to kill the complainant. She complained to the police, and after she signed an affidavit, the police arrested the husband appellant and brought him before a magistrate to inquire into the alleged breach of the interdict.

The Minister of Justice and the Commission for Gender Equality intervened in the action, challenging the High Court's decision on three grounds. First, they felt the "alleged violators should not be considered 'accused persons' entitled to the presumption of innocence."[146] Second, even if they were to be treated as such, the sections of the Criminal Procedure Act under review should not be interpreted as imposing a reverse onus. Third, if the proper interpretation of those sections

---

142   Penelope E. Andrews, *Violence against Women in South Africa: The Role of Culture and the Limitations of the Law, supra* Note 40; *see also* CRIMINAL JUSTICE: VIOLENCE AGAINST WOMEN IN SOUTH AFRICA, SHADOW REPORT ON BEIJING + 15 (POWA and others, March 2010) at: *www.powa.co.za/files/ SouthAfricaShadowReportMarch2010.pdf.*

143   *S v Baloyi and Others* 2000 (1) BCLR 86. Section 3 (5) of the Prevention of Family Violence Act 133 of 1993.

144   The case was first brought in the Pretoria High Court where the appellant argued that the section in question imposed an unfair onus on him to disprove that he had committed the crime. The High Court upheld his contention. Counsel for the Minister of Justice and The Commission For Gender Equality appealed to the Constitutional Court.

145   Section 3 (5) of the Prevention of Family Violence Act provides as follows: "The provisions of the Criminal Procedure Act, 1977 (Act. No. 51 of 1977), relating to the procedure which shall be followed in respects of an enquiry referred to in Section 170 of that Act shall apply mutatis mutandis in respect of an enquiry under subsection (4)."

146   *S v Baloyi, supra* Note 143 at 10.

involved the imposition of a reverse onus, "then the limitation of the presumption of innocence involved could be justified."[147]

The Court began its discussion by addressing the Constitution's express reference to the problem of domestic violence.[148] Justice Albie Sachs, writing for the majority in a unanimous decision, embarked on a thoughtful analysis of the need to deal comprehensively and effectively with the problem of domestic violence. He described the unique "hidden, repetitive character" of domestic violence, its ubiquity in cutting across class, race, culture, and geographic boundaries, and the deleterious consequences of its persistence for society. Moreover, because of the gender-specific nature of domestic violence, it mirrored and mimicked patriarchal domination in a particularly abhorrent manner.[149]

Justice Sachs explored the banality and perceived inevitability of domestic violence and the imperatives on the government to stem it. He contextualized the problem as embedded in patriarchy and the continued subordination of women. He noted that in their research, women's organizations have uncovered high levels of domestic abuse across all sectors of South African society.[150] These disturbing numbers confirm the Court's assessment of the certain normalcy or banality of domestic violence. In his analysis, Justice Sachs detailed the effects of domestic violence on its victims, including the shame and stigma left with the victim. Moreover, he noted that the collusion of the state in failing to eliminate domestic violence undermined the state's promise of gender equality and non-discrimination so clearly articulated in the Constitution.[151] Such inaction on the part of the government also contradicted South Africa's international and regional obligations, including those contained in the General Assembly Declaration on the Elimination of Violence Against Women, the Convention on the Elimination of All Forms of Discrimination Against Women, and the African Charter on Human and Peoples' Rights.[152]

Dealing with the constitutional presumption of innocence, Justice Sachs cited a list of Constitutional Court decisions that reiterated this right. He then elaborated on the hybrid (public/private) nature of the Prevention of Family Violence Act and

---

147   *Ibid.*

148   "Domestic and family violence is a pervasive and frequently lethal problem that challenges society at every level. Violence in families is often hidden from view and devastates its victims physically, emotionally, spiritually and financially. It threatens the stability of the family and negatively impacts on all family members, especially the children who learn from it that violence is an acceptable way to cope with stress or problems or to gain control over another person. It violates our communities' safety, health, welfare, and economies by draining billions annually in social costs such as medical expenses, psychological problems, lost productivity and intergenerational violence." *Ibid* at 11.

149   *Ibid.* at 12.

150   *Ibid.* at 19, Footnote 46.

151   *Ibid.* at 12.

152   *Ibid.* at 13.

analyzed the complications that surface when the private (family) domain intersects with the public through the interdict provisions. The interdict proceedings in the Act are situated somewhere between family and criminal law remedies; their purpose is to supplement and enforce those remedies.

Citing feminist scholarship on this issue, Justice Sachs stressed the unique character of domestic violence as a legal problem because of the "strange alchemy of violence within intimacy."[153] Innovative legal skills and methods are therefore essential in combating the problem and to some extent the interdict provisions of the Prevention of Family Violence Act create the legal space for such a possibility. These provisions require that police officers and other actors in the legal system temporarily jettison stereotypical and often negative attitudes about the appropriateness and need to interfere in private family matters.[154] In a country where victims of domestic violence have largely experienced the police as either hostile or ambivalent to their predicament, these provisions are imperative if the attitudinal shift in policing domestic violence is to occur. Justice Sachs observed that the interdict provisions are intended as an "accessible, speedy, simple and effective" process, a proactive mechanism aimed at preventing further violence without being punitive.[155] In the words of Justice Sachs, "it seeks preventive rather than retributive justice."[156]

Justice Sachs then went on to deal with the three grounds on which the Act was challenged. The first was whether the alleged violator was "an accused person" and therefore entitled to the presumption of innocence. Counsel for the appellant husband had argued on the basis of precedent that the proceedings under the Act were "essentially civil in character" and that "the arrested person was not an accused person entitled to the protection of the section in question."[157] A case cited had dealt with the procedural consequences of the failure to testify when a legal duty to do so had been established. That case held that "the recalcitrant examinee who, on refusing or failing to answer a question, triggers the possible operation of the imprisonment provisions of section 189(1) [of the Criminal Procedure Act] is not, in my view, an 'accused person'."[158] The judge in that case described the imprisonment provisions of Section 189 as "nothing more than process in aid."[159]

Justice Sachs, however, distinguished *Baloyi* from the precedent case by pointing out the punitive nature of Section 6 of the Prevention of Family Violence Act, which provided for the imposition of a fine or imprisonment for breach of the interdict provisions. Whereas the examinees in the cited case carried "the keys of

---

153   *Ibid.* at 16.
154   *Ibid.*
155   *Ibid.* at 17.
156   *Ibid.*
157   *Ibid.* at 20.
158   *Ibid.* at 20. (Citing *Nel v. Le Roux And Others* 1996 (3) SA 562 (CC) at 11).
159   *Ibid.*

their prison in their own pockets,"[160] no such situation existed with violators of the interdict provisions of the Act. According to Justice Sachs, once the inquiry into the alleged violation of the Act commences, the complainant essentially has abdicated control of the proceedings to the state. The Court concluded that the alleged violator of the interdict was an "accused person," and therefore entitled to the presumptions of innocence.

The Court then went on to discuss whether Section 3 (5) of the Prevention of Family Violence Act imposed a reverse onus. Commenting on the "obscure" nature of the words used in Section 3 of the Family Violence Act and Section 170 of the Criminal Procedure Act, Justice Sachs examined three possible interpretations of the actions under review. They are summarized in the judgment as interpretations A, B, and C.

Interpretation A, emphasizing the word "procedure," allowed only the importation of the summary procedure, and not a reverse onus. In other words, the protections guaranteed in the Criminal Procedure Act were not suspended; there was therefore no reverse onus interfering with the presumption of innocence. As the Court pointed out, this interpretation lent itself to the approach mandated in Section 39 (2) of the Constitution: "when interpreting any legislation ... every court ... must promote the spirit, purport and objects of the Bill of Rights."[161]

Interpretation B embodied the High Court's position that Section 170 "provides for a procedure which incorporates a reverse onus as a central element."[162]

Interpretation C provided for a reverse onus, but only once the "accused person" had proved lack of willfulness on his part. The Court articulated interpretation C as follows:

> It presupposes that the judicial officer must first be satisfied beyond reasonable doubt that the interdict has in fact been breached and that only then is the onus placed on the alleged violator to prove on a balance of probabilities a lack of wilfulness on his part. There is a reverse onus, but its reach would be restricted because it would be triggered only after a breach of the interdict has been proved beyond a reasonable doubt.[163]

Finding that interpretation C was too "strained," and not persuaded by the High Court's position (interpretation B), the Court adopted interpretation A as stating the correct legal position. Distinguishing the substantive law question from the procedural law question, Justice Sachs pointed out that Section 170 (2) of the Criminal Procedure Act provides for conviction for failure to attend court proceedings "unless the accused satisfies the court that his failure was not due to

---

160 *Ibid.* at 21.
161 *Ibid.* at 25.
162 *Ibid.* at 27.
163 *Ibid.* at 28.

fault on his part."[164] This shifting of the burden to the accused renders the issue one of substantive law, and therefore, the procedures of the Criminal Procedure Act are no longer apposite. In short, the presumption of innocence is left undisturbed.

Justice Sachs referred to the need to provide the legislature with latitude in dealing with intransigent social problems that find their way to the courts. But he also emphasized that while such latitude exists within constitutionally appropriate limits, fairness to the complainant is pre-eminent. This requires that the proceedings are "speedy and dispense with the normal process of charge and plea," something akin to a bail hearing.[165]

This judgment follows the *Hugo* decision discussed earlier in contextualizing the contemporary reality of South African women. There is widespread recognition that private violence against women is a cause for great concern and, as some have argued, such violence constitutes a continual violation of women's human rights. The Court recognized the need to eradicate such violence but was constrained to abide by the constitutional rights of the alleged perpetrators.

Socio-Economic Rights Cases

I now turn from individual rights claims such as the preceding to how the courts are dealing with socio-economic rights the Constitution provides. The Constitutional Court's decisions regarding the enforcement of socio-economic rights have shown how these rights can bring about meaningful relief, especially to the poorest in the country.

In 2000 the Constitutional Court decided a case involving the right to housing as incorporated in Section 26 of the Constitution, the section that provides for access to housing.[166] Although the Court had decided a somewhat comparable case a few years before concerning the right to health, and delineated some of the governing legal principles, this housing case was awaited with great anticipation.[167] Today, it is widely regarded internationally as a celebrated test case on the enforceability of social and economic rights, although the case is not without its critics.[168]

---

164   *Ibid.* at 29.

165   *Ibid.* at 31.

166   Section 26 provides as follows: "Everyone has the right to have access to adequate housing.

(2) The state must take reasonable legislative and other measures, within its available resources, to achieve the progressive realisation of this right.

(3) No one may be evicted from their home, or have their home demolished, without an order of court made after considering all the relevant circumstances. No legislation may permit arbitrary evictions."

167   *Government of the Republic of South Africa v Grootboom and Others* (2001) (1) 46 (CC).

168   *See* D.M. Davis, *Adjudicating the Socio-Economic Rights in the South African Constitution: Towards "Deference Lite"?*, 22 SOUTH AFRICAN JOURNAL OF HUMAN

The case concerned an application for temporary shelter brought by a group of people, including a number of children, who were without shelter following their brutal eviction from private land on which they were squatting. The conditions under which the community lived were deplorable; they had access to one tap and no sanitation facilities.[169]

In its decision, the Constitutional Court affirmed the government's duty under Section 26 of the Constitution to adopt reasonable policy, including legislative and budgetary measures, to provide relief for people who have no access to land, no roof over their heads, and who are living in intolerable conditions. Justice Yacoob, writing for a unanimous court noted:

> I am conscious that it is an extremely difficult task for the state to meet these obligations in the conditions that prevail in our country. This is recognized by the Constitution, which expressly provides that the state is not obliged to go beyond available resources or to realize these rights immediately. I stress however, that despite all these qualifications, these are rights, and the Constitution obliges the state to give effect to them. This is an obligation that courts can, and in appropriate circumstances, must enforce.[170]

Although this decision has been widely hailed as setting an important precedent for the enforcement of socio-economic rights at both the local and global level, many commentators have expressed disappointment in the Court's focus on "reasonableness."[171] They instead argue that the Court should have applied the "minimum core approach" as adopted in the interpretation of the International Covenant on Economic, Social and Cultural Rights.[172]

The right of access to health care was explored in the *Treatment Action* case.[173] In this case, an appeal to the Constitutional Court was directed at reversing orders made in a provincial High Court against the government because of perceived shortcomings in its response to an aspect of the HIV/AIDS challenge. The Court found that the government had not reasonably addressed the need to reduce the

---

RIGHTS (2006) 301.

169   *Government of the Republic of South Africa v Grootboom, supra* Note 167.

170   *Ibid.* at 94.

171   *See* Stuart Wilson and Jackie Dugard, *Taking Poverty Seriously: The South African Constitutional Court and Socio-Economic Rights*, 22 STELLENBOSCH LAW REVIEW (2011) 664; *see also* DAVID BILCHITZ, POVERTY AND FUNDAMENTAL RIGHTS: THE JUSTIFICATION AND ENFORCEMENT OF SOCIO-ECONOMIC RIGHTS (2007).

172   Marius Pieterse, *Resuscitating Socio-Economic Rights: Constitutional Entitlement to Health Care Service*, 22 SOUTH AFRICAN JOURNAL ON HUMAN RIGHTS (2006) 473.

173   *Minister of Health and Others v Treatment Action Campaign and Others* 2002 (5) SA 721 (CC).

risk of HIV-positive mothers' transmitting the disease to their babies at birth.[174] More specifically, the finding was that the South African government had acted unreasonably in (a) refusing to make an anti-retroviral drug called *nevirapine* available in the public health sector where the attending doctor considered it medically indicated, and in (b) not setting out a time frame for a national program to prevent mother-to-child transmission of HIV.[175] This case gave some teeth to the right of access to health. The *Grootboom* case mentioned earlier also gave teeth to the right of access to housing, but not in as definite and certain a way with respect to individual applicants.

The right of access to housing and health cases can be interpreted as cases involving positive socio-economic rights, that is, the obligation of the state to provide certain benefits. There are also claims that can be characterized as negative socio-economic rights. One case characterized in this manner involved the protection of a tenant against eviction who had been in the middle of executing a judgment on debts. The Court held that such a process violated the constitutional right to housing.[176] It constituted what seemingly might be termed in the U.S. a retaliatory eviction.

Interpreting the Common Law and Customary Law to Embrace Constitutional Principles

Section 39 of the Constitution provides that "when developing the common law or customary law" that courts and tribunals "must promote the spirit, purport and objects of the Bill of Rights."[177] In furtherance of this mandate, the Constitutional Court in 2001, in a landmark decision, decided a case involving the duty of the police to protect individuals from those who are dangerous threats to them.[178] This case has profound ramifications for development of the common law as a result of superintending constitutional provisions. In this case, the Constitutional Court considered a claim by a woman who had been attacked and seriously injured by a man who was at the time awaiting trial for rape.

In spite of a previous conviction for indecent assault and a history of violent behavior towards women, the assailant had been released unconditionally on his own recognizance in the rape matter—despite repeated requests by the victim and other members of the community to keep him in custody.[179] The victim sued the

---

174   *Ibid.*

175   *Ibid.* at 14–15.

176   *Gundwana v Steko Development CC and Others* 2011 (3) SA 608 (CC).

177   THE CONSTITUTION, *supra* Note 32, Section 39 (2).

178   *Carmichele v Minister of Safety and Security and Others* 2001 (1) SA 489 (CC).

179   *Ibid.* For a discussion of the need for decisions like *Carmichele, see* Helene Combrinck, *The Dark Side of the Rainbow: Violence against Women in South Africa after 10 Years of Democracy,* in ADVANCING WOMEN'S RIGHTS: THE FIRST DECADE OF DEMOCRACY (Christina Murray and Michelle O'Sullivan eds. 2005) 171.

police and prosecution for their negligent failure to take proactive steps to protect her as a potential further victim. A unanimous court stated that the Constitution embodies an objective, normative value system that must shape the common law, in this case the common law of negligence.[180]

The Court held that the Constitution obliged the state to respect, protect, promote, and fulfill the rights in the Bill of Rights, including the right of women to have their safety and security protected. The Constitutional Court found in the victim's favor, namely, that the state officials had a legal duty to take steps to prevent further violent actions by the perpetrator, and referred the matter back to the trial court for determination of further issues in the tort claim. At the later trial the Supreme Court of Appeal found for the plaintiff and ruled that the state was indeed liable.[181]

Later cases have analyzed the effect on women's rights of cultural and traditional rights guaranteed to indigenous communities by the Constitution.[182] As stated earlier, the Constitution guarantees the rights of cultural communities but also provides that such rights are not to impair the rights of women to gender equality.

In March, 2004, the Constitutional Court considered cases raising this conflict. It involved challenges to the legal principle of male primogeniture as it applies to the African customary law of succession, the Intestate Succession Act, and the Black Administration Act and regulations flowing therefrom.[183]

The applicants in one case were the two minor daughters of the deceased. In the other case, the applicant was a sister of an unmarried deceased brother. All three applicants had been denied the right to be declared heirs; male representatives instead stood to inherit the property of the deceased.

Other applicants were parties to the case but they were intervenors. One intervenor was the Women's Legal Center Trust, a women's legal advocacy organization in Cape Town, the other was the South African Human Rights Commission, a state institution mandated by South Africa's Constitution to pursue human rights in South Africa. Both parties intervened in the case in support of the claim that the statutes in question, as well as the principle of primogeniture violated the South African Constitution by unfairly discriminating against women in that it violated their right to dignity and equality and by denying children their constitutionally guaranteed protections to safety and security.

---

180   *Carmichele v Minister of Safety and Security and Others, supra* Note 178.

181   *Minister of Safety and Security and Another v Carmichele* 2004 (3) SA 305 (SCA). For a discussion of the *Carmichele* case in comparative perspective, *see* HELEN SCOTT, THE LIABILITY OF POLICE FOR FAILING TO PREVENT CRIMES IN ENGLISH AND SOUTH AFRICAN LAW, PAPER DELIVERED AT ST. ANNE'S COLLEGE, OXFORD, July 14, 2010 at: *http://www.privatelaw.uct.ac.za/usr/private_law/attachments/Police%20Liability.pdf.*

182   *Bhe & Others v The Magistrate, Khayelitsha, supra* Note 113; *Gumede (Born Shange) v President of the Republic of South Africa & Others* (2001) (1) 46 (CC).

183   *Bhe & Others v The Magistrate, Khayelitsha, supra* Note 113, at 594–600, 621–2.

Thus, the two central issues in the cases revolved around the constitutional validity of Section 23 of the Black Administration Act, the law which administered the intestate deceased estates of Africans. This section provided that,

> all movable property belonging to a Black and allotted by him or accruing under Black law or custom to any women with whom he lived in a customary union, or to any house, shall upon his death devolve and be administered under Black law and custom.[184]

The second issue was a constitutional challenge to the principle of primogeniture. The thrust of this rule is that only a male who is related to the deceased may inherit in the absence of a will. Women could inherit when named in a will.

In practice this meant that generally it was the eldest son, or the father or male cousins and uncles who were entitled to become heirs. The principle mirrors other aspects of indigenous law in which women are treated as perpetual minors, always under the tutelage of a male.[185] The rationale underpinning the exclusion of women was based on the fact that:

> (W)omen were always regarded as persons who would eventually leave their original family on marriage, after the payment of roora/lobola, to join the family of their husbands. It was reasoned that in the new situation—a member of the husband's family—they could not be heads of their original families, as they were more likely to subordinate the interests of the original family to those of their new family. It was therefore reasoned that in their new situation they would not be able to look after the original family.[186]

In its judgment the Court examined the place of indigenous law in South Africa's constitutional framework, recognized its importance in South Africa's culturally diverse society, held it both subject to and protected by the Constitution, and considered that it was to be "accommodated, not merely tolerated."[187] Referring to the neglect of the positive aspects of customary law, including its inherent flexibility, its preference for consensus-seeking and co-operation and its "nurturing of healthy communitarian traditions,"[188] the Court was respectful of its historic significance and importance in the day to day lives of many people but held that customary law was nonetheless subject to the Bill of Rights.

---

184   BLACK ADMINISTRATION ACT, Section 23(1).

185   Penelope Andrews, *Who's Afraid of Polygamy? Exploring the Boundaries of Family, Equality and Custom in South Africa*, 11 UNIVERSITY OF UTAH LAW REVIEW (2009) 303, 318.

186   *Bhe & Others v The Magistrate, Khayelitsha, supra* Note 113 at 646.

187   *Ibid.* at 604.

188   *Ibid.* at 606.

On the issue of constitutionality of Section 23 of the Black Administration Act, the Court held that in light of its history and context, the section is part of an Act which was a "cornerstone of racial oppression, division and conflict"[189] and that South Africans will take years to eviscerate its legacy. The Court gave short shrift to the argument that Section 23 reflects the pluralist nature of South African society by giving recognition to customary law. The Court noted its racist and destructive roles in entrenching division and subordination, a role which "could not be justified in any open and democratic society."[190]

In the course of its opinion, the Court examined the evolution of the rule of male primogeniture and particularly its place within indigenous communities. The Court held that the rule unfairly discriminated against women and illegitimate children and declared it unconstitutional. While recognizing the importance of the rule in traditional indigenous societies, the court found that this was no longer the setting in which the rules existed. Nonetheless, the communitarian context within which customary rules or succession developed, with its "safeguards to ensure fairness in the context of entitlements, duties and responsibilities" and its aim to "contribute to the communal good and welfare," was noteworthy.[191]

The Court pointed to the ensuing hardship that results from the application of the rule "in circumstances vastly different from their traditional setting."[192] The Court in its judgment cited the importance of customary law in the organization of communal societies, while acknowledging both the changing nature of indigenous communities, particularly the role of urbanization in restructuring traditional relationships. The Court also recognized the evolutionary nature of indigenous law which continues to evolve and develop "to meet the changing needs of the community."[193] In its remedy, the Court ordered that all intestate estates must now be administered under the Intestate Succession Act, thereby creating a non-racial uniform system across the country. The Court made the order retrospective to April 27, 1994, the day when the first Constitution of South Africa came into effect.

In a recent judgment, the Court rendered an opinion on the constitutionality of a section of the Recognition of Customary Marriages Act that precluded wives in customary marriages entered into before the passage of the Act from the benefits and protections offered in the Act.[194] The disputed section of the Act provided

---

189   *Ibid.* at 612–13.

190   *Ibid.* at 616.

191   *Ibid.* at 617.

192   *Ibid.* at 619.

193   *See Ibid.* at 618 (quoting *Alexkor Ltd & Another v The Richtersveld Community & Others* 2004 (5) SA 460 (CC)) at 53. This view reflects the holdings in courts in other parts of Africa. *Ibid.* at 650. For example, the Nigerian Court of Appeal struck down an Igbo succession rule which discriminated against women. *Ibid.* [citing *Mojekwu V Mojekwu* [1997] 7 N.W.L.R. 305 (C.A.) (Nigeria)].

194   *See Gumede (Born Shange) v President of the Republic of South Africa & Others, supra* Note 182.

that "the proprietary consequences of a customary marriage entered into" before the passage of the Act "continue to be governed by customary law."[195] While the property regime of marriages entered into after the promulgation of the Act was in community of property, marriages governed by customary law provided that the family head (the male) is the owner of all the family property, and has full control over such property.

The applicant in the case, who had entered into a customary marriage in 1968, and therefore outside of the Act's protections, and who had instituted divorce proceedings against her husband, claimed that the property regime of customary marriages violated her rights to equality under the Constitution. A lower court had found in her favor, and the Constitutional Court confirmed that finding, holding that the impugned section of the Act, as well as the customary law provisions, "patently limits the equality dictates of our [the] Constitution."[196] Writing for the majority, Justice Moseneke observed the,

> ... patriarchal domination over, and the complete exclusion of, the wife in the owning or dealing with family property unashamedly demeans and makes vulnerable the wife concerned and is thus discriminatory and unfair. It has not been shown to be otherwise, nor is there any justification for it.[197]

The decisions discussed above suggest that the Constitutional Court, although mindful of the need to respect the cultural rights of all South Africans, is committed to ensuring that all members of indigenous communities enjoy those rights without distinction or discrimination.[198] This is the case as well with the Court's decisions on equality and violence against women. With regard to violence against women, there is a general, societal consensus that private violence, indeed any violence, against women is odious, and the state is obligated to deal with this problem aggressively.[199]

But despite these very impressive judgments on these key issues relating to the situation of women, there is still a large gap, however, between ubiquitous cultural attitudes about women, fueled by a particular brand of South African masculinity that gives rise to discrimination and violence against women, and the laudable statements of the Court. Closing this gap will require a recognition that the structural and attitudinal impediments to the "right to be free from private violence" as articulated in the Constitution can only be eradicated by a combination

---

195   RECOGNITION OF CUSTOMARY MARRIAGES ACT 120 of 1998, Section 7(1).

196   *Gumede (Born Shange) v President of the Republic of South Africa & Others, supra* Note 182 at 46.

197   *Ibid.*

198   Penelope E. Andrews, *Violence against Women in South Africa: The Role of Culture and the Limitations of the Law, supra* Note 40.

199   *Ibid.*

of governmental assaults which include education, access to resources, and continued vigilance regarding the extent and persistence of violence. In addition, the promises of a substantive equality so forcefully articulated by the Court needs to be internalized in relationships and interactions between men and women—in the family, workplace, and elsewhere. The Constitutional Court, at least, is doing its part, but it needs to be bolstered by other institutional arrangements that will include both legal and extra-legal measures.

Chapter 6
Afghanistan and Gender Equality

... there is no real question here of women's status. The "second sex" did not exist. The only concern was to be assured of procreation and work: reproduce and produce. Any and all ideas of autonomy, emancipation, desire, or awakening were taboo, repressed, and dangerous. Women had a function but no destiny, unless it was taking the deadly risk of challenging the customary order that combines the male code of honor and Islamic law so as to increase the subjugation.[1]

We will insist that women play prominent roles as planners, implementers and beneficiaries of the reconstruction of Afghanistan.[2]

Introduction

In June, 2011 during a weekend visit to London, I attended two exhibitions on Afghanistan. One exhibition, entitled, *Afghanistan: Crossroads of the Ancient World*, at the British Museum, featuring pieces from the National Museum of Afghanistan, highlighted the vast treasures of Afghan culture, "its immense fragility and its remarkable place in world history."[3] The other was an exhibition of photographs of the two Afghan wars at the Tate Modern entitled, *Burke and Norfolk, Photographs from the War in Afghanistan*. This was an exhibition of the photographs of contemporary British photographer, Simon Norfolk, who traced the photographs of John Burke, who had photographed the second Anglo-Afghan war between 1878 and 1880. Norfolk exhibited his own photographs and was also the curator of the earlier photographs taken by Burke.[4]

---

1 ISABELLE DELLOYE, WOMEN OF AFGHANISTAN (2003) xii.

2 *Powell and Dobriansky on Afghan Women's Crucial Role*, RELIEFWEB, November 19, 2001 at: *http://reliefweb.int/node-90366.pdf*.

3 *See* BRITISH MUSEUM, *What's on*, at : *http://www.britishmuseum.org/whats_on/exhibitions/afghanistan.aspx*.

4 *See* TATE MODERN at: *http://www.tate.org.uk/modern/exhibitions/burkeandnorfolk/default.shtm*. A blog describes the photographs of these two men as follows: "Because Burke also photographed groups and portraits, Norfolk does too. These are some of Norfolk's most disturbing photographs, again in their juxtaposition, their dialogue as he calls it, with Burke's. The group portraits are powerful and searing in their critique because they are subtle, unsettling because they are so different from the way that war is photographed

These two exhibitions captured for me the essence of Afghanistan in the global imagination. On the one hand, Afghanistan is a country that conjures up images of a vast exotic cultural past, and on the other, it is a country at war with itself, ravaged by decades of violence and seeming anarchy. This existential contradiction, as it were, raises some dilemmas for me as an observer and scholar, because Afghanistan's history and its contemporary reality bear on my analysis of the situation of women, as well as my suggestions for legal reform that I explore in this book.

Since I embarked on this book project I have been a keen observer of contemporary political developments in Afghanistan, as well as a student of the country's history, both ancient and modern.[5] Afghanistan is also an incredibly beautiful and diverse country, one that embodies a multitude of regions and geographical characteristics.[6] The country's history reflects the trajectory of an ancient civilization that has generated an exquisite artistic and cultural heritage, but also one confronting successive waves of conquest and war.[7]

Afghanistan's tumultuous past, in many ways dictated by its peculiar geography and topography, is almost a cliché. A landlocked country, bordering six countries—Pakistan, Iran, China, Tajikistan, Uzbekistan, and Turkmenistan— with mountain ranges that effectively divide the country into three regions, and a climate that ranges from extreme cold to sweltering heat.[8] Historically serving as a trading link and transport route between Central Asia, the Middle East and the Indian sub-continent, Afghanistan's geography has, since the period of Alexander the Great, made it a site of struggle and conflict.[9]

To the outsider, Afghanistan feels a bit like a country in waiting—waiting for peace, waiting for autonomy, waiting for economic development, waiting to be part of the international community. This sense of a country in waiting has been heightened by the last military encounter since the events of September 11,

---

in the twenty-first century. And so they enable us to look at this war that we have seen countless times before, from a completely different angle." *See http://fxreflects.blogspot. com/2011/06/burke-norfolk-photographs-from-war-in.html.*

5   I am using the word "student" very loosely here, and I do not wish to suggest that I have academic credentials directly attributable to the formal study of Afghan history, politics or law. I am very interested in Afghanistan mostly because of my interest in the situation of women in that country.

6   One of the most compelling accounts of the vast geographical diversity of Afghanistan is relayed by Rory Stewart in his account of his hiking trip from Kandahar to Kabul in 2002, a few months after the invasion began. *See* RORY STEWART, THE PLACES IN BETWEEN (2003).

7   DAVID ISBY, AFGHANISTAN: GRAVEYARD OF EMPIRES: A NEW HISTORY OF THE BORDERLAND (2011).

8   *See* LOUIS DUPREE, AFGHANISTAN (2002). This book, first published in 1973, contains charts and maps.

9   *See* THOMAS BARFIELD, AFGHANISTAN: A CULTURAL AND POLITICAL HISTORY (2010).

2001, and has a profound influence on the aspirations and lives of the country's population.

The Situation of Women

Afghanistan ranks as one of the poorest countries in the world, with a life expectancy of 44.6 years.[10] The wretchedness of this situation is borne disproportionately by women and girls.[11] A lethal combination of extraordinary economic deprivation coupled with demeaning political, social, and cultural attitudes towards women have created the most dire conditions for women. Arguably this situation is akin to the ravages created by other historically unjust societies like apartheid South Africa and its treatment of the majority black population, or the Khmer Rouge in Cambodia and their alarming fear of, among other traits of their citizenry, intellectual autonomy, indeed, intellectual capacity of any kind.[12]

Much has been written about the situation of women in Afghanistan, particularly the spectacularly brutal suppression of their rights during the reign of the Taliban.[13] Yet despite the overthrow of the Taliban, the repression continues.[14] There is almost nothing new that can be added to the litany of brutal oppression and subjugation of women. But in an international context Afghanistan occupies a special place in the annals of horror that have and continue to be visited upon women.[15]

Seen by the Taliban as "a temptation, an unnecessary distraction,"[16] the unimaginable conditions within which women found themselves had been

---

10   In the United Nations Human Development Report, Afghanistan ranks 173rd out of 177 countries in terms of development, and as the 3rd poorest country in the world.

11   *See* Eve McCabe, *The Inadequacy of International Human Rights Law to Protect the Rights of Women as Illustrated by the Crisis in Afghanistan*, 5 UCLA JOURNAL OF INTERNATIONAL LAW AND FOREIGN AFFAIRS (2001) 419, 447–8.

12   *See* CHANRITHY HIM, WHEN BROKEN GLASS FLOATS: GROWING UP UNDER THE KHMER ROUGE (2001) and JOHN ALLEN, APARTHEID SOUTH AFRICA: AN INSIDER'S OVERVIEW ON THE ORIGIN AND EFFECTS OF SEPARATE DEVELOPMENT (2005).

13   *See*, for example, HUMAN RIGHTS WATCH, HUMANITY DENIED: SYSTEMATIC VIOLATIONS OF WOMEN'S RIGHTS IN AFGHANISTAN (2001), at *http://www.hrw.org/reports/2001/afghan3/*.

14   HUMAN RIGHTS WATCH, "WE WANT TO LIVE AS HUMANS": REPRESSION OF WOMEN AND GIRLS IN WESTERN AFGHANISTAN (2002).

15   Organizations like Human Rights Watch and Amnesty International regularly report on the range of violence to which women and girls are regularly subjected to with impunity, from the systemic rape of young girls and women in the senseless war in the Congo, to the cavalier killings of women who violate the "honor" of families in Pakistan, to the trafficking into sexual slavery of girls and young women in Peru. *See www.hrw.org*.

16   AHMED RASHID, TALIBAN: MILITANT ISLAM, OIL AND FUNDAMENTALISM IN CENTRAL ASIA (2000) at 33.

initiated by the mujahedeen after the defeat of the Russians in 1992, in the wake of a decade-long occupation.[17] In fact, all Afghans, men, women, and children, have been subjected for several decades to the horror of war and occupation, a casualty of Cold War politics in which the Western allies headed by the United States, supported an array of forces to defeat the Soviet occupation of Afghanistan.[18] Afghanistan became a surrogate for Cold War conflict, and the country was awash with arms and ammunition for several decades.[19] The United States became directly involved in Afghanistan after the Soviet invasion of the country, and at the height of the conflict in 1986 the United States had channeled more than $3 billion dollars to the mujahedeen, an amount surpassed only by a major United States ally, Saudi Arabia.[20] This was one of the largest covert operations of the United States during the Cold War, so cynically portrayed in the book and movie *Charlie's Wilson's War*.[21] Indeed it has been persuasively argued that the foundations for Taliban rule were laid during the conflict that raged within the country, since most of the professional, skilled, and educated population had left the country by the time the Taliban came to power. Referring to the extent of the level of destruction in Afghanistan during the years of conflict, one scholar has noted:

> You know, the scale of this is different from the scale of the Guatemalan death squads or apartheid in South Africa. To some extent, this was carnage, at least for Afghanistan, on the scale of what we saw in the Second World War. Everywhere we could go, we would find horrors: it is like an archaeology of horrors. It was layer upon layer of victims and victimizers.[22]

It follows therefore that any debate about reconstruction has to center on the issue of security—the ability of Afghans, and particularly Afghan women, to be safe in their persons and property.

---

17   *Ibid.* at 243.

18   *See* JOHN FULLTERTON, THE SOVIET OCCUPATION OF AFGHANISTAN (1983); *see also* HELSINKI WATCH, ASIA WATCH, TO DIE IN AFGHANISTAN (December 1985).

19   *See* WILLIAM MALEY, FUNDAMENTALISM REBORN? AFGHANISTAN AND THE TALIBAN (1998); *see also* GEORGE CRILE, CHARLIE WILSON'S WAR: THE EXTRAORDINARY STORY OF THE LARGEST COVERT OPERATION IN HISTORY (2004).

20   Charles Hirschkind and Saba Mahmood, *Feminism, the Taliban, and Politics of Counter-Insurgency*, 75 ANTHROPOLOGICAL QUARTERLY (2002) 339, 342.

21   *See* GEORGE CRILE, CHARLIE WILSON'S WAR, *supra* Note 19; *see also* STEVE COLL, GHOST WARS: THE SECRET HISTORY OF THE CIA, AFGHANISTAN, AND BIN LADEN, FROM THE SOVIET INVASION TO SEPTEMBER 10, 2001 (2005).

22   Questions, Answers and Comments, *Reluctant National Building: Promoting the Rule of Law in Post-Taliban Afghanistan*, 17 CONNECTICUT JOURNAL OF INTERNATIONAL LAW (2002) 461, 462.

Although they were not recognized as a legitimate government by the United Nations, once the Taliban came to power in late 1996, they refined and reinforced a system that oppressed and subordinated women in the most grotesque manner. The enforcement of a strict interpretation of the Koran by the Taliban provided the *raison d'être* for the austere behavioral codes enforced upon women. Indeed, the goal of the Taliban legal code was "to create a pure Islamic society free from crime, vice and Western influence."[23] The nature, extent, and consequences of this system for women have been documented in great detail.[24] They included the systemic and brutal violations of women's rights across the spectrum of life, including education, health, employment, marriage, and family. They also included a systemic and complete erasure of women from public life, and total subordination in public.

The documentation of the Taliban's brutal suppression of women has been met with unprecedented alarm, a profound sense of hopelessness, and despair in the global community, but also a sense of determination to support and work with Afghan women to stem the continued violation of their rights. As has been noted:

> It is hard for people in other countries to believe that we women in Afghanistan are beaten everyday by the Taliban. The sadness in our story is endless. I know that they (the Taliban) beat us, lash us, and lock us up in our homes all because they want to destroy the dignity of women. But all these crimes against us will not stop our struggle. Will other women in the world join with us?[25]

A Kafkaesque system of control and regulation, requiring permission from husbands and other male relatives dominated women's lives, creating one of the most brutally infantilizing and dependency-creating societies on earth.[26] In addition, the decades of war has spawned one of the largest populations of widows in the world. These absolute strictures on women have therefore had the most

---

23 Shefali Desai, *Hearing Afghan Women's Voices: Feminist Theory's Re-Conceptualization of Women's Human Rights*, 16 ARIZONA JOURNAL OF INTERNATIONAL AND COMPARATIVE LAW (1999) 805.

24 *See*, for example, ISABELLE DELLOYE, WOMEN OF AFGHANISTAN (2003); SAIRA SHAH: THE STORYTELLER'S DAUGHTER (2003); ASNE SEIERSTAD, THE BOOKSELLER OF KABUL (2004); NELOFER PAZIRA, A BED OF RED FLOWERS: IN SEARCH OF MY AFGHANISTAN (2005).

25 Shannon A. Middleton, *Women's Rights Unveiled: Taliban's Treatment of Women in Afghanistan*, 11 INDIANA INTERNATIONAL AND COMPARATIVE LAW REVIEW (2001) 421.

26 ROSEMARY SKAINE, THE WOMEN OF AFGHANISTAN UNDER THE TALIBAN (2002).

deleterious impact on these women, for whom there are no males who could act as their providers or protectors, however inadequately.[27]

9/11 and the "Reconstruction" of Afghanistan

As I indicated in the introduction to this book, my interest in the plight of Afghan women surfaced in the wake of September 11, 2001 and the military invasion by the United States military and the allied forces under the umbrella of NATO. I was particularly struck by the attention paid to the rights of women in the narrative that accompanied the invasion, and the invocation of the rights of women in many national and international venues.[28] As the then Secretary of State, Colin Powell, noted:

> The women of Afghanistan have been the backbone of Afghan society. It is in large measure thanks to their endurance, their courage, that their country has survived. The recovery of Afghanistan must entail the restoration of the rights of Afghan women. Indeed, it will not be possible without them. The rights of the women of Afghanistan will not be negotiable.[29]

What particularly captured my attention were the possibilities for women's rights that the invasion and subsequent political developments engendered. Indeed, for many years before the events of 9/11, Mavis Leno, the wife of the famous talk show host, Jay Leno, was a board member and major advocate and fundraiser for the Feminist Majority Foundation and their campaign for the rights of Afghan women. In addition to successfully lobbying the Clinton Administration and ultimately the United Nations not to recognize the Taliban as the legitimate government of Afghanistan, in 1998 the Feminist Majority Foundation successfully pressured the American energy company, UNOCAL, to cease negotiations with the Taliban for the construction of a natural gas pipeline across Afghanistan to neighboring Turkmenistan.[30] The campaign allowed for immense publicity amongst the media and celebrities, although it was not without its critics.[31] Having been involved with the transition to democracy in South Africa, and having been intensely caught up with constitutional developments there, I saw great possibilities for the women of

---

27   *See* ASNE SEIERSTAD, THE BOOKSELLER OF KABUL, *supra* Note 24; *see also* ANN JONES, KABUL IN WINTER: LIFE WITHOUT PEACE IN AFGHANISTAN (2003).

28   ROSEMARY SKAINE, WOMEN OF AFGHANISTAN IN THE POST-TALIBAN ERA: HOW LIVES HAVE CHANGED AND WHERE THEY STAND TODAY (2008).

29   *Powell and Dobriansky on Afghan Women's Crucial Role*, *supra* Note 2.

30   *See* Janelle Brown, *A Coalition of Hope*, 12 MS. MAGAZINE 2 (Spring 2002) 63.

31   Charles Hirschkind and Saba Mahmood, *Feminism, the Taliban, and Politics of Counter-Insurgency*, *supra* Note 20.

Afghanistan if a new political, legal, and constitutional framework was to emerge from the war and violence.

Despite what was perceived as an unremittingly bleak situation, the plight of women in Afghanistan has rallied the support of huge numbers of women around the world, with some referring to the plight of women there as representing "gender apartheid."[32] Indeed, the plight of Afghanistan's women was ostensibly one of the primary reasons for the United States and its allies invading that country in the fall of 2001.[33]

The celebration of International Women's Day at the United Nations in March 2002 was celebrated in the wake of the American-led NATO invasion of Afghanistan. There is no doubt that successive Afghan governments, and particularly the Taliban, oppressed women in the most grotesque manner. There is also no doubt that the commitment to the reconstruction of Afghanistan has to incorporate the needs and aspirations of women—and in this respect the legacy of the current Karzai government is rather mixed.[34]

In writing this chapter I considered various analytical perspectives that might capture the stark reality of the contemporary condition of Afghan women, one that fully and candidly described their identity, role, and status, an identity that appeared to be constantly in the shadow of the ubiquitous burqa. The most profound impression one has of Afghan women is one of subjugation and a systemic erasure from public space, stripped of identity, voice, and mobility. Any analysis of the political, legal, or economic situation in Afghanistan, any discussion of the government, or its security forces—all seem to be conducted through a male prism. It is as if women are not involved in the political, legal, social, and economic transformation of the society. Just a minor example will suffice: President Karzai's wife, Zinat Karzai, although a medical professional in her own right, is almost never seen in public. Her absence from public life may be related to security concerns, but there appears to be a much more sinister explanation, namely, the seclusion of women as part of Afghan recent history, particularly under the Taliban, and which continues in contemporary Afghan society.

The situation of Afghan women raises complex impressions. Before the events of 9/11 catapulted Afghan women into the global spotlight, one observed the picture of two sets of women: on one side, poor and rural women, and on the other, urban elite women. Before the takeover by the Taliban in 1996, it has been

---

32 *See* CAMPAIGN FOR AFGHAN WOMEN AND GIRLS, at: *http://www.feminist. org/afghan/facts.html*.

33 The former United Nations Secretary General referred to the condition of Afghan women as "an affront to all standards of dignity, equality and humanity." *See* SILENCE IS VIOLENCE: END THE ABUSE OF WOMEN IN AFGHANISTAN (United Nations Mission in Afghanistan and the United Nations High Commissioner for Human Rights, 2009) at 6.

34 NICK B. MILLS, KARZAI: THE FAILING AMERICAN INTERVENTION AND THE STRUGGLE FOR AFGHANISTAN (2007).

estimated that women worked in huge numbers as teachers, doctors, lawyers, and in a host of other professions.[35] In addition, women were schooled at more or less the same rates as men, and attended universities in significant numbers. Indeed, their social, economic, and political realities did not differ significantly from other similarly situated countries.[36]

A friend who is a law professor tells me the story of her long-term travel agent, an Afghan woman, who used to be a senior executive at a financial institution. She comes from an Afghan family of diplomats and is educated, funny, and worldly. When my friend enquired about Afghanistan after the Taliban blew up the Buddha statues at Bamiyan, her agent shrugged off the events. It was as if she denied any association with such cultural barbarism, but also any expression of solidarity with Afghan people. To her everything about Afghanistan was all in the past. She would insist that, "… all my people have left," or "I don't know those people," as if to signal that Afghanistan today is inhabited by different people in a different world.[37]

Although I initially saw these sentiments as a reflection of class differences, it became increasingly clear that even middle-class and elite women were not immune to the human rights violations committed under the mujahedeen and Taliban. Whereas in other societies class and elite status provide some protection for women from gender repressive regimes, this was not the case in Afghanistan. All women experienced an extreme loss of freedom.

But despite the dire impressions of Afghan women that I outline above, I had hoped to capture the experiences of women as agents of their political, economic, and social destiny, beyond the stereotypical images of victims of widespread violence, subordination, and discrimination.

The Bonn Agreement

In Afghanistan, incremental change is occurring. At least since 2001, a more equality-based notion of human rights, and particularly women's rights, is emerging. The December 2001 Bonn Agreement set the preconditions for moving

---

35   The Mujahedeen also started eroding women's rights in the most brutal manner, but it was the Taliban that instituted an absolute ban on women in employment. *See* MALALAI JOYA, A WOMAN AMONG WARLORDS: THE EXTRAORDINARY STORY OF AN AFGHAN WHO DARED TO RAISE HER VOICE (2011).

36   *See* DEBORAH ELLIS, WOMEN OF THE AFGHAN WAR (2000) at 62.

37   Not all Afghan expatriates necessarily share her perspective. For example, the Oakland Tribune reported a 2003 trip to Afghanistan by Taiyaba Hosseini, who was a "well-respected" official in the Afghan Ministry of France during the 1970s and 1980s, and who fled the country in 1989. The story reported on her enthusiasm for, and engagement with her country of birth, and her determination to contribute her skills to bolstering democracy in Afghanistan. *See* Melissa Evan, *Bay Area Women's Group Visits Afghanistan,* OAKLAND TRIBUNE, March 3, 2003.

Afghanistan towards a stable and democratically elected government within three years, that is, by 2004.[38] The Bonn Agreement specifically acknowledges "the right of the people of Afghanistan to freely determine their own political future in accordance with the principles of Islam, democracy, pluralism and social justice."[39] Moreover, the Bonn Agreement notes that the interim arrangements provided for are a "first step towards the establishment of a broad based, *gender-sensitive*, multi-ethnic and fully representative government."[40] In addition, the Bonn Agreement mandates that the emergency Loya Jirga to be convened "will ensure the participation of women as well as the equitable representation of all ethnic and religious communities."[41]

A key government department established to promote gender equality and women's human rights, namely, the Ministry of Women's Affairs, has worked closely with the United Nations Assistance Mission in Afghanistan and the United Nations Development Fund for Women. The Ministry has pursued five strategic areas of operation, namely, legal services and advocacy; education; vocational training; women's health and communication; and planning and international relations.[42]

The *New York Times* on March 9, 2009 reported a story about Afghan women having access to women's shelters for the first time.[43] This is a significant development in a country that has always seen women as property, and where women resisting tyrannical husbands often are forced by culture and custom to remain in oppressive marriages. As Manizha Naderi, Director of women for Afghan women, states:

> The problems they are confronting are deeply ingrained in a culture that has been mainly governed by tribal law. But they [women's shelters] are changing the lives of young women .... Simply put, this is a patriarchal society .... Women are the property of men. This is tradition.[44]

---

38 *See* AGREEMENT ON PROVISIONAL ARRANGEMENTS IN AFGHANISTAN PENDING THE RE-ESTABLISHMENT OF PERMANENT GOVERNMENT INSTITUTIONS (2001) at: *http://www.afghangovernment.com/AfghanAgreementBonn.htm.*

39 *Ibid.*

40 *Ibid.* (emphasis added). The Agreement demarcated the powers and obligations of the Interim Authority which consisted of a Special Independent Commission for Convening an Emergency Loya Jirga.

41 *Ibid.* The definition of "Loya Jirga" is a grand council or grand assembly used to resolve political conflicts or other national problems.

42 DEMOCRATIZATION AND CIVIL SOCIETY EMPOWERMENT PROGRAMME, UNITED NATIONS DEVELOPMENT PROGRAMME, AFGHANISTAN COUNTRY OFFICE (March 2007).

43 Kirk Semple, *Afghan Women Slowly Gaining Protection*, NEW YORK TIMES, March 3, 2009.

44 *Ibid.*

Reports in the last few years have also indicated progress in the number of girls who have been and are attending school. In addition, hairdressing and other beauty-related feminine occupations are being pursued in huge numbers. A rather poignant television program about the number of beauty salons that are operating in Kabul has been shown in the U.S.A.[45] So too have stories been written about Afghanistan women's soccer teams, and other sporting endeavors embarked upon by Afghan women.[46] These are radical developments in a country that was held captive by an almost medieval system of government and society imposed by the Taliban, and before them several mujahedeen factions, for nearly three decades.

Since the United States invasion in 2002, although life has changed somewhat for women in the major urban centers such as Kabul, Herat, and Mazar-e-Sharif, in the rural and more remote areas women are still imprisoned by feudal attitudes because so many men have internalized the attitudes of the Taliban.[47] In Kabul, for instance, women have the relative freedom not to wear the burqa, even though they still cover their heads, and they hold jobs and girls attend schools relatively freely. Nasrine Gross, who runs a non-governmental organization in Kabul, reports that hundreds of women are employed in the public sector—in health, education, and communications, among others. But for their rural counterparts, the invasion has barely altered their cloistered existences.[48] Practices such as forced marriages of young girls (to older men) continue, ostensibly to bring money into households or to settle disputes between families. Women continue to be stoned to death for adultery and other "honor" crimes, often only on the words of local clerics. They are forced to wear the burqa. In addition, in these places women continue to experience disturbing patterns of domestic violence. In response to the dehumanizing and intolerable conditions of domestic violence, some women attempt suicide by dousing themselves with kerosene and setting themselves on

---

45   THE BEAUTY ACADEMY OF KABUL captures a group of American hairdressers who travel to Afghanistan to open a series of beauty schools there. *See also,* DEBORAH RODRIGUEZ AND KRISTIN OHLSON, BEAUTY SHOP IN KABUL: AN AMERICAN WOMAN GOES BEHIND THE VEIL.

46   *See* Rod Nordland, *For a Women's Soccer Team, Competing Is a Victory,* NEW YORK TIMES, December 8, 2010, at: *http://www.nytimes.com/2010/12/09/world/ asia/09kabul.html.*

47   For example, a 2003 United Nations Report notes: "Despite positive developments regarding women's rights, intimidation and violence by regional and local commanders against women continue unabated ... In many rural areas, especially in the more conservative tribal belt, the situation of women has not changed to any great extent since the removal of the Taliban. The prevalence of conservative attitudes limits the full, equal and effective participation of women in civic, cultural, economic, political and social life throughout the country at all levels of society." THE SITUATION OF WOMEN AND CHILDREN IN AFGHANISTAN at: *http://www.reliefweb.int/w/rwb.nsf/UNID/12954335D77EODDDC12 56CDF00482910?OpenDocument.*

48   *See* SILENCE IS VIOLENCE: END THE ABUSE OF WOMEN IN AFGHANISTAN, *supra* Note 33.

fire.[49] Most disturbingly, however, local warlords continue to run most of the country, with a mixture of violence and misogyny.[50]

Hundreds of women stood in line to vote in the nation's first parliamentary elections for three decades, held in September 2005. The names of hundreds of women were on the ballot. As a British journalist observed:

> In the elections held in Afghanistan last weekend, many reporters concentrated on the extraordinary spectacle of women queuing, their blue burkas billowing, at the polling station. George Bush also hit upon this as proof of the success of the American presence in Afghanistan. He stated that the first person to vote in the election was a 19 year old woman ....[51]

The first government established after the Bonn Agreement consisted of three female ministers (the Minister of Women's Affairs, the Minister of Public Health, and the Minister of State for Women's Affairs) and four Deputy-Ministers, and two of the nine Commissioners appointed to the Constitutional Drafting Committee were women.[52]

On March 8, 2003, 1,500 women from Kabul and throughout the country gathered for a public event to celebrate International Women's Day. The Minister for Women's Affairs, Habiba Sarabi, noted that this was "a big change in Afghan women's life, as well as a significant sign of their interest in social affairs."[53] New voting laws enacted in May 2005 provided for the reservation of 25 percent of national and provincial seats to be set aside for women in the national parliament and in the provincial councils.[54] As Dr. Nazdama, a hospital administrator who is Pashtun, and one of two hundred women delegates who joined 1,400 male delegates to the first Loya Jirga noted: "Afghanistan has come out of a very dark and terrible graveyard."[55] The women delegates "determinedly used the platform

---

49   *See* ANN JONES, KABUL IN WINTER, *supra* Note 27.

50   HUMAN RIGHTS WATCH, ALL OUR HOPES ARE CRUSHED: VIOLENCE AND REPRESSION IN WESTERN AFGHANISTAN (2002); *see also* HUMAN RIGHTS WATCH, "WE HAVE THE PROMISES OF THE WORLD": WOMEN'S RIGHTS IN AFGHANISTAN (2009) at: *http://www.wluml.org/sites/wluml.org/files/hrw_report_2009.pdf.*

51   Natasha Walte, *Comment and Analysis: The US and Britain Used the Oppression of Afghan Women to Justify Their Intervention,* THE GUARDIAN (London), October 12, 2004.

52   Catherine A. Fitzpatrick, *Afghanistan Women: Progress and Unmet Promises,* RADIO FREE EUROPE/RADIO LIBERTY AFGHAN REPORT, 27 March 2003.

53   *Ibid.*

54   Masuda Sultan, *From Rhetoric to Reality: Afghan Women on the Agenda for Peace,* WOMEN WAGING PEACE POLICY COMMISSION (2005) at: *http://www.iiav. nl/epublications/2005/from_rhetoric_to_reality.pdf.*

55   Carlotta Gall, *Afghan Women in Political Spotlight,* NEW YORK TIMES, June 28, 2002.

to show Afghanistan that women want peace, not war, education, not guns, construction and jobs, not poverty."[56]

But even in the urban centers, and despite the reservation of seats for women parliamentary candidates, a combination of the security situation and deeply entrenched patriarchal attitudes, sometimes life-threatening, to individual candidates have precluded their taking advantage of voting laws.[57] Dr. Sima Samar, a former Minister and Deputy-President in the first Karzai government, and now head of the Afghan Independent Human Rights Commission, was forced out of her post by religious fundamentalist politicians because of their opposition to her advocacy for women's rights.[58]

Afghan female politicians, including those who are parliamentary candidates, are increasingly attacked by the Taliban and other armed groups.[59] For example, Amnesty International reported that in March 2011, Member of Parliament Fawzia Kofi was shot and injured while travelling from Jalalabad to Kabul. The following month, Nadia Kayyani, a member of the Provincial Council was critically injured in a drive-by shooting in the city of Pul-e-Khumri in Northern Afghanistan.[60] Malalai Joya, one of the youngest persons elected to the Loya Jirga in 2005, was forced to resign because she criticized the warlords who continue to run Afghanistan. She has survived several assassination attempts, and has been forced to seek the protection of armed security guards.[61] In addition, a combination of fear for their own safety, and reticence about the role of women in a democratic Afghanistan, has meant that male family members often do not support the candidacy of their female family members.[62] Moreover, women who carry voter-registration cards in

---

56   *Ibid.*

57   *See* SILENCE IS VIOLENCE: END THE ABUSE OF WOMEN IN AFGHANISTAN, *supra* Note 33 at 10.

58   *Ibid.* For a chilling account of the targeting of female politicians and women in public life, *see* Kim Sengupta, *Women Who Took on the Taliban – and Lost*, INDEPENDENT (UK), October 3, 2008.

59   AMNESTY INTERNATIONAL, ANNUAL REPORT 2011: THE STATE OF THE WORLD'S HUMAN RIGHTS at: *http://www.amnesty.org/en/region/afghanistan/report-2011#page.*

60   *Ibid.*

61   *See* MALALAI JOYA, A WOMAN AMONG WARLORDS, *supra* Note 35.

62   Indeed, family members may also be a target of the violence. Recently a Commissioner at the Afghan Independent Human Rights Commission and members of his family were killed in a bombing at a supermarket in Kabul. The supermarket was used by foreigners, so it is unclear whether he was the target of the bombing. *See* REPORT OF THE SPECIAL RAPPORTEUR ON EXTRAJUDICIAL, SUMMARY OR ARBITRARY EXECUTIONS, CHRISTOF HEYNS (May 27, 2011), 8 at: *http://www2.ohchr.org/english/bodies/hrcouncil/docs/17session/A.HRC.17.28 add.0_en.pdf. See also* SILENCE IS VIOLENCE: END THE ABUSE OF WOMEN IN AFGHANISTAN, *supra* Note 33.

an attempt to exercise their newly-acquired right to vote, often face danger from radical males who do not want to change the conservative status quo.[63]

In the face of widespread opposition, women have used innovative techniques to encourage both males and females to vote for them. For example, they appeal to the religiosity of their constituents by engaging with the major tenets of Islam, attempting to illustrate an Islam that is amenable to a more engaged participation of women in public life.[64] During election rallies, they quote from the Koran, drawing examples from the prophet Muhammad's life, where women had an important role in Islamic society.

Women's groups throughout the country focused on bolstering and sustaining the network of women's councils, called *shuras*, in the villages surrounding the urban centers. The purpose of these *shuras* was to allow women to engage in dialogue outside the presence and supervision of men. In addition, performing the function of women's co-operatives, these *shuras* provide financial assistance to women to set up small businesses, particularly various cottage industries within their homes. Some funding for these *shuras* have been provided by international support groups, such as Women for Afghan Women in the U.S.A. and the Afghan Women's Mission.[65]

In addition, since 2002 a range of state and non-state organs have been set up to pursue a human rights agenda, and particularly an agenda that furthers the human rights of women. Under the Bonn Agreement, the Judicial Reform Commission (JRC) was set up in November 2002 with the express purpose of re-establishing the rule of law in Afghanistan and rebuilding Afghan's legal system.[66] Central to the success of the JRC was the education and training of judges, prosecutors, and other key actors in the legal system. The JRC was also established to develop and strengthen Afghanistan's permanent judicial structures, including the Ministry of

---

63 "WE HAVE THE PROMISES OF THE WORLD": WOMEN'S RIGHTS IN AFGHANISTAN, *supra* Note 50.

64 *See* Meri Melissi Hartley-Blecic, *The Invisible Women: The Taliban's Oppression of Women in Afghanistan*, 7 ILSA JOURNAL OF INTERNATIONAL AND COMPARATIVE LAW (2001) 553, who states: "The Muslim Women's League points out that the Koran gave women rights almost 1400 years ago, such as the right to sell property. The Muslim Women's League claims that the religion of Islam promotes equality among men and women to facilitate the economic growth of society, and that it mandates education for all Muslims, including women." *Ibid* at 576.

65 *See* their websites at: *http://www.womenforafghanwomen.org* and *http://www. afghanwomensmission.org*.

66 AGREEMENT ON PROVISIONAL ARRANGEMENTS IN AFGHANISTAN PENDING THE RE-ESTABLISHMENT OF PERMANENT GOVERNMENT INSTITUTIONS, *supra* Note 38.

Justice, the Attorney-General's office, and the Supreme Court, and local judicial mechanisms and processes.[67]

Another human rights body established subsequent to the Bonn Agreement was the Afghan Independent Human Rights Commission (AIHRC), to promote and strengthen the support of human rights within the Afghan population, and to monitor and investigate human rights violations. Since its establishment it has been headed by Dr. Sima Samar, a medical doctor and one of Afghanistan's most prominent human rights figures.[68] The Constitutional Commission was established to draft the Afghanistan Constitution after the meeting of the first emergency constitutional Loya Jirga. The Commission was terminated after the drafting of Afghanistan's Constitution and its signing by President Karzai in 2004.[69]

In June 2003 President Karzai established the Anti-Corruption Commission to tackle the issues of corruption, nepotism, and bureaucratic inertia and inefficiency. It was primarily designed to promote a competent, responsive, and dedicated civil service to support the work of the Afghan government. Although this was one of several anti-corruption initiatives instigated by the Afghan government, the problem of corruption in Afghanistan seems intractable to some.[70]

The Afghan Constitution

After the Bonn Agreement of 2002, the constitutional drafting process included demarcated structures, roles, and timetabling. The Bonn agreement was very clear about the need to include women in the process of drafting the Constitution, as well as the inclusion of rights for women in the final document.[71]

---

67   *Afghanistan: Judicial Reform and Transitional Justice*, THE INTERNATIONAL CRISIS GROUP (2003) at: *http://unpan1.un.org/intradoc/groups/public/documents/apcity/unpan016653.pdf.*

68   *Ibid.*

69   Cornelia Schneider, *Striking a Balance in Post-Conflict Constitution Making: Lessons from Afghanistan for the International Community*, 7 PEACE, CONFLICT AND DEVELOPMENT: AN INTERDISCIPLINARY JOURNAL (2005) 174 at: *http://www.peacestudiesjournal.org.uk/dl/July05Schneider.pdf.*

70   *See* FIGHTING CORRUPTION IN AFGHANISTAN: A ROADMAP FOR STRATEGY AND ACTION (Asian Development Bank and Others, February 16, 2007) at: *http://www.unodc.org/pdf/afg/anti_corruption_roadmap.pdf; see also, Afghan Force to Fight Corruption*, BBC NEWS, November 16th 2009 at: *http://news.bbc.co.uk/2/hi/americas/8363148.stm.*

71   AGREEMENT ON PROVISIONAL ARRANGEMENTS IN AFGHANISTAN PENDING THE RE-ESTABLISHMENT OF PERMANENT GOVERNMENT INSTITUTIONS, *supra* Note 38. Noting that these interim agreements are intended as the first step towards the establishment of a broad-based, gender-sensitive, multi-ethnic and fully representative government.

Just as South African women presented their demands in a Charter of Rights to ensure that women's rights were incorporated in the South African Constitution drafting process, Afghan women also lobbied to ensure that women's rights were not ignored in the new constitutional framework. The Afghan Constitution that was drafted in the wake of the Bonn Agreement contains several provisions that give effect to women's rights.[72]

In 2003 women leaders from all over Afghanistan met in Kandahar at a conference entitled "Women and the Constitution," to draft and sign the Afghan Women's Bill of Rights, which they presented to the Minister of Women's Affairs, Habiba Sarabi, the Constitutional Commission of the Transitional Islamic State of Afghanistan, and President Hamid Karzai.[73] This was a seminal event held outside of Kabul in the former Taliban stronghold of Kandahar, and it brought together a large number of women from several ethnic groups, community leaders, and prominent women's and human rights advocates, including elite women and those who were not educated, from all parts of the country, including rural and urban areas. The document reflected a process of debate, engagement and consensus from all the participants, "with each right debated and its wording unanimously agreed upon before inclusion into the document."[74] The conference participants saw the Bill of Rights as an important vehicle through which to educate communities throughout the country about women's and human rights.

They listed the rights as follows:

1. Mandatory education for women through secondary school and opportunities for all women for higher education.
2. Provision of up-to-date health services for women with special attention to reproductive rights.
3. Protection and security for women: the prevention and criminalization of sexual harassment against women publicly and in the home, of sexual abuse of women and children, of domestic violence, and of "bad blood-price" (the use of women as compensation for crimes by one family against another).
4. Reduction of the time before women can remarry after their husbands have disappeared, and mandatory government support of women during that time.
5. Freedom of speech.
6. Freedom to vote and run for election to office.
7. Rights to marry and divorce according to Islam.

---

72 THE CONSTITUTION OF AFGHANISTAN (2004) [HEREINAFTER "THE AFGHAN CONSTITUTION"].

73 *Afghan Women's Bill of Rights Presented to President Hamid Karzai by Women's Rights Groups*, WOMEN FOR AFGHAN WOMEN at *http://www.womenforafghanwomen.org/publications.php?ID=pubs.html*.

74 *Ibid.*

8. Equal pay for equal work.
9. Right to financial independence and ownership of property.
10. Right to participate fully and to the highest levels in the economic and commercial life of the country.
11. Mandatory provision of economic opportunities for women.
12. Equal representation of women in the Loya Jirga and Parliament.
13. Full inclusion of women in the judiciary system.
14. Minimum marriageable age set at 18 years.
15. Guarantee of all constitutional rights to widows, disabled women, and orphans.
16. Full rights of inheritance.[75]

In January 2004 President Karzai signed into law a new constitution that the Loya Jirga had ratified.[76] The Preamble to the Constitution promises,

> [the] creation of a civil society free of oppression, atrocity, discrimination, and violence based on the rule of law, social justice, protection of human rights, and dignity, and ensuring the fundamental rights and freedoms of the people .... For strengthening of political, social, economics, and defensive institutions of the country .... For ensuring a prosperous life, and sound environment for all those residing in this land.[77]

The Constitution is committed to human rights and equality and explicitly recognizes equal rights for both men and women as citizens. Indeed, in addition to enumerated rights listed in Chapter 2, the Constitution also makes clear that Afghanistan will abide by the United Nations Charter, the Universal Declaration of Human Rights, and other international treaties and conventions that Afghanistan

---

75   Additional demands affecting the lives of women:

1. Disarmament and national security.

2. Trials of war criminals in international criminal courts and the disempowerment of warlords.

3. A strong central government.

4. A commitment to end government corruption.

5. Decisive action against foreign invasion and protection of the sovereignty of Afghanistan. *See* Afghan Women's Bill of Rights, *Ibid.*

76   THE AFGHAN CONSTITUTION, *supra* Note 72.

77   *Ibid.* Preamble Sections 8 to 10. The Preamble also makes clear the belief of the Afghan people in the "Sacred religion of Islam." Article two reiterates that the state religion is Islam, with the provision that those who follow "other religions are free to exercise their faith and perform their religious rites within the limits of the provisions of law."

has signed.[78] Since many of these documents address women's rights directly or indirectly, this section is potentially of enormous benefit to women.[79]

Chapter 2 lists an extensive array of civil and political rights, including the right to freedom of expression, association, the right to vote, the right to protest, the right to travel, and the right of access to information. This chapter also provides for a range of economic and social rights, including the right to property, health, free public education until the end of a bachelor's degree, and the right to work and choice of occupation. Discrimination is outlawed, and everyone, male and female, is offered "equal rights and duties before the law."[80] This chapter also specifies the right to life, dignity, and liberty, stating that the right to liberty "has no limits unless affecting the rights of others or public interests which are regulated by law."[81] Chapter 2 also lists the presumption of innocence and the prohibition of torture, as well as "punishment contrary to human integrity."[82]

Of enormous significance for women is the constitutional mandate to ensure the "physical and psychological well being of family, especially of child and mother," as well as the "elimination of traditions contrary to the principles of ... Islam."[83] The Human Rights Commission is mandated to investigate complaints of violations, and may refer such violations to "the legal authorities" and may assist the complainant who is pursuing redress of the violation.[84] Beyond this, however, despite the wide range of rights listed in Chapter 2, there is very little provision for strong institutions to promote and protect those rights. This is unlike the situation in South Africa, where a range of bodies are mandated to promote and fulfill the rights enunciated in the Constitution.

Chapter 7 contains the provisions related to the judiciary. This section outlines the organization and structure of the judicial authorities and courts, and provides for the appointment of judges. It affirms the principle of the independence of the judiciary, but is completely silent on the issue of diversity of the bench, especially gender diversity. The appropriate qualifications include age (those under the age of 40 are not eligible), citizenship, education, "high ethical standards and a reputation for good deeds," no criminal record, and no political affiliation during the term of office.[85] This chapter makes no provision for an independent authority to appoint

---

78   *Ibid.* Article 7.

79   The international documents include THE INTERNATIONAL CONVENTION ON THE ELIMINATION OF ALL FORMS OF DISCRIMINATION AGAINST WOMEN, THE INTERNATIONAL COVENANT ON CIVIL AND POLITICAL RIGHTS and THE INTERNATIONAL COVENANT ON ECONOMIC, SOCIAL AND CULTURAL RIGHTS.

80   THE AFGHAN CONSTITUTION, *supra* Note 72, Article 22.

81   *Ibid.* Articles 23 and 24.

82   *Ibid.* Articles 25 and 29.

83   *Ibid.* Article 54.

84   *Ibid.* Article 58.

85   *Ibid.* Article 118. Interestingly, the requirement of educational qualifications include both "higher education in law or in Islamic jurisprudence."

judges, except providing that judges will be appointed "with the recommendation of the Supreme Court and approval of the President."[86] The President administers the following oath to the judges of the Supreme Court before they take office:

> In the name Allah, the Merciful and the Compassionate I swear in the name of God Almighty to support justice and righteousness in accord with the provisions of the sacred religion of Islam and the provisions of the Constitution and other laws of Afghanistan, and to execute the duty of being a judge with utmost honesty, righteousness and nonpartisanship.[87]

Although on the face of it, this provision appears to commit Supreme Court judges to "support justice and righteousness," this requirement is subject to judges' interpretation of Islam, the Constitution, and relevant laws in a way that comports with notions of equality and human rights. If a judge holds particularly odious views of women, his interpretation of "justice and righteousness" may be at odds with universally accepted notions of equality and human rights. Similarly, the Constitution provides that courts in Afghanistan shall apply Shia law in personal matters to those are who followers of the Shia sect, and unless there are constitutional and legal provisions to the contrary, Shia law will be applied in non-personal matters if both parties are members of the Shia sect.[88] This provision seems to suggest that Shia women might be afforded less protection than other women if the application of Shia law is particularly conservative regarding women's issues.

Obstacles to Women's Equality

But despite the gains mentioned above, in particular the Constitution that provides a measure of rights for women, perusal of the lives of women in Afghanistan suggest that their situation has barely changed since the military invasion in early 2002, and that in fact for the majority of women, the situation has become progressively worse.[89] Ann Jones, an author who has spent years in Afghanistan, notes warily that,

> ... an unsentimental look at the record reveals that for all the fine talk of women's rights since the US invasion, equal rights for Afghan women have been illusory all along, a polite feel-good fiction that helped to sell the American enterprise

---

86   *Ibid.* Article 132.
87   *Ibid.* Article 119.
88   *Ibid.* Article 131.
89   HUMAN RIGHTS WATCH, "I HAD TO RUN AWAY": THE IMPRISONMENT OF WOMEN AND GIRLS IN AFGHANISTAN (March 2012).

at home and cloak in respectability the misbegotten government we installed in Afghanistan.[90]

In addition, a report by Human Rights Watch issued in 2009 cited disturbing trends in Afghanistan despite promises made in the Bonn Agreement.[91] For example, they noted the reconfiguration of a Vice and Virtue Squad named "Islamic Teaching," consisting of a team of about ninety women within the Ministry of Religious Affairs, who were ostensibly mandated to curb female "un-Islamic behaviour."[92]

Whereas initially the concerns of women appear to have been central to the reconstruction of the new government, it has become increasingly clear that those concerns have been relegated to the margins of political preoccupation in Afghanistan. Indeed, the situation for women has for the most part changed only minimally. Some statistics will make the point: Before the Taliban took control in 1996, a significant proportion of women in Afghanistan were educated and employed. For example, 50 percent of the students and 60 percent of the teachers at Kabul University were women.[93] Seventy percent of school teachers, 50 percent of civilian government workers, and 40 percent of doctors in Kabul were women. Today, Afghanistan has the world's second highest death rate in women during pregnancy and childbirth. For every 100,000 births, 1,600 mothers die (compared to 1 to 12 in affluent countries).[94]

Ms. Azfhar, a midwife from Afghanistan, notes that women "are dying because society has yet to make the decision that their lives are worth saving."[95] Average life expectancy for women is under forty years, and the illiteracy rate for women is 80 percent.[96] A recent report has shown that Afghanistan is one of the ten most dangerous countries for women. The report notes,

... the average Afghan girl will live to only 45—one year less than an Afghan male. After three decades of war and religion-based repression, an overwhelming number of women are illiterate. More than half of all brides are under 16, and

90   Ann Jones, *Remember the Women?*, THE NATION, November 9, 2009.

91   HUMAN RIGHTS WATCH, "WE HAVE THE PROMISES OF THE WORLD": WOMEN'S RIGHTS IN AFGHANISTAN, *supra* Note 50.

92   *Ibid.*

93   Kenneth J. Cooper, *Kabul Women under Virtual House Arrest*, WASHINGTON POST, October 7, 1996: CNN, March 9, 1997.

94   In the remote province of Badakhshan, 6507 mothers die for every 100,000 births, according to the British medical journal, *Lancet. See* Denise Grady, *In War and Isolation: A Fighter for Afghan Women*, NEW YORK TIMES, July 28, 2009. The *Lancet* further reports that most of these deaths are preventable.

95   *Ibid.*

96   STATEMENT BY SIMA WALI, PRESIDENT, REFUGEE WOMEN IN DEVELOPMENT ON THE OCCASION OF INTERNATIONAL WOMEN'S DAY, NEW YORK, 8 MARCH, 2002 at: *http://www.un.org/events/women/2002/wali.htm.*

one woman dies in childbirth every half hour. Domestic violence is so common that 87 per cent of women admit to experiencing it. But more than one million widows are on the streets, often forced into prostitution. Afghanistan is the only country in which the female suicide rate is higher than that of males.[97]

This latest report echoes several earlier ones that have pointed out the harsh consequences for women stemming from the lack of security, abuses by powerful regional and local warlords, and ineffective law enforcement mechanisms.[98] As Amnesty International stated in a 2003 report:

> Women and girls are vulnerable to rape, sexual violence and abduction. The burning of a number of girls' schools has demonstrated the threat to provision for the realization of the rights of women .... The prevailing insecurity has directly impacted on attempts by women to engage in political activities and ensure integration of women's rights in the process of reconstruction.[99]

President Karzai provoked international outrage two years ago when it was disclosed that he had signed off on draconian "Taliban-like restrictions" on women, specifically on allowing the passage of laws that restrict women's autonomy and that "permit marital rape."[100] The disclosure came as President Obama and European leaders were meeting at a NATO summit to push for an increase in NATO troop numbers in Afghanistan. Some observers speculated that the passage of the draconian laws would provide an excuse for wavering European governments to commit more troops.

97　　*The Ten Worst Countries for Women*, FEMINIST EZINE, at: *http://www. feministezine.com/feminist/international/Ten-Worst-Countries-for-Women.html.*

98　　*See*, for example, HUMAN RIGHTS WATCH, "KILLING YOU IS A VERY EASY THING FOR US": HUMAN RIGHTS ABUSES IN SOUTHEAST AFGHANISTAN (July 2003),; *see also We Want to Live as Humans: Repression of Women and Girls in Southeast Afghanistan* (December 2002).

99　　AMNESTY INTERNATIONAL, AFGHANISTAN: "NO ONE LISTENS TO US AND NO ONE TREATS US AS HUMAN BEINGS": JUSTICE DENIED TO WOMEN (October 2003) at: *http://amnesty.org/en/library/asset/ASA11/023/2003/en/39a4c8fd-d693-11dd-ab95-a13b602c0642/asa110232003en.pdf.* In its 2011 STATE OF THE WORLD'S HUMAN RIGHTS ANNUAL REPORT, Amnesty International noted: "Afghan women and girls continued to face endemic violence and discrimination at home and in the public sphere. The Afghanistan Independent Human Rights Commission documented 1,891 cases of violence against women, but the true number may be higher." Annual Report at: *http://www.amnesty.org/en/region/afghanistan/report-2011#page.*

100　　*See, Afghan Anti-Women Law Attacked*, BBC NEWS, April 1, 2009 at: *http://news.bbc.co.uk/2/hi/south_asia/7977293.stm*; *see also* Dexter Filkins, *Afghan Women Protest New Restrictive Law*, NEW YORK TIMES, April 15, 2009 at: *http://www.nytimes.com/2009/04/16/world/asia/16afghan.html?_r=1&emc=etal1.*

Although the issue of women's rights in Afghanistan has been waning and waxing in the Western media and amongst American advocates for some time, since 2001 it has captured the attention of Western feminists. "Liberating" the women of Afghanistan has largely been seen to be the primary goal and ultimately to be the biggest winner in a democratic Afghanistan. However, the narrative and statistics that I outline above indicate that the goal of gender equality in Afghanistan is fraught.

Since 2002, the plight of women in Afghanistan has received notable attention; unfortunately, it has also given rise to some political opportunism. For example, in his State of the Union Address in January 2002, then President Bush referred to the need to free the women of Afghanistan, directly linking the invasion of Afghanistan to restoring women's rights and equality.[101] But it is widely known that the United States, in its attempts to thwart the Soviet occupation of Afghanistan, supported an array of anti-Soviet groups, most particularly the mujahedeen, who embarked on a concerted campaign against women's rights, which the Taliban later refined in the most cynical and brutal way. This is despite the valiant efforts by women's rights activists in the U.S.A. who engaged in widespread campaigns during the 1990s to draw attention to the plight of Afghan women.[102]

Notwithstanding official rhetoric and lofty sentiments about equality and dignity for women, women's rights and concerns are often relegated to second place as most post-conflict societies embark on political and legal transformation. Ample evidence of this marginalization is apparent when one scours the legacy of most newly-independent societies. Afghanistan provides one contemporary example. Regardless of the promises of freedom, liberty, and equality made to Afghan women, their situation appears to have only marginally improved. As the business of constructing a new government has captured the attention of the politicians, overwhelmingly male, women's rights appear to have once again become of secondary concern. Even valiant attempts by Afghan women and their non-Afghan supporters have been disappointingly derailed in the face of intransigent patriarchal attitudes that appear hard to dislodge.[103]

Since the American and NATO intervention in 2002, it was thought that things would overall improve for Afghan people, and particularly for Afghan women. But despite changes that have occurred as a result of the agitation and activism of Afghan women and their allies elsewhere, a decade since the last military

---

101   *See* President George W. Bush, State of the Union Address (January 29, 2002), at: *allpolitics/01/29/bush.speech.txt/index.html.*

102   *See*, for example, *Afghan Apartheid*, 2 THE WOMEN'S WATCH 2, International Women's Rights Action Watch (Spring 1997).

103   Ann Jones provides a thoughtful and sobering account of attempts to pursue projects and programs for women in the face of official ineptitude and indifference. *See* ANN JONES, KABUL IN WINTER, *supra* Note 27. *See also* Ann Jones, *Remember the Women?*, *supra* Note 90.

invasion, and waning interest on the part of the international community, the situation certainly demands greater urgency.[104]

So in the midst of these rather bleak observations and statistics, how does one not just concentrate on the contemporary situation of Afghan women, but also think through some policy and practical approaches that should be considered to change such reality? In other words, there is plenty of empirical, statistical, and impressionistic evidence to suggest that the situation of women in Afghanistan is so absolutely dismal that a listing of such evidence seems to be an exercise in futility. As tort lawyers observe when arguing the obvious: *res ipsa loquitur* [the facts speak for themselves]. I could cover pages listing the incidence and consequences of stoning, forced marriages, child bride practices, domestic violence, rape, and other forms of private and public violence against women. I could tabulate the economic hardships that result when women are not allowed to work outside the home, or when they are not provided with the resources needed to make reproductive choices. I could highlight the enforced impoverishment of widows, who in addition to suffering emotional trauma, are prohibited from seeking work outside the home. I could list the utter humiliation of being forced to travel always accompanied by a male family member, even in cases of medical emergencies, and to completely cover oneself in public. I could describe the generic fear which was the currency of Taliban and mujahedeen rule, and which persists in many parts of Afghanistan today. I could describe a totalitarian masculinist universe in which women are not second class, but without class at all. But these facts and statistics would be the mere listing of a litany of subjugation, oppression, discrimination, and the persistent denial of rights.

Without meaning to treat this with levity, the comedian Bill Maher, in referring to the situation of women in Afghanistan notes:

> What if there were black men in some white country? Black men being beaten for showing an ankle or wrist? Black men dying because it was against the law for them to receive medical attention? Black men starving to death because they were not allowed to work or stoned to death for having sex?[105]

This situation constitutes gender apartheid.

---

104   This has been made clear in a report issued by USAID in 2011. *See* USAID/ AFGHANISTAN EVALUATION OF THE AMBASSADOR'S SMALL GRANTS PROGRAM (ASGP) TO SUPPORT GENDER EQUALITY IN AFGHANISTAN (August 19, 2011).

105   BILL MAHER, WHEN YOU RIDE ALONE YOU RIDE WITH BIN LADEN (2002).

Gender Apartheid

For the past twenty-three years I have anguished over how to explain the untold suffering, oppression, grief, and outrage that the women of Afghanistan have endured. Throughout this period, Afghan women not only have been subject to the generalized horrors of war, and the daunting and unending circle of violence which has confronted everyone in Afghan society, but, in addition, in a historically unprecedented way, became the targets of a new kind of war. The ferocity of the attacks against Afghan women have been so severe and draconian, that a new term, "gender-apartheid," was coined to describe the extent of the new kind of horror aimed directly at them.[106]

The rights of women that are violated with regularity in Afghanistan are to be found in the Universal Declaration of Human Rights,[107] the International Covenant on Civil and Political Rights,[108] the International Covenant on Economic, Social and Cultural Rights,[109] and the Convention on the Elimination of all Forms of Discrimination Against Women.[110] These rights include the right to freedom of movement, freedom of association, the right to equality, the right to life, liberty and security of the person, the right to work and free choice of employment, and a range of other civil, political, and economic rights. In addition, the right of individuals to be free from torture, as outlined in the Convention Against Torture,[111] are regularly violated, as evidenced by the horrendous statistics of violence against women, including stoning those women who "commit adultery."[112]

To conscript an alternative vision that contrasts with the reality of the lives of most Afghan women today, I want to argue once again (as the Feminist Majority Foundation and others have done) that the treatment of women by the government and male civil society in Afghanistan since the 1970s (the end of the communist era) amounted to a crime against humanity, in the same way that the United Nations, by the passage of the Apartheid Convention, deemed

---

106　STATEMENT BY SIMA WALI, PRESIDENT, REFUGEE WOMEN IN DEVELOPMENT ON THE OCCASION OF INTERNATIONAL WOMEN'S DAY, *supra* Note 96. Ms. Wali was referring to AMBER SCHNEEWEIS, GENDER APARTHEID IN AFGHANISTAN at: *http://www.public.iastate.edu/~rhetoric/105H17/aschneeweis/cof.html*.

107　*Supra* Chapter 3, Note 8.

108　*Supra* Chapter 3, Note 9.

109　*Supra* Chapter 3, Note 10.

110　CEDAW, *supra* Chapter 2, Note 9.

111　CONVENTION AGAINST TORTURE AND OTHER CRUEL, INHUMAN AND DEGRADING TREATMENT OR PUNISHMENT, Adopted and opened for signature, ratification and accession by General Assembly Resolution 39/46 of December 10, 1984, entry into force June 26, 1987.

112　*See* Dr. Huma Ahmed-Ghosh, *A History of Women in Afghanistan: Lessons Learnt for the Future or Yesterdays and Tomorrow: Women in Afghanistan*, 4 JOURNAL OF INTERNATIONAL WOMEN'S STUDIES (May 2003) 1.

apartheid a crime against humanity.[113] When one reads the Apartheid Convention closely, and replaces "gender" with "race/apartheid," a compelling argument can be made that the situation of women is in some ways identical to the plight of black South Africans under apartheid. In fact, the definition provided for in the Apartheid Convention draws strong parallels between the situation of women in Afghanistan and the situation of black South Africans under apartheid. My argument consequently is that one way of thinking about constructing a genuine alternative to the contemporary realities of women's lives in Afghanistan is to think about the way the international community confronted the eradication of apartheid in South Africa.

To illustrate the point, if one adds the term "gender" to apartheid, and replaces the term "racial group" with "gendered group" in the definition section of the Convention on the Suppression of the Crime of Apartheid, and also replace "Southern Africa" with "Afghanistan," the term "gender apartheid" is apparent. The definition of " gender apartheid" in the "Apartheid Convention" will read as follows:

> For the purpose of the present Convention, the term "the crime of gender apartheid," which shall include similar policies and practices of gender segregation and discrimination as practised in Afghanistan, shall apply to the following inhuman acts committed for the purpose of establishing and maintaining domination by one gendered group of persons over any other gendered group of persons and systematically oppressing them:
>
> (a) Denial to a member or members of a gendered group or groups of the right to life and liberty of person:
>
> (i) By murder of members of a gendered group or groups;
>
> (ii) By the infliction upon the members of a gendered group or groups of serious bodily or mental harm, by the infringement of their freedom or dignity, or by subjecting them to torture or to cruel, inhuman or degrading treatment or punishment;
>
> (iii) By arbitrary arrest and illegal imprisonment of the members of a gendered group or groups;
>
> (c) Any legislative measures and other measures calculated to prevent a gendered group or groups from participation in the political, social, economic and cultural life of the country and the deliberate creation of conditions preventing the full development of such a group or groups, in

---

113   INTERNATIONAL CONVENTION ON THE SUPPRESSION AND PUNISHMENT OF THE CRIME OF APARTHEID, *supra* Chapter 5, Note 94.

particular by denying to members of a gendered group or groups basic human rights and freedoms, ...

(f) Persecution of organizations and persons, by depriving them of fundamental rights and freedoms, because they oppose gender oppression, subordination and discrimination.

Reports from the United Nations Mission in Afghanistan, United Nations Women, Human Rights Watch, Amnesty International, the Afghan Independent Human Rights Commission, and other international and Afghan bodies have documented the systemic violence and deprivation of human rights that would fit the definition of gender apartheid as defined above. For example, women are regularly mutilated when they run away from intolerant domestic situations involving abusive husbands or in-laws.[114] Any woman suspected of adultery may be stoned to death, assaulted, or sent to prison on trumped up charges. In fact women's prisons are full of women and their children who languish there in appalling conditions for merely trying to avoid child marriage or rape or other forms of violence.[115] In 2010, the Taliban stoned to death a couple who chose to marry, and eloped—against the wishes of their parents.[116] In August 2011, a similar incident occurred.[117] Women have been stoned to death for traveling with men who were not their relatives, or for not being properly dressed. The prohibition of war widows from working has resulted in tens of thousands of families in destitution. Because women make up a large proportion of the Afghan population, and because so many men have died during several decades of war, widows are disproportionately represented as a total of the Afghan population. As a consequence, many international development and aid efforts are increasingly being focused on the widows of Afghanistan.[118]

---

114   For example, in 2010 the disfigured face of Bibi Aisha appeared on the cover of *Time* magazine after her nose was cut off when she ran away from her abusive in-laws. *See Bibi Aisha, Disfigured Afghan Woman Featured on "Time" Cover, Visits US*, NPR NEWSBLOG, October 13, 2010 at: *http://www.npr.org/blogs/thetwo-way/2010/10/13/130527903/bibi-aisha-disfigured-afghan-woman-featured-on-time-cover-visits-u-s.*

115   HUMAN RIGHTS WATCH, "I HAD TO RUN AWAY," *supra* Note 89.

116   AMNESTY INTERNATIONAL 2011 REPORT at: *http://www.amnesty.org/en/region/afghanistan/report-2011#page.*

117   This incident was reported to me by the Canadian human rights advocate, Susan Bazilli, who traveled to Afghanistan for three weeks in July and August, 2011.

118   *See Afghan Widows Find Employment*, USAID/AFGHANISTAN, March 7, 2012 at: *http://afghanistan.usaid.gov/en/USAID/Article/2581/Afghan_Widows_Find_Employment.* Since 9/11, several charities have been set up to assist widows in Afghanistan. They include the Alia Foundation at *www.aliafoundation.com* and Beyond the 11th at *www.beyondthe11th.org.*

Another example of the denial of fundamental human rights is the number of maternal deaths, shocking by global standards: 593 out of 100,000 live births.[119] The custom of giving birth at home, underpinned by the requirement that women need their husband's permission to seek medical treatment, compounds the situation.[120] In addition, an average of 1,600 women die in Afghanistan for every 100,000 live births.[121] In one province, the rate is 6,500 per 100,000, making Afghanistan one of the worst places in the world for women to give birth.[122] A socially engineered very high illiteracy rate among women reinforces the tragedy, such illiteracy making it very hard for women to access useful information about their health and well-being, let alone legal and constitutional rights.[123]

All these obstacles to women enjoying their human rights are found in deeply ingrained masculinist cultural values and attitudes that have been ossified through continuous cycles of war and violence, economic hardships, and a lack of national political and security structures that could serve as moderating factors on such values and attitudes.[124] In addition, these values and attitudes have been intertwined with an interpretation of Islam that is at its core hostile to the needs and aspirations of women. Such interpretations therefore make it harder for women to reject their families or communities because their religion is important to them.[125] As the Iranian legal scholar, Lisa Ayoub, has noted:

> Social customs and norms are the real problem in the economic oppression of women. These social norms and customs put a strain on Afghan women's economic opportunities and not the Shari'a itself. Studies conducted among Muslim women in Israel, Egypt and the West Bank show that the customs of society are the main elements that limit women's employment opportunities. Therefore, one must be able to comprehend the difference between Islamic law and social norms to understand Afghan's economic future. Islamic feminists

---

119   PHYSICIANS FOR HUMAN RIGHTS REPORT (2002) at: *https:// s3.amazonaws.com/PHR_Reports/afghanistan-herat-maternal-mortality-2002.pdf.*

120   *Ibid.*

121   *Afghan Women and Their Newborns Immunized for Tetanus,* UNICEF, January 31, 2003 at: *http://www.unicef.org/media/media_7353.html.*

122   *Afghanistan: The Worst Place in the World to Give Birth,* OXFAM at: *http://www. oxfam.org/en/campaigns/health-education/afghanistan-worst-place-world-give-birth.*

123   *See* Valentine Moghadam, *Meeting Practical Needs and Strategic Gender Interests: Women and Development in Afghanistan,* PAPER PRESENTED TO FULBRIGHT CONFERENCE ON WOMEN IN THE GLOBAL COMMUNITY, Bogazici University, Istanbul, September 18–21, 2002.

124   *Ibid.*

125   Lisa M. Ayoub, *The Crisis in Afghanistan: When Will Gender Apartheid End?,* 7 TULSA JOURNAL OF COMPARATIVE AND INTERNATIONAL LAW (2000) 513.

that understand the difference between the social norms and Shari'a believe that rejecting the oppression of women does not mean that they must reject Islam.[126]

A recognition that the systemic subordination of and discrimination against women in Afghanistan constituted gender apartheid, would demand a more concerted effort to ensure that the lackluster performance on the part of the Afghan government and international community since 2002 to fundamentally transform the lives of Afghan women has been wholly inadequate.

A strong argument can be made that in addition to the enactment of the constitution and the establishment of formal structures, such as the Women's Ministry, to promote and pursue gender equality and human rights for women, a kind of Truth Commission ought to be established to unearth the layers of violence against women that have and continue to permeate Afghan society. Such a process would at least give public acknowledgement to the issue—and allow women to expose publicly the ways in which their humanity and dignity are assailed regularly and with impunity. I do not wish to suggest that this process would be an easy one, or that consensus will be reached in the near future as to its establishment. It is likely that under the present conditions, men, from whom acceptance for such a commission would be crucial, will not agree. But if media accounts are accurate, moves are afoot to have some negotiation with the Taliban about a future Afghanistan (since a military victory on the part of the United States and NATO now appears elusive).[127] If that is the case, then part of that negotiation should include a transitional process that, unlike the Bonn Agreement, provides for a process like a Truth Commission.[128] As a human rights advocate who recently traveled to Afghanistan notes:

> Negotiation is real and many people I met say that the Taliban is already in control in most places outside the cities of Kabul, Herat and Mazar. American military, when I was there, were quoted as saying they fight them by day and meet to negotiate by night.[129]

---

126   *Ibid.*

127   Stephen Lee Myers *et al.*, *Against Odds, Path Opens up for US-Taliban Talks*, NEW YORK TIMES, January 11, 2012 at: *http://www.nytimes.com/2012/01/12/world/asia/quest-for-taliban-peace-talks-at-key-juncture.html?pagewanted=all.*

128   These issues are canvassed in a 2004 law article. *See* Mark Drumbl, *Rights, Culture and Crime: The Role of the Rule of Law for the Women of Afghanistan*, WASHINGTON AND LEE PUBLIC LAW AND LEGAL THEORY RESEARCH PAPER SERIES, January 2004 at: *http://ssrn.com/abstract=452440.*

129   Comment by Susan Bazilli (on file with the author).

A Future Committed to Women's Human Rights

It is hard to engage in a discussion of constitution making, law enforcement, and security in the context of the continuing insecurity and chaos in Afghanistan. In fact, largely to talk about institutions in Afghanistan is to talk about Kabul, since the rest of the country is almost unreachable by road. Today it appears that the Taliban has made a comeback. And the American adventures in Iraq, as well as a severe economic crisis in the U.S.A., have surely curbed the possibility of making the kind of 100 percent commitment that was promised post 9/11.[130]

But despite this dire situation, that may or may not continue indefinitely, can lessons be learned from other fractured nations, or nations coming together in the wake of conflict? Or are the culture and political institutions of Afghanistan so unique? In other words, is Afghanistan sui generis? What are the possibilities of reviving Afghan indigenous institutions of dispute resolution and other law making institutions? Could they be modernized and incorporated into the new legal system?

Is Afghanistan as heterogeneous culturally or politically as we think it is? Is the country doomed to its apparent fate of tribal factions, conflict, and war? Are there not different groups or communities that have similar priorities or interests that could constitute what we consider national interests? If beyond the formal structures of government and the legislative process, are tribal leaders the ones who set the rules? Where do they derive the right to do so? Who represents communities and the many cultures of Afghanistan? Could it not be stated that Afghanistan's history is in effect a history of the clash between traditionalists and modernists, between the rural and urban areas, between religious leaders who fear the intrusion of secular values on their society, between those who favor economic development and those who fear the deleterious or negative consequences of economic development?

The general sentiment appears to be that building or rebuilding legal institutions is bedeviled by the notion that justice in Afghanistan has been more local and tribal, than national. No doubt there is mistrust at the local level of over-reaching on the part of the national state (a concern not confined to Afghanistan but other developed and less developed states). And if there is a distrust of the national, the distrust of the international (who appear to be imposing their will on the Afghan people) is even more pronounced. Public international law, especially human rights law, depends on the concept of nation and state that might be rather unfamiliar to Afghanistan in light of its history.

---

130   Sarah Chayes, *Afghanistan's Future, Lost in the Shuffle*, NEW YORK TIMES, July 1, 2003 at A23; Khaled Hosseini, *Desperation in Kabul*, NEW YORK TIMES, July 1, 2003 at A23 and Scott Baldauf, *Letter from Afghanistan*, THE NATION, April 28, 2003 at 24; Susan Page, *Poll: Half of Americans Back Faster Pullout from Afghanistan*, USA TODAY, March 14, 2012 at: *http://www.usatoday.com/news/washington/story/2012-03-14/ poll-afghanistan-pullout/53529896/1.*

Lessons for Afghanistan from Other Transitional Societies Like South Africa?

What political and legal lessons could be drawn for the women of Afghanistan from the transition in South Africa? One answer may be found in the manner in which South African women maneuvered to create the conditions so that the project of gender equality became a key focus of the constitutional and legal transition.[131] To make this possible, South African women across the political and racial divide, and from rural and urban locations, drew up a Women's Charter that incorporated their aspirations. Once women's issues were incorporated into the transitional political and legal agenda, women could utilize the political skills they had developed in the decades of struggle against apartheid to influence the new constitutional arrangement. For example, in the decades leading up to the constitutional talks in South Africa, women had been involved in major debates in international venues and at home in South Africa regarding the shape and content of constitutional protections of women's rights. Women's organizations, academics, female members of the major political parties, and women's trade union groups lobbied hard for the incorporation of gender equality into the transitional Constitution and the successes of these lobbying efforts are evident in the final constitutional framework and constitutional text.

Women presented their demands in a charter of women's rights, which embodied the priorities of women throughout the country. These demands included contractual, property, and inheritance rights that had been denied to women under both the South African legal system and indigenous law.

In the same vein, while the political negotiations for a Transitional Authority were taking place in Bonn in December, 2001, Afghan women organized a summit in Brussels to which Afghan expatriate women, as well as those living in Afghanistan, were invited. At the conclusion of the summit they presented a list of demands to the post-Bonn government to ensure that women's concerns would be taken into account. Similarly, in 2003 women leaders from all over Afghanistan met in Kandahar at a conference entitled "Women and the Constitution," to draft and sign the Afghan Women's Bill of Rights. The rights demanded included the right to education, protection and security, freedom of speech, rights to marry, equal pay for equal work, freedom to vote, right to financial autonomy and ownership of property, and a range of others.[132]

As I have pointed out elsewhere in this book, in South Africa, at the dawn of the new democracy, an openness towards the project of gender equality emerged when it was clear that women's needs are in fact national needs. Similarly the invasion of Afghanistan and the creation of the Transitional Authority, and later a permanent government there, have provided the discursive space for women to reiterate that women's needs are intertwined with national needs. It is apparent that

---

131   *See* Chapter 4 for a discussion of the South African constitutional drafting process.

132   *See* AFGHAN WOMEN'S BILL OF RIGHTS *supra* Note 73.

women in Afghanistan want a restructuring of the political, economic, and social relations that continue to subordinate and oppress them.

One can assume that Afghan women, particularly those who live in the rural areas, for the most part, want their lives to be guided by the values of Islam. One can also assume that despite the distortions of sharia law by religious fundamentalists, the legitimacy of Islamic law in rural communities remains intact. But should a commitment to religious principles exclude a commitment to gender equality?

The reality of Islamic law and principles is apparent in the daily lives of Afghans. So any consideration of future steps to consider a more equitable social arrangement for women needs to accommodate this reality. Some Islamic feminists have argued that interpretations of Islam that promote gender equality are possible, particularly those that allow a "progressive" as opposed to a "literalist" interpretation of sharia law.[133]

With this in mind, Afghan rural communities and individuals, including women, are renegotiating traditional practices, albeit with extraordinary challenges, to accommodate the changing political, economic, and cultural environment. The Bonn Agreement made possible the drafting of a constitution and laws that commit the society to gender equality and human rights. But in order for the rights enshrined in the Constitution and national laws to have any possibility of transforming the lives of women, they must be bolstered by widespread attitudinal change.

Shortly after the American and NATO invasion of Afghanistan, great faith was placed in the capacity of military intervention to achieve human rights for women. Indeed, a few months after the invasion, in March 2002, the United Nations dedicated the celebration of International Women's Day to the women of Afghanistan. And throughout the day the impassioned speeches of several prominent women paid tribute to the struggles of Afghan women, and their aspirations. But I recall listening to all the speeches with an acute sense of déjà vu.

In my lifetime, I have witnessed the continuous commemoration of women's struggles and women's achievements. Since my student days in South Africa in the late 1970s and early 1980s, the celebration of women's contribution to national liberation in a host of postcolonial situations has been featured rather prominently. For example, I can wistfully recall when we hailed the women of Zimbabwe, when that country was on the brink of democracy in 1980, and Robert Mugabe was then praised for his revolutionary leadership. In just over two decades we have witnessed the decline of a promising democracy, with women bearing the brunt of such decline.

I also remember in the mid-1970s the support for the women of Mozambique; those brave women fighting alongside men to unseat the spectacularly brutal Portuguese colonialists. Except for a discrete global constituency, the situation of women in Mozambique goes largely unnoticed. In the 1980s some celebrated the women of Nicaragua, sharing the euphoria which greeted the establishment

---

133   SHAHEEN SARDAR ALI, GENDER AND HUMAN RIGHTS IN ISLAM AND INTERNATIONAL LAW: EQUAL BEFORE ALLAH, UNEQUAL BEFORE MAN (2002).

of the Sandinista government there. That euphoria has largely been replaced by indifference, also a feature of the postcolonial landscape.

I reflect on these examples not to display weariness about the ebb and flow of our attention. That is almost inevitable in a global context in which those living in the global North have for the most part been spectators to some or other political makeover. I mention them to illustrate how women's contributions to national political struggles somehow come to represent the values and aspirations of societies in transformation. The celebration of women's contributions also serve to indicate the future path of that particular society; if not predicated on gender equality, at least formally embracing the role that women played in the overall political transformation. In these contexts it seems as if the female becomes the romanticized icon of the "revolution." She becomes the mythical figure around which the new democracy rallies and she is embraced by a broad array of interest groups, many opportunistically trading on her symbolism. She is also the lynchpin for the solidarity of the global human rights movement, the metaphor of the noble victim in dire need of rescue. For example, during the struggle to unseat apartheid in South Africa, Winnie Mandela embodied both the collective suffering of the victims of apartheid, and the virtues associated with womanhood. She was the "mother of the nation," wife of the pre-eminent political icon of the twentieth century, Nelson Mandela, and at times it did appear as if she was "holding up half the sky."

The struggle for women's rights in Afghanistan is not only over the interpretation of religious laws or cultural values, but also about the economic subordination and disadvantage that such interpretation may spawn. Severe economic suffering occurs for Afghan women who are denied the right to own property, to inherit, to participate in any kind of commercial activity, or be recognized as heads of households. In short, they are not treated like full human beings. Therefore interpretations of religious or cultural imperatives that disadvantage women contribute to the cycle of poverty and despair that plague Afghan women. In addition, the patriarchal basis of traditional authorities excludes women from becoming engaged in activities at the local community level and making decisions that will have a profound effect, not only on their own lives, but on their communities as a whole. As a young Afghan human rights advocate has noted:

While the education of women in Afghanistan is to some extent restricted by cultural beliefs and misinterpretations of Islam, the lack of educational opportunities, including schools, female teachers, school buildings, security for female teachers and students—and extreme poverty—all contribute to the lack of education. Influenced by economic inequalities, many families cannot afford to pay for the educational needs of their sons and daughters. Because of the need for labour in agricultural fields and the large number of children in families, paying for stationery, lunch money or food, and transportation for all children is impossible for many in farming communities. This is complicated even more by the lack of safety and secure transport in most rural areas of the country.[134]

Moreover, any attempt to change the role and status of women has to be accomplished with the recognition of the importance of the majority of women in Afghanistan who live in the rural areas. It is in the rural areas that tribal powers, and the myriad complexities and conflicts between tribal powers, so integral to the role and status of women, are entrenched. A perusal of the struggle for women's rights in Afghanistan in the last century demonstrates that rural tribal powers have shown the major resistance to attempts to modernize gender relations and improve the conditions of women.[135] As the scholar, Dr. Ahmed-Ghosh notes:

> Social traditionalism and economic underdevelopment or rural Afghanistan have repeatedly contested the center (Kabul), thus a better understanding of tribal controlled areas is essential to empower women in these regions. For women in rural Afghanistan, control over their lives and gender roles is determined by patriarchal kinship arrangements These kinship relationships are derived from the Quran and tribal traditions where men exercise unmitigated power over women.[136]

These struggles illustrate the need for a strong response from the central authorities to give effect to the rights embodied in the Afghan Constitution. In addition to those substantive constitutional rights, the criminal justice system will need to be utilized in a much more effective and forceful manner, indeed, to play a key role in promoting human rights for Afghan women. The criminal justice system has to be central in providing redress to victims of human rights abuses by bringing accused people to justice in accordance with the constitutional commitment to due process and an impartial trial.

The United States and the NATO forces are working hard at rebuilding the crucial parts of the legal system in Afghanistan, especially the judicial system and the criminal justice system.[137] Great effort and resources are being spent to build the capacity of the police force, a vital part of the legal armory required to stem violations of the human rights of women.[138] But despite these almost Sisyphean

---

134   Noorjahan Akbar, *Despite Widening Opportunities, Schooling Is Still The Preserve Of The Few*, ALJAZEERA.NET at: *http://english.aljazeera.net/indepth/opinion/profile/2011726102930470716.html*, 28 July 2011.

135   *See* Dr. Huma Ahmed-Ghosh, *A History of Women in Afghanistan: Lessons Learnt for the Future or Yesterdays and Tomorrow: Women in Afghanistan*, *supra* Note 112.

136   *Ibid.*

137   Gintautas Zenkevicius, *Post-Conflict Reconstruction: Rebuilding Afghanistan – Is That Post-Conflict Reconstruction?*, 9 BALTIC SECURITY AND DEFENCE REVIEW (2007) 28.

138   Randall Garrison, *Rebuilding Justice? The Challenges of Accountability in Policing in Post-Conflict Afghanistan*, PAPER PRESENTED AT THE CONFERENCE OF

efforts, to date the criminal justice system in Afghanistan has been woefully inadequate in providing relief to victims of crime, particularly those harmed by the hands of relatives. In fact, what has happened has been a persistent criminalization of victims themselves through the practice of *zina* and other kinds of "honor" crimes. It is clear that impunity for violators and failure to provide protection and justice for women is still very much the status quo, since those very violators do not consider themselves criminals.[139]

Furthermore, the Afghan Constitution is silent on the issue of addressing directly the need to involve more women in all levels of the legal, judicial, and criminal justice systems, particularly the appointment of judges and increasing the number of women in the police force. Moreover, even where women are employed in these capacities, reports suggest that there has not been sufficient attention paid to discrimination that women may experience in these roles.[140]

Ultimately the key to change in Afghanistan is a concerted nation-building effort that is able to accommodate the decentralized notion of governance that has typified Afghan existence for so long. Such an arrangement must have as its targets security, employment, and the provision of governmental resources such as education and health. This will have notable impact on the lives of Afghan women.

THE INTERNATIONAL SOCIETY FOR THE REFORM OF CRIMINAL LAW, August 8–12, 2004 at: *www.isrcl.org/Papers/2004/Garrison.pdf.*

139 *See* SILENCE IS VIOLENCE: END THE ABUSE OF WOMEN IN AFGHANISTAN, *supra* Note 33.

140 NEAMAT NOJUMI, DYAN MAZURANA AND ELIZABETH STITES, AFGHANISTAN'S SYSTEM OF JUSTICE: FORMAL, TRADITIONAL AND CUSTOMARY (June 2004) at: *www.gmu.edu/depts/crdc/neamat1.pdf.*

Chapter 7

Obstacles to the Pursuit of Women's Rights: Conditional Interdependence Revisited

The South African experience demonstrates that the creation of extensive legal rights for women and others, though of supreme importance, is not decisive for guaranteeing political and social success for women or eliminating economic deprivations for them.

Post-apartheid developments in South Africa shows that the trajectory pursued for gender equality exhibits profound contradictions. On the one hand, South Africa ranks as one of the top democracies in the world with respect to women's representation in Parliament. There are an impressive number of ministers, deputy ministers, and parliamentarians. The speaker of Parliament is a woman, and several women hold top ambassadorial posts.[1]

These impressive statistics, however, exist alongside other statistics showing an excessively large number of women, and children, are in extreme poverty, and that violence against women is severe, pervasive, and virtually uncontrolled. Indeed, the research indicators suggest that widespread rape and domestic violence against women has in fact reached epidemic proportions.[2] This apparent contradiction between the representation of women in governance and the dire straits of women in economic terms and as victims of violence is troubling. Moreover, violence against women is one of many obstacles to economic development overall as well as to the ability of women to enjoy to the fullest the benefits of rights accorded them in the Constitution.

South Africa has taken steps to improve the plight of women such as provision of housing and improved access to education and other benefits, but these interventions, despite their aggressive nature, have failed to substantially reverse the legacy of apartheid and its disproportionate impact upon black women. The gap between the expansive provisions in South Africa's Constitution and the underlying reality of the lives of the majority of South Africa's women, and men, poses a significant danger to democracy. At a theoretical level, the gap raises the question about how a country with an admirable Constitution and Bill of Rights

---

1 *See* Mavivi Manzini Mayakayaka, *Political Party-Quotas in South Africa*, in THE IMPLEMENTATION OF QUOTAS: AFRICAN EXPERIENCES (Julie Ballington ed. 2004), at: *http://www.idea.int/loader.cfm?url=/commonspot/security/getfile.cfm&pageid=7841*.

2 *See* Penelope E. Andrews, *Learning to Love after Learning to Harm: Post-Conflict Reconstruction, Gender Equality and Cultural Values*, 15 MICHIGAN STATE JOURNAL OF INTERNATIONAL LAW (2007) 41.

could leave the majority of its women in the lurch.[3] This question is even more perplexing in light of a decade of extraordinary equality jurisprudence generated by the Constitutional Court. The Court has committed itself, though not always successfully, to a transformative vision that centers on women's equality and the right to dignity.[4] In addition, the Court has provided an overarching framework for creative legal advocacy to address the problem of poverty amongst women.

The interlinking of economic and social factors are obviously complex. They include patterns of wealth distribution, the wealth of the country, and issues of patriarchy and masculinity that are in part by-products of colonial occupation and violence. Issues of masculinities embodying indigenous and Western forms of patriarchy persist despite the constitutional commitment to equality.[5] This dilemma is not peculiar to South Africa or Afghanistan, for these two countries are in many ways a microcosm of other societies, particularly those in the developing world that confront tensions, conflicts, and ambiguities in pursuing rights for women. These contradictions also are present in affluent societies, but the reality of pervasive poverty and weak state institutions bedevils the quest for equality in poorer countries. Afghanistan and South Africa's ongoing attempts to pursue rights for women therefore are constantly challenged, and often compromised, by a deeply embedded patriarchal and male ethos that constitutional guarantees can only erode so far.

The link between poverty and gender inequality has been established.[6] Case studies and examples from almost every country, particularly those countries in the global South, consistently demonstrate that gender-based poverty and economic inequality constrain women's human rights and development, as well as those of the communities within which they live. These factors also impede national economic growth.[7] South Africa's legislative and executive branches of government have attempted to approach gender-based economic inequality

---

3   For a very interesting reflection on the challenges to addressing poverty as a constitutional imperative, *see* Lucy A. Williams, *Issues and Challenges in Addressing Poverty and Legal Rights: A Comparative United States/South African Analysis*, 21 SOUTH AFRICAN JOURNAL ON HUMAN RIGHTS (2005) 436.

4   For a critique of the Constitutional Court's equality jurisprudence, *see* Cathi Albertyn and Beth Goldblatt, *Facing the Challenge of Transformation: Difficulties in the Development of an Indigenous Jurisprudence of Equality*, 14 SOUTH AFRICA JOURNAL OF HUMAN RIGHTS (1998) 248; *see also* D.M. Davis, *Equality: The Majesty of Legoland Jurisprudence*, 116 SOUTH AFRICAN LAW JOURNAL (1999) 398.

5   Indeed, Constitutional Court Justice Albie Sachs has referred to patriarchy as the "only truly non-racial institution in South Africa."

6   Stephanie Seguino, *Gender Inequality and Economic Growth: A Cross-Country Analysis*, 28 WORLD DEVELOPMENT (2000) 1211.

7   *See*, for example, Alan Gelb, *Gender and Growth: Africa's Missed Potential*, WORLD BANK INSTITUTE (2001) at· *http://www.devoutreach.com/spring01/SpecialReport/tabid/1067/Default.aspx.*

and poverty by focusing on economic management and priority setting through "gender budget initiatives" and the publication of an annual "women's budget."[8] These budgets,

> examine the efficiency and equity implications of budget allocations and the policies and programs that lie behind them. This would encourage public spending priorities to focus on investment in rural infrastructure and labor-saving technologies.[9]

In addition to the previously mentioned factors, the HIV/AIDS epidemic and its collateral consequences severely impede the quest for women's equality. It is extremely difficult for women caught in a cycle of economic dependency and powerlessness to prevent HIV infection or to gain access to treatment for AIDS. Furthermore, many rights are compromised by women's inability to access economic resources.

The Road Ahead

The preceding chapters have dealt with many issues. The overall focus has been on achieving and sustaining a regime of women's rights and gender equality. I have suggested constitutional developments in South Africa as a model while noting deficiencies in the functioning of the TRC and in relying solely upon law as the prime means of attaining these goals. I have also noted that in Afghanistan, the adoption of a Constitution and Bill of Rights, although not as comprehensive or potentially transformative as South Africa's, nonetheless marked an important formal shift from the Taliban's rule of totalitarianism and "gender apartheid" to equality and rights for all. Furthermore, I have emphasized in these pages the importance of the support that international covenants and women activists around the world have provided in the struggle for women's rights and gender equality. Along the way, I have sought to identify structural and cultural obstacles in achieving gender equality and women's rights. And I have warned against assuming that there is one size that fits all nations for meeting these goals. I have used the concept of conditional interdependence as one way to avoid falling into the trap of one size fits all. In this regard, I have also stressed that there are a variety of perspectives that women have on these issues, and that not infrequently women activists in developing countries see the issue of women's rights and gender equality through prisms that are different from those of women activists in the West. But I have also argued that, although women are differently situated and their realities contextualized, there are universal approaches that capture the

---

8　Debbie Budlender, *South Africa: The Women's Budget*, 12 SOUTHERN AFRICA REPORT (1996) 16.

9　Alan Gelb, *Gender and Growth*, *supra* Note 7.

essence of women's experiences, and that these universal approaches, and not morally relativist approaches, should guide our thinking. Finally, I have noted the reservations of many who believe either that a discourse based upon rights functions to displace needed discourse on economic inequalities and progressive politics or that the rights discourse has supplanted "all other ethical languages" or both.

I cannot agree with Janet Halley that we should take a break from feminism.[10] The feminist enterprise and feminist goals have barely touched too large a section of the world's female population. There are too many unresolved problems women face. But I do agree with her exhortation to look at feminism from the outside—and rethink feminist methodologies and feminist epistemologies. On the latter, she states:

> Perhaps my ultimate point is that we can't make decisions about what to do with legal power in its many forms responsibly without taking into account as many interests, constituencies, and uncertainties as we can acknowledge.[11]

South Africa, as a young constitutional democracy, is a place where feminism has a foothold and is a place where, in advancing the cause of women's rights and gender equality, feminism must compete with other interests and constituencies such as nationalism, indigenous population groups, cultural traditions antagonistic to women's interests, men who only see masculinity as a way to control women, and jurists and other actors in the legal system who would restrain the Constitutional Court's expansive interpretations of socio-economic constitutional provisions. All these factors are at play in South Africa, and the legions of women who have been empowered by the Constitution and the national liberation movement are worthy adversaries for the competition. The annual women's budget by female parliamentarians, inasmuch as it identifies the impact of budgetary choices and allocations on the lives of women, could function, in part, as a measure for gauging the progression of the competition.

In many countries, including South Africa, Afghanistan, and others with a long history of colonialism and subordination, the political transition raises profound questions about the nature of the new democratic regime. Sometimes the course of the feminist project faces more bumps in the road because it was injected into the political deliberations fairly late in the process, as was the case in South Africa.[12]

Constitutional negotiation occurs against the backdrop of ongoing contestations about the meaning, purpose, and ideology of the newly established democracy and its constitution. The resulting constitution naturally reflects a compromise that mediates competing discourses of liberation. In South Africa the Constitution did

---

10   JANET HALLEY, SPLIT DECISIONS: HOW AND WHY TO TAKE A BREAK FROM FEMINISM (2006).

11   *Ibid* at 9.

12   *See* PUTTING WOMEN ON THE AGENDA (Susan Bazilli Ed. 1991); *see also* THE CONSTITUTION OF SOUTH AFRICA FROM A GENDER PERSPECTIVE (Sandra Liebenberg Ed. 1994) 64.

so by recognizing indigenous institutions, and prioritizing the principle of equality. In Afghanistan, the principle of equality was rendered secondary to the tenets of Islam. These constitutional compromises to some extent occur against a debate that has occupied human rights advocates for some decades, and that has spawned a vast literature about the role and status of religious and indigenous institutions in contemporary constitutional frameworks that enshrine principles of gender quality and women's rights. Conversely, the push for the absolute primacy of equality with respect to race or gender reflects not just the agitation of advocates belonging to the groups benefiting from the equality but also those, of whatever gender or race, involved in the constitution drafting process.

In both South Africa and Afghanistan, the new constitutional framework embraced, to a greater or lesser extent, the vision of a pluralistic society that strives to incorporate historically marginalized legal systems and institutions, including those of indigenous and religious minorities. The modernist project of constitutionalism and human rights that includes the recognition of gender equality, cultural and religious rights, signals a commitment to full citizenship for women. Very often this citizenship also includes female representation in government.[13] Election of female politicians does not, however, automatically translate into a commitment to women's rights and gender equality. The first generation of female politicians is often groomed by male mentors on the basis of party political affiliation and loyalty to that party, and this may impair the ability and willingness of the women politicians to make a full commitment to women's rights and gender equality.

Female representation also presents questions about different perspectives among women. What is to be done when there are genuine differences amongst women, that is, between those who accept that a particular cultural practice does not lead to inequality, or does not violate women's rights and those women representatives who believe otherwise? "False consciousness" is surely not an appropriate response.[14] Who dictates the outcomes of competing claims to truth? These questions point to ongoing tensions in the global feminist project, namely, attempting to respect the differences among women while at the same time describing the collective experiences of women to mobilize for political change.

---

13   For example, in Afghanistan, women were elected to office in the first round of democratic elections. In Rwanda, women enjoy the highest percentage of electoral representation in the world, holding 49 percent of parliamentary seats. Germany elected its first female chancellor (twice), and in the United States, the number of women elected to office continues to climb. *http://oldsite.womensenews.org/article.cfm/dyn/aid/2498/context/archive.*

14   *See* Denis Patterson, *Postmodernism/Feminism/Law*, 77 CORNELL LAW REVIEW (1991–1992) 254. "The term 'false consciousness' refers to the Gramscian notion of 'cultural hegemony' that states that women 'although they believe they are making choices [are in reality] ... unwitting accomplices in the maintenance of existing inequalities ...'." *Ibid* at 293–4.

This is where conditional interdependence may provide space to negotiate the conflicts and tensions.

In the final analysis, by actively engaging with the state, civil societies, their communities, and families, women have to find the ways and the resources to control their own circumstances. They have to be the authors of their own lives.

Feminist legal theorists aim to connect the academic world with social change. Their agenda must therefore continue to connect academic endeavors with the broader social movements advocating for women's rights and gender equality. As mentioned in Chapter 2, feminist legal theorists have presented, described, and analyzed the lives of women and their intersection with the law. The challenge is to continue to generate strategies for improving those lives. In many ways, the feminist legal agenda is antithetical to notions of cultural relativism. But it has to be mindful of the cultural context because cultural traditions and institutions have great power. Successful legal strategies depend on all aspects of the contexts in which women must struggle for their rights. To ensure that human rights groups take proper account of women's rights, Rebecca Cook has argued for the inclusion of,

> women's voices, interests, and concerns into the mainstream human rights law-
> making arena so that the diversity of women's experiences in different cultures
> is introduced into international human rights law.[15]

In contexts like South Africa and Afghanistan, the goals of feminism, and the challenges to feminist approaches to legal transformation, have to be evaluated against the goals and purposes of national liberation movements. This is so whether those movements locate their transformative goals in political ideology, as in South Africa, or see the nation state as one embracing the major tenets of the relevant religion, as in the Islamic Republic of Afghanistan.

Often what is at tension in this evaluation is the relationship between the individual (and her family) and the larger community, and, more importantly, the relationship of the society to the international claims of human rights and democracy. The moral philosopher Gail Linsenbard explores ways in which to blend universal human rights norms with those that are culturally specific. She deconstructs the power dynamics that exist even in isolated communities that regard themselves as egalitarian, and reveals how supposedly shared moral or philosophical standards and views are not necessarily widely shared, but typical only of those with power and influence.[16] Her views have not been universally accepted by scholars, particularly by male human rights scholars. Former human

---

15   Rebecca J. Cook, *Women's International Human Rights Law: The Way Forward*, in HUMAN RIGHTS OF WOMEN: NATIONAL AND INTERNATIONAL PERSPECTIVES (Rebecca Cook ed. 1994).

16   Gail Linsenbard, *Women's Rights as Human Rights: An Ontological Grounding*, in WOMEN'S RIGHTS AS HUMAN RIGHTS: ACTIVISM AND SOCIAL CHANGE IN AFRICA (Diana J. Fox and Naima Hasci eds. 1999) 65.

rights scholar and now politician, Michael Ignatieff, has taken the view that the "secularism" of the premises of the Universal Declaration of Human Rights "is ever more open to doubt in a world of resurgent religious conviction."[17] Ignatieff argues that the idea of rights is in many ways religious. He says it is only because each human being is sacred that provides the persuasive reason "that their dignity should be protected with rights."[18] Whatever past truth this statement may once have had, it is today a contested view, and an example of what Linsenbard probably meant when she said that supposedly widely shared moral or philosophical perspectives are often not so widely shared.

Referring specifically to the human rights project in Africa, the Kenyan-American scholar, Makau Mutua, frames the question of rights as one involving conceptual contradictions. Mutua points out that in the affluent countries, mostly the West, the language of rights has primarily been articulated as legal claims against the state.[19] These claims are grounded in the idea of a right, for which there is an individual remedy for a wrong caused. The African language of rights also incorporates the idea of a duty. As the African Charter of Human and People Rights makes clear, while people have rights, these rights are also accompanied by duties.[20]

The South African Constitution incorporates this idea of right and duties through the inclusion of notions of *ubuntu* and dignity.[21] Now, rights are correlatives of duties, and vice versa. A person has a right against another only if that other has a duty towards the person. Although rights and duties thus technically have the same meaning in terms of legal relationships, they approach the relationship from opposing ends. Sometimes, the statement of the right–duty relationship will be better understood depending upon whether it is stated in terms of the person owning the right or the person owing the duty. The idea of conditional interdependence is broad enough to embraces this correlative, or reciprocal, relationship.

Conclusion

In the final analysis, the existence of an expansive constitution is only a precondition for legal and other changes. Scholars and advocates have noted that despite laudable efforts by women's groups to incorporate women's rights into the democratic legal framework and agenda, much work still needs to be done.

---

17   Michael Ignatieff, *Human Rights: The Midlife Crisis*, NEW YORK REVIEW OF BOOKS, May 20, 1999, 58 at 60.

18   *Ibid.*

19   Makau wa Mutua, *The Banjul Charter and the African Cultural Fingerprint: An Evaluation of the Language of Duties*, 35 VIRGINIA JOURNAL OF INTERNATIONAL LAW (1995) 344.

20   AFRICAN CHARTER OF HUMAN AND PEOPLES RIGHTS (1981).

21   *Ubuntu* refers to the African concept that our humanity is interconnected.

The constitutional and legal foundations have provided a framework for some possibilities to transform, or at least alter, women's lives for the better. However, the privatized nature of most economies and the imperatives of a market driven agenda may undermine aspects of the transformative possibilities of a constitution. Women suffer disproportionately from the failure of government to provide adequately for health, education, social welfare services, and other needs of a society. Women also suffer disproportionately when government cutbacks occur. A constitution, as has become plainly obvious in South Africa, is not a vehicle adequate for fundamentally challenging a government's economic policies. In South Africa, the most that the Constitutional Court has been able to do in the enforcement of socio-economic provisions of the Constitution has been merely to ensure that government policy takes account of its constitutional mandate. Consequently, although the South African Constitution can be invoked to keep the South African government from ignoring certain economic inequalities, it cannot force the government to eliminate the inequalities, particularly those that afflict millions of women in South Africa today.

To ensure gender equality, a constitution with a bill of rights helps. But it is not enough. It needs to be bolstered by an overarching vision that seeks to transform institutions, laws, and practices that subjugate women. In addition, it needs to be accompanied by a cultural shift across all sectors of society—a shift that can be invoked to help eradicate gender inequality in the social, political, and economic spheres.

In writing this book, I hoped not to end up simplifying, discounting, ignoring, or overshadowing the complexities of the pursuit of women's rights and gender equality. I have focused on the generalities of women's lives, finding meaning in outwardly observable shared patterns, trends or experiences, without occluding the particularized realities of individual women or groups of women, and the inner lives and spiritual, psychological, and emotional choices that guide them. I am acutely aware that in order to analyze the existence and causes of inequality, local conditions need to be scrutinized. Because the peculiarities of each country or local geographical location is premised on its history, geography, culture, and economic status, the enquiry about women at the local level is arguably the preeminent one. It follows therefore that the investigation of women's human rights and gender equality, and the relevant response to these issues requires a focus on local conditions. However, in seeking responses, our engagement with the global, and particularly international human rights law as it pertains to women, necessarily entails sweeping with a general brush. The widespread coincidence and overlap of the experiences of women, whether through violence, subordination, discrimination, or other forms of gender oppression, necessarily makes that general brush appropriate, certainly as a theoretical matter.[22]

---

22 For a thoughtful discussion on the implications of global feminist initiatives for local organization, *see* L. Amede Obiora, *Feminism, Globalization, and Culture: After Beijing*, 4 INDIANA JOURNAL OF GLOBAL LEGAL STUDIES (1997) 355.

Bibliography

Books

RICK ABEL, POLITICS BY OTHER MEANS: LAW IN THE STRUGGLE AGAINST APARTHEID (Taylor and Francis Ltd., December 2002).

RANDY ALBEIDA AND CHRIS TILLY, GLASS CEILINGS AND BOTTOMLESS PITS: WOMEN'S WORK, WOMEN'S POVERTY (South End Press, July 1999).

SHAHEEN SARDAR ALI, GENDER AND HUMAN RIGHTS IN ISLAM AND INTERNATIONAL LAW: EQUAL BEFORE ALLAH, UNEQUAL BEFORE MAN (Brill Academic Publishers, Inc. January 2000).

JOHN ALLEN, APARTHEID SOUTH AFRICA: AN INSIDER'S OVERVIEW ON THE ORIGIN AND EFFECTS OF SEPARATE DEVELOPMENT (IUniverse, Inc. June 2005).

AMNESTY INTERNATIONAL, JUSTICE DENIED TO WOMEN (2003).

MARGOT BADRAN, FEMINISTS, ISLAM, AND NATION: GENDER AND THE MAKING OF MODERN EGYPT (Princeton University Press 1996).

JUDITH A. BAER, OUR LIVES BEFORE THE LAW: CONSTRUCTING A FEMINIST JURISPRUDENCE (Princeton University Press 1999).

FAREDA BANDA, WOMEN, LAW AND HUMAN RIGHTS: AN AFRICAN PERSPECTIVE (Hart Publishing April 2005).

THOMAS BARFIELD, AFGHANISTAN: A CULTURAL AND POLITICAL HISTORY (Princeton University Press March 2012).

BRIAN BARRY, CULTURE AND EQUALITY (Harvard University Press, October 2002).

DERRICK BELL, FACES AT THE BOTTOM OF THE WELL: THE PERMANENCE OF RACISM (Basic Books, October 1993).

CHERYL BERNARD, VEILED COURAGE (2002).

HILDA BERNSTEIN, FOR THEIR TRIUMPH AND THEIR TEARS (Brill Academic Publishers, Inc. April 1985).

SURJIT S. BHALLA, IMAGINE THERE'S NO COUNTRY: POVERTY, INEQUALITY AND GROWTH IN THE ERA OF GLOBALIZATION (Peterson Institute for International Economics, November 2002).

MEENA K. BHAMRA, THE CHALLENGES OF JUSTICE IN DIVERSE SOCIETIES: CONSTITUTIONALISM AND PLURALISM (Ashgate Publishing, April 2011).

DAVID BILCHITZ, POVERTY AND FUNDAMENTAL RIGHTS: THE JUSTIFICATION AND ENFORCEMENT OF SOCIO-ECONOMIC RIGHTS (Oxford University Press, April 2007).

VIRGINIA L. BLUM, FLESH WOUNDS: THE CULTURE OF COSMETIC SURGERY (University of California Press, October 2003).

SUSAN R. BORDO, UNBEARABLE WEIGHT: FEMINISM, WESTERN CULTURE AND THE BODY (University of California Press, September 1993).

JUSTICE STEPHEN BREYER, ACTIVE LIBERTY: INTERPRETING OUR DEMOCRATIC CONSTITUTION (Knopf Doubleday Publishing Group, October 2006).

CHILLA BULBECK, RE-ORIENTING WESTERN FEMINISMS: DIVERSITY IN A POSTCOLONIAL WORLD (Cambridge University Press, January 1998).

IAN BURUMA AND AVISHAI MARGALIT, OCCIDENTALISM: THE WEST IN THE EYES OF ITS ENEMIES (Penguin, March 2004).

MARTHA CHAMALLAS, INTRODUCTION TO FEMINIST LEGAL THEORY (Wolters Kluwer Law & Business, May 2003).

MARTIN CHANOCK, THE MAKING OF SOUTH AFRICAN LEGAL CULTURE 1902–1936: FEAR, FAVOUR AND PREJUDICE (Cambridge University Press, February 2007).

MARTIN CHANOCK, LAW, CUSTOM AND SOCIAL ORDER: THE COLONIAL EXPERIENCE IN MALAWI AND ZAMBIA (Cambridge University Press, June 1995).

ERWIN CHEMERINSKY, CONSTITUTIONAL LAW: PRINCIPLES AND POLICIES (Wolters Kluwer Law & Business, June 2011).

ANINKA CLAASSENS AND BEN COUSINS, LAND, POWER AND CUSTOM (Ohio University Press, January 2009).

STEVE COLL, GHOST WARS: THE SECRET HISTORY OF THE CIA, AFGHANISTAN, AND BIN LADEN, FROM THE SOVIET INVASION TO SEPTEMBER 10, 2001 (Penguin Group (USA), December 2004).

REBECCA J. COOK AND SIMONE CUSACK, GENDER STEREOTYPING: TRANSNATIONAL LEGAL PERSPECTIVE (University of Pennsylvania Press, December 2009).

TYLER COWEN, CREATIVE DESTRUCTION: HOW GLOBALIZATION IS CHANGING THE WORLD'S CULTURES (Princeton University Press, March 2004).

GEORGE CRILE, CHARLIE WILSON'S WAR: THE EXTRAORDINARY STORY OF THE LARGEST COVERT OPERATION IN HISTORY (Grove Atlantic, Inc. March 2003).

SIMONE DE BEAUVOIR, THE SECOND SEX (1949).

ISABELLE DELLOYE, WOMEN OF AFGHANISTAN (Ruminator Books, June 2003).

DEMOCRATIZATION AND CIVIL SOCIETY EMPOWERMENT PROGRAMME, UNITED NATIONS DEVELOPMENT PROGRAMME, AFGHANISTAN COUNTRY OFFICE (2007).

VANAJA DHRUVARAJAN AND JILL VICKERS, GENDER, RACE AND NATION: A GLOBAL PERSPECTIVE (University of Toronto Press, June 2002).

SUSAN J. DOUGLAS, WHERE THE GIRLS ARE: GROWING UP FEMALE WITH THE MASS MEDIA (Times Books, April 1994).

JOHN DUGARD, HUMAN RIGHTS AND THE SOUTH AFRICAN LEGAL ORDER (Princeton University Press, 1978).

LOUIS DUPREE, AFGHANISTAN (Oxford University Press, July 2002).

TASLIM OLAWALE ELIAS, THE NATURE OF AFRICAN CUSTOMARY LAW (Manchester University Press, January 1956).

DEBORAH ELLIS, WOMEN OF THE AFGHAN WAR (Praeger, April 2000).

BUCHI EMECHETA, SECOND-CLASS CITIZEN (George Braziller Inc. February 1983).

EVE ENSLER, THE GOOD BODY (Villard, November 2004).

CATHERINE ESCHLE AND BICE MAIGUASHCA, MAKING FEMINIST SENSE OF THE GLOBAL JUSTICE MOVEMENT (Rowman & Littlefield Publishers, November 2010).

NANCY ETCOFF, SURVIVAL OF THE PRETTIEST (Doubleday, February 1999).

ELIZABETH WARNOCK FERNEA, IN SEARCH OF ISLAMIC FEMINISM: ONE WOMAN'S GLOBAL JOURNEY (Doubleday, December 1997).

FINAL REPORT OF THE TRUTH AND RECONCILIATION COMMISSION (2004).

CAROLINE A. FORELL AND DONNA M. MATTHEWS, A LAW OF HER OWN: THE REASONABLE WOMAN AS A MEASURE OF MAN (NYU Press, January 2000).

BETTY FRIEDAN, THE FEMININE MYSTIQUE (Dell Delacorte Press 1963).

FROM BEIJING TO BEIJING +5: REVIEW AND APPRAISAL OF THE IMPLEMENTATION OF THE BEIJING PLATFORM FOR ACTION, United Nations (2001).

JOHN FULLTERTON, THE SOVIET OCCUPATION OF AFGHANISTAN (Routledge, June 2011).

ANTHONY GIDDENS, RUNAWAY WORLD: HOW GLOBALIZATION IS RESHAPING OUR LIVES (Routledge, April 2000).

SIRI GLOPPEN, SOUTH AFRICA: THE BATTLE OVER THE CONSTITUTION (Dartmouth Publishing Co. December 1997).

ADRIAN GUELKE, RETHINKING THE RISE AND FALL OF APARTHEID: SOUTH AFRICA AND WORLD POLITICS (Palgrave Macmillan, January 2005).

ANDREW HACKER, TWO NATIONS: BLACK AND WHITE, SEPARATE, HOSTILE, UNEQUAL (Maxwell Macmillan, 1992).

C.R.D. HALISI, BLACK POLITICAL THOUGHT IN THE MAKING OF SOUTH AFRICAN DEMOCRACY (Indiana University Press, January 2000).

JANET HALLEY, SPLIT DECISIONS: HOW AND WHY TO TAKE A BREAK FROM FEMINISM (Princeton University Press, July 2006).

HELSINKI WATCH, ASIA WATCH, TO DIE IN AFGHANISTAN (1985).

JEFFREY HERBST, STATES AND POWER IN AFRICA: COMPARATIVE LESSONS IN AUTHORITY AND CONTROL (Princeton University Press, March 2000).

CHANRITHY HIM, WHEN BROKE GLASS FLOATS: GROWING UP UNDER THE KHMER ROUGE (W.W. Norton & Co. April 2001).

HUMAN RIGHTS WATCH, "I HAD TO RUN AWAY": THE IMPRISONMENT OF WOMEN AND GIRLS IN AFGHANISTAN (2012).

HUMAN RIGHTS WATCH, "WE HAVE THE PROMISES OF THE WORLD": WOMEN'S RIGHTS IN AFGHANISTAN (2009).

HUMAN RIGHTS WATCH, SOLDIERS WHO RAPE, COMMANDERS WHO CONDONE: SEXUAL VIOLENCE AND MILITARY REFORM IN THE DEMOCRATIC REPUBLIC OF CONGO (2009).

HUMAN RIGHTS WATCH, SWEPT UNDER THE RUG: ABUSES AGAINST DOMESTIC WORKERS AROUND THE WORLD (2006).

HUMAN RIGHTS WATCH, STRUGGLING TO SURVIVE: BARRIERS TO JUSTICE FOR RAPE VICTIMS IN RWANDA (2004).

HUMAN RIGHTS WATCH, "KILLING YOU IS A VERY EASY THING FOR US": HUMAN RIGHTS ABUSES IN SOUTHEAST AFGHANISTAN (2003).

HUMAN RIGHTS WATCH, "WE WANT TO LIVE AS HUMANS": REPRESSION OF WOMEN AND GIRLS IN WESTERN AFGHANISTAN (2002).

HUMAN RIGHTS WATCH, ALL OUR HOPES ARE CRUSHED: VIOLENCE AND REPRESSION IN WESTERN AFGHANISTAN (2002).

HUMAN RIGHTS WATCH, HUMANITY DENIED: SYSTEMATIC VIOLATIONS OF WOMEN'S RIGHTS IN AFGHANISTAN (2001).

HUMAN RIGHTS WATCH, VIOLENCE AGAINST WOMEN IN SOUTH AFRICA: STATE RESPONSE TO DOMESTIC VIOLENCE AND RAPE (1995).

MARK HUNTER, LOVE IN THE TIME OF AIDS: INEQUALITY, GENDER, AND RIGHTS IN SOUTH AFRICA (Indiana University Press, October 2010).

DAVID ISBY, AFGHANISTAN: GRAVEYARD OF EMPIRES: A NEW HISTORY OF THE BORDERLAND (Pegasus, April 2010).

RUTH, IYOB, THE ERITREAN STRUGGLE FOR INDEPENDENCE: DOMINATION, RESISTANCE, NATIONALISM 1941–1993 (Cambridge University Press, May 1995).

TOSHIHIKO IZUTSU, ETHICO-RELIGIOUS CONCEPTS IN THE QURAN (McGill University Press 1966).

THOMAS E. JACKSON, FROM CIVIL RIGHTS TO HUMAN RIGHTS (University of Pennsylvania Press, December 2006).

INDIRA JAISING, MEN'S LAWS, WOMEN'S LIVES: A CONSTITUTIONAL PERSPECTIVE ON RELIGION, COMMON LAW, AND CULTURE IN SOUTH INDIA (Kali/Women Unlimited 2005).

JUTTA M. JOACHIM, AGENDA SETTING, THE U.N. AND NGOs: GENDER VIOLENCE AND REPRODUCTIVE RIGHTS (Georgetown University Press, July 2007).

ANN JONES, KABUL IN WINTER: LIFE WITHOUT PEACE IN AFGHANISTAN (Metropolitan Books, March 2006).

MALALAI JOYA, A WOMAN AMONG WARLORDS: THE EXTRAORDINARY STORY OF AN AFGHAN WHO DARED TO RAISE HER VOICE (Scribner, October 2009).

MARGARET E. KECK AND KATHRYN SIKKINK, ACTIVISTS BEYOND BORDERS: ADVOCACY NETWORKS IN INTERNATIONAL POLITICS (Cornell University Press, March 1998).

MARK KENDE, CONSTITUTIONAL RIGHTS IN TWO WORLDS: SOUTH AFRICA AND THE UNITED STATES (Cambridge University Press, March 2009).

ALICE KESSLER-HARRIS, IN PURSUIT OF EQUITY: WOMEN, MEN, AND THE QUEST FOR ECONOMIC CITIZENSHIP IN 20TH CENTURY AMERICA (Oxford University Press, February 2003).

HEINZ KLUG, THE CONSTITUTION OF SOUTH AFRICA (Hart Publishing, January 2010).

NICHOLAS KRISTOF AND CHERYL WUDUNN, HALF THE SKY: TURNING OPPRESSION INTO OPPORTUNITY FOR WOMEN WORLDWIDE (Knopf Doubleday Publishing Group, June 2010).

ANTJE KROG, THE COUNTRY OF MY SKULL: GUILT, SORROW AND THE LIMITS OF FORGIVENESS IN THE NEW SOUTH AFRICA (Crown Publishing, February 1999).

ROBIN TOLMACH LAKOFF AND RAQUEL L. SCHERR, FACE VALUE: THE POLITICS OF BEAUTY (1984).

CATHARINE A. MACKINNON, WOMEN'S LIVES, MEN'S LAWS (Harvard University Press, February 2005).

CATHARINE A. MACKINNON, ARE WOMEN HUMAN? AND OTHER INTERNATIONAL DIALOGUES (Harvard University Press, October 2007).

CATHARINE A. MACKINNON, TOWARD A FEMINIST THEORY OF THE STATE (Harvard University Press, September 1989).

CATHERINE A. MACKINNON, THE SEXUAL HARASSMENT OF WORKING WOMEN: A CASE OF SEX DISCRIMINATION (Yale University Press, September 1979).

BILL MAHER, WHEN YOU RIDE ALONE YOU RIDE WITH BIN LADEN (Phoenix Books Incorporated, November 2002).

CHARLES S. MAIER, DISSOLUTION: THE CRISIS OF COMMUNISM AND THE END OF EAST GERMANY (Princeton University Press, April 1997).

WILLIAM MALEY, FUNDAMENTALISM REBORN? AFGHANISTAN AND THE TALIBAN (NYU Press, March 1998).

AMINA MAMA, BEYOND THE MASKS: RACE, GENDER AND SUBJECTIVITY (Routledge, August 1995).

ANTHONY W. MARX, LESSONS OF STRUGGLE: SOUTH AFRICAN INTERNAL OPPOSITION 1960–1990 (Oxford University Press, March 1992).

MIRIAMA MBA, SO LONG A LETTER (Heinemann, June 1989).

NORRIE MCQUEEN, COLONIALISM (Longman, September 2007).

SALLY ENGLE MERRY, HUMAN RIGHTS AND GENDER VIOLENCE: TRANSLATING INTERNATIONAL LAW INTO LOCAL JUSTICE (University of Chicago Press, December 2005).

ANNE ELIZABETH MEYER, ISLAM AND HUMAN RIGHTS: TRADITION AND POLITICS (Westview Press, September 1998).

JOEL MIGDAL, STRONG SOCIETIES AND WEAK STATES: STATE-SOCIETY RELATIONS AND STATE CAPABILITIES IN THE THIRD WORLD (Princeton University Press, December 1988).

NICK B. MILLS, KARZAI: THE FAILING AMERICAN INTERVENTION AND THE STRUGGLE FOR AFGHANISTAN (Wiley, August 2007).

MARTHA MINOW, BETWEEN VENGEANCE AND FORGIVENESS: FACING HISTORY AFTER GENOCIDE AND MASS VIOLENCE (Beacon Press, November 1998).

VALENTINE M. MOGHADAM, GLOBALIZING WOMEN: TRANSNATIONAL FEMINIST NETWORKS (The Johns Hopkins University Press, January 2005).

VALENTINE MOGHADAM, MODERNIZING WOMEN: GENDER AND SOCIAL CHANGE IN THE MIDDLE EAST (Lynne Riencr Publishers, May 2003).

CHANDRA TALPADE MOHANTY, FEMINISM WITHOUT BORDERS: DECOLONIZING THEORY, PRACTICING SOLIDARITY (Duke University Press, February 2003).

NAJMA MOOSA, UNVEILING THE MIND: A HERSTORY OF THE HISTORICAL EVOLUTION OF THE LEGAL POSITION OF WOMEN IN ISLAM (Juta 2004).

MARY JANE MOSSMAN, THE FIRST WOMEN LAWYERS: A COMPARATIVE STUDY OF GENDER, LAW AND THE LEGAL PROFESSIONS (Hart Publishing, May 2006).

MARIE-HELENE MOTTIN-SYLLA AND JOELLE PALMIERI, CONFRONTING FEMALE GENITAL MUTILATION: THE ROLE OF YOUTH AND ICTS IN CHANGING AFRICA (Pumbazuka Press, July 2011).

MAKAU MUTUA, HUMAN RIGHTS: A POLITICAL AND CULTURAL CRITIQUE (University of Pennsylvania Press, October 2008).

AZAR NAFISI, READING LOLITA IN TEHRAN (Random House, 2003).

UMA NARAYAN, DISLOCATING CULTURES: IDENTITIES, TRADITIONS AND THIRD WORLD FEMINISM (Routledge, July 1997).

MARTHA NUSSBAUM, CREATING CAPABILITIES: THE HUMAN DEVELOPMENT APPROACH (Belknap Press, March 2011).

MARTHA C. NUSSBAUM, SEX AND SOCIAL JUSTICE (Oxford University Press, February 1999).

PATRICE OPPLIGER, GIRLS GONE SKANK: THE SEXUALIZATION OF GIRLS IN AMERICAN CULTURE (McFarland, April 2008).

ARZOO OSANLOO, THE POLITICS OF WOMEN'S RIGHTS IN IRAN (Princeton University Press, March 2009).

OUR GLOBAL NEIGHBORHOOD: THE REPORT OF THE COMMISSION ON GLOBAL GOVERNANCE (Oxford University Press, February 1995).

RHIAN PARKER, WOMEN, DOCTORS AND COSMETIC SURGERY: NEGOTIATING THE "NORMAL" BODY (Palgrave Macmillan, April 2010).

NELOFER PAZIRA, A BED OF RED FLOWERS: IN SEARCH OF MY AFGHANISTAN (Free Press, September 2005).

KATHY PEISS, HOPE IN A JAR: THE MAKING OF AMERICA'S BEAUTY CULTURE (University of Pennsylvania Press, August 2011).

REILAND RABAKA, AGAINST EPISTEMIC APARTHEID: W.E. DU BOIS AND THE DISCIPLINARY DECADENCE OF SOCIOLOGY (Lexington Books, May 2010).

WAPULA NELLY RADITLOANENG, WOMEN, POVERTY AND LITERACY: A CASE STUDY IN BOTSWANA (Lap Lambert Academic Publishing, July 2010).

AHMED RASHID, TALIBAN: MILITANT ISLAM, OIL AND FUNDAMENTALISM IN CENTRAL ASIA (Yale University Press, 2000).

STEVE REDHEAD, UNPOPULAR CULTURES: THE BIRTH OF LAW AND POPULAR CULTURE (Manchester University Press, June 1995).

DEBORAH RODRIGUEZ AND KRISTIN OHLSON, KABUL BEAUTY SCHOOL: AN AMERICAN WOMAN GOES BEHIND THE VEIL (Random House, December 2007).

GERALD ROSENBERG, THE HOLLOW HOPE: CAN COURTS BRING ABOUT SOCIAL CHANGE? (University of Chicago Press, May 2008).

SUSAN DELLER ROSS, WOMEN'S HUMAN RIGHTS: THE INTERNATIONAL AND COMPARATIVE LAW CASEBOOK (University of Pennsylvania Press, August 2009).

KUMKUM ROY, THE POWER OF GENDER AND THE GENDER OF POWER (2011).

FATIMA SADIQUI AND MOHA ENNAJI, WOMEN IN THE MIDDLE EAST AND NORTH AFRICA: AGENTS OF CHANGE (2011).

EDWARD SAID, ORIENTALISM (1979).

WILLARD CROMPTON SAMUEL, NELSON MANDELA: ENDING APARTHEID IN SOUTH AFRICA (2007).

BOAVENTURA DE SOUSA SANTOS, TOWARD A NEW COMMON SENSE: LAW SCIENCE AND POLITICS IN THE PARADIGMATIC TRANSITION (1995).

ANN SCALES, LEGAL FEMINISM: ACTIVISM, LAWYERING AND LEGAL THEORY (NYU Press, May 2006).

JONI SEAGER, THE PENGUIN ATLAS OF WOMEN IN THE WORLD (Penguin, April 2003).

ASNE SEIERSTAD, THE BOOKSELLER OF KABUL (Back Bay Books, October 2004).

AMARTYA SEN, DEVELOPMENT AS FREEDOM (Knopf, September 1999).

AYELET SHACHAR, MULTICULTURAL JURISDICTIONS: CULTURAL DIFFERENCES AND WOMEN'S RIGHTS (Cambridge University Press, October 2001).

SAIRA SHAH: THE STORYTELLER'S DAUGHTER (Knopf, September 2003).

HAROLD JACK SIMONS, AFRICAN WOMEN: THEIR LEGAL STATUS IN SOUTH AFRICA (1986).

ROSEMARY SKAINE, WOMEN OF AFGHANISTAN IN THE POST-TALIBAN ERA: HOW LIVES HAVE CHANGED AND WHERE THEY STAND TODAY (McFarland, September 2008).

ROSEMARY SKAINE, THE WOMEN OF AFGHANISTAN UNDER THE TALIBAN (McFarland, November 2001).

ALLISTER SPARKS, TOMORROW IS ANOTHER COUNTRY: THE INSIDE STORY OF SOUTH AFRICA'S ROAD TO CHANGE (University of Chicago Press, July 1996).

RORY STEWART, THE PLACES IN BETWEEN (Mariner Books, May 2006).

JOSEPH E. STIEGLITZ, GLOBALIZATION AND ITS DISCONTENTS (W.W. Norton & Co. June 2002).

BETTY W. TAYLOR, SHARON RUSH AND ROBERT J. MUNRO, FEMINIST JURISPRUDENCE, WOMEN AND THE LAW: CRITICAL ESSAYS, RESEARCH AGENDA, AND BIBLIOGRAPHY (Fred B. Rothman & Co. October 1998).

NGUGI WA THIONG'O, THE RIVER BETWEEN (Longman, August 2008).

HAKAN THORN, ANTI-APARTHEID AND THE EMERGENCE OF A GLOBAL CIVIL SOCIETY (Palgrave Macmillan, May 2006).

MARGARET THORNTON, DISSONANCE AND DISTRUST: WOMEN IN THE LEGAL PROFESSION (Oxford University Press, June 1996).

MARGARET THORNTON, THE LIBERAL PROMISE (Oxford University Press, February 1994).

NAHID TOUBIA, FEMALE GENITAL MUTILATION: A CALL FOR GLOBAL ACTION (Rainbo, 1995).

AILI MARI TRIPP, ISABEL CASIMIRO, JOY KWESIGA AND ALICE MUNGWA, AFRICAN WOMEN'S MOVEMENTS: TRANSFORMING POLITICAL LANDSCAPES (Cambridge University Press, November 2008).

UNIFEM, PROGRESS OF THE WORLD'S WOMEN (2005).

USAID/AFGHANISTAN EVALUATION OF THE AMBASSADOR'S SMALL GRANTS PROGRAM (ASGP) TO SUPPORT GENDER EQUALITY IN AFGHANISTAN (August 19, 2011).

ALICE WALKER, WARRIOR MARKS: FEMALE GENITAL MUTILATION AND THE SEXUAL BLINDING OF WOMEN (Harcourt Brace & Co. October 1993.

GEORGINA WAYLEN, ENGENDERING TRANSITIONS: WOMEN'S MOBILIZATION, INSTITUTIONS, AND GENDER OUTCOMES (Oxford University Press, July 2007).

PETER WILLETTS, NON-GOVERNMENTAL ORGANIZATIONS IN WORLD POLITICS (Routledge, February 2011).

PATRICIA WILLIAMS, THE ALCHEMY OF RACE AND RIGHTS (Harvard University Press, April 1991).

PAUL D. WILLIAMS, WAR AND CONFLICT IN AFRICA (Polity, October 2011).

WILLIAM JULIUS WILSON, TRULY DISADVANTAGED: THE INNER CITY, THE UNDERCLASS AND PUBLIC POLICY (University of Chicago Press, October 1990).

JOHN WITTE, JR., THE REFORMATION OF RIGHTS: LAW, RELIGION AND HUMAN RIGHTS IN EARLY MODERN CALVINISM (Cambridge University Press, February 2008).

NAOMI WOLF, THE BEAUTY MYTH: HOW IMAGES OF BEAUTY ARE USED AGAINST WOMEN (Anchor Books, February 1991).

NIGEL WORDEN, THE MAKING OF MODERN SOUTH AFRICA: CONQUEST, APARTHEID, DEMOCRACY 4th Ed. (Wiley-Blackwell, August 2007).

ERIC K. YAMAMOTO, INTERRACIAL JUSTICE, CONFLICT AND RECONCILIATION IN POST CIVIL-RIGHTS AMERICA (NYU Press, January 1999).

MUHAMMAD YUNUS, BANKER TO THE POOR (Public Affairs, October 2003).

SUSAN M. ZIMMERMAN, SILICONE SURVIVORS: WOMEN'S EXPERIENCE WITH BREAST IMPLANTS (Temple University Press, April 1998).

Edited Volumes

AFRICAN WOMEN: A POLITICAL ECONOMY (Meredeth Turshen Ed. Palgrave Macmillan, October 2010).

AT THE BOUNDARIES OF LAW: FEMINISM AND LEGAL THEORY (Martha Albertson Fineman and Nancy Sweet Thomadsen Eds. Routledge, December 1990).

AUSTRALIAN FEMINISM: A COMPANION (Barbara Caine *et al.* Eds. Oxford University Press, March 1999).

BEYOND THE MAGIC BULLET: NGO ACCOUNTABILITY AND PERFORMANCE IN THE POST-COLD WAR WORLD (Michael Edwards and David Hulme Eds. Kumarian Press, March 1996).

BRITISH FEMINISM IN THE 20TH CENTURY (Harold L. Smith Ed. University of Massachusetts Press, January 1990).

BUILDING FEMINIST MOVEMENTS AND ORGANIZATIONS: GLOBAL PERSPECTIVES (Lydia Alpizar *et al.* Eds. Zed Books, May 2007).

CIVIL SOCIETIES AND SOCIAL MOVEMENTS: DOMESTIC, TRANSNATIONAL AND GLOBAL (Ronnie D. Lipschutz Ed. Ashgate, October 2006).

COMMISSIONING THE PAST: UNDERSTANDING SOUTH AFRICA'S TRUTH AND RECONCILIATION COMMISSION (Deborah Posel and Graeme Simpson Eds. Witwatersrand University Press, February 2003).

CONSTITUTING EQUALITY: GENDER EQUALITY AND COMPARATIVE CONSTITUTIONAL LAW (Susan H. Williams Ed. Cambridge University Press, August 2011).

CRITICAL RACE FEMINISM: A READER (Adrien Wing Ed. NYU Press, March 1997).

DIVIDING THE DOMESTIC: MEN, WOMEN AND HOUSEHOLD WORK IN CROSS-NATIONAL PERSPECTIVE (Judith Treas and Sonja Drobnic Eds. Stanford University Press, February 2010).

ENGENDERING HUMAN RIGHTS: CULTURAL AND SOCIO-ECONOMIC REALITIES IN AFRICA (Obioma Nnaemeka and Joy Ezeilo Eds. Palgrave Macmillan, April 2005).

FEMINISM AND ANTIRACISM: INTERNATIONAL STRUGGLES FOR JUSTICE (France Winddance Twine and Kathleen M. Blee Eds. NYU Press, August 2001).

FEMINISM AND ISLAM: LEGAL AND LITERARY PERSPECTIVES (Mai Yamani Ed. NYU Press, December 1996).

FEMINISM AND POSTCOLONIAL THEORY: A READER (Reina Lewis and Sara Mills Eds. Routledge, July 2003).

FEMINIST CONSTITUTIONALISM: GLOBAL PERSPECTIVES (Beverley Baines *et al.* Eds. 2012).

FEMINIST LEGAL THEORY (Nancy E. Dowd and Michells S. Jacobs Eds. NYU Press, January 2003).

FOR LESBIANS ONLY: A SEPARATIST ANTHOLOGY (Sarah Hoagland and Julia Penelope Eds. Onlywomen Press, April 1992).

GENDER AND THE NEW SOUTH AFRICAN LEGAL ORDER (Christina Murray Ed. Juta, December 1994).

GENDER EQUALITY: DIMENSIONS OF WOMEN'S EQUAL CITIZENSHIP (Linda C. McClain and Joanna L. Grossman Eds. Cambridge University Press, July 2009).

GENDERING THE STATE IN AN AGE OF GLOBALIZATION: WOMEN'S MOVEMENTS AND STATE FEMINISM IN POSTINDUSTRIAL DEMOCRACIES (Melissa Hausmann *et al.* Eds. Rowman & Littlefield Publishers, May 2007).

GLOBAL CRITICAL RACE FEMINISM: AN INTERNATIONAL READER (Adrien Wing Ed. NYU Press, May 2000).

HUMAN RIGHTS IN AFRICA: CROSS-CULTURAL PERSPECTIVES (Abdullah Ahmed An-Naim and Francis Deng Eds. Brookings Institution Press, August 1990).

HUMAN RIGHTS OF WOMEN: NATIONAL AND INTERNATIONAL PERSPECTIVES (Rebecca Cook Ed. University of Pennsylvania Press, January 1994).

HUMAN RIGHTS WATCH WOMEN'S RIGHTS PROJECT, VIOLENCE AGAINST WOMEN IN SOUTH AFRICA: THE STATE RESPONSE TO DOMESTIC VIOLENCE AND RAPE (Bronwen Manby and Dorothy Q. Thomas Eds. 1995).

ISLAM, GENDER AND SOCIAL CHANGE (Yvonne Yzabeck Haddad and John L. Esposito Eds. Oxford University Press, December 1997).

MUSLIM WOMEN'S CHOICES: RELIGIOUS BELIEF AND SOCIAL REALITY (Cammillia Fawzi El-Solh and Judy Mabro Eds. Berg Publishers, February 1994).

NORMS IN INTERNATIONAL RELATIONS: THE STRUGGLE AGAINST APARTHEID (Audie Klotz and Peter J. Katzenstein Eds. Cornell University Press, January 1999).

ON THE FRONTLINES: GENDER, WAR, AND THE POST-CONFLICT PROCESS (Fionnuala Ni Aolain *et al.* Eds. Oxford University Press, November 2011).

PROMOTING THE RULE OF LAW ABROAD (Thomas Carothers Ed. Carnegie Endowment for International Peace, January 2006).

PUTTING WOMEN ON THE AGENDA (Susan Bazilli Ed. Ravan Press, July 1992).

READINGS IN GENDER IN AFRICA (Andrea Cornwall Ed. Indiana University Press, February 2005).

RECONCEIVING REALITY: WOMEN AND INTERNATIONAL LAW (Dorinda G. Dallmeyer Ed. The American Society of International Law, 1993).

RELIGION IN INTERNATIONAL RELATIONS (Fabio Petito and Pavlos Hatzopoulos Eds. Palgrave Macmillan, June 2003).

REMAKING WOMEN: FEMINISM AND MODERNITY IN THE MIDDLE EAST (Lila Abu-Lughod Ed. Princeton University Press July 1998).

RETHINKING EQUALITY PROJECTS IN LAW: FEMINIST CHALLENGES (Rosemary Hunter Ed. Hart Publishing, August 2008).

SEGREGATION (James H. Carr *et al.* Eds. Routledge, February 2008).

SILENCE IS VIOLENCE: END THE ABUSE OF WOMEN IN AFGHANISTAN (United Nations Mission in Afghanistan and the United Nations High Commissioner for Human Rights 2009).

SLAVERY (Stanley Engeran *et al.* Eds. Oxford University Press, May 2001).

SOUTH AFRICA: TWELVE PERSPECTIVES ON THE TRANSITION (Helen Kitchen and J. Coleman Kitchen Eds. Praeger, October 1994).

SPIRITUAL PRACTICES AND ECONOMIC REALITIES: FEMINIST CHALLENGES (Renata Jambresic Kirin and Sandra Prlenda Eds. Heinrich Boll Stufting, February 2011).

STRUGGLES FOR SOCIAL RIGHTS IN LATIN AMERICA (Susan Eva Eckstein and Timothy P. Wickham-Crowley Eds. Routledge, November 2002).

THE CONSTITUTION OF SOUTH AFRICA FROM A GENDER PERSPECTIVE (Sandra Liebenberg Ed. David Philip 1995).

THE GENDER FACE OF ASIAN POLITICS (Azaar Ayaz and Andrea Fleschenberg Eds. Oxford University Press, June 2009).

THEORETICAL PERSPECTIVES ON GENDER AND DEVELOPMENT (Jane L. Parpart *et al.* Eds. IDRC Books, June 2000).

THE POLITICS OF SURVIVAL IN SUB-SAHARAN AFRICA (Gwendolyn Mikell Ed. University of Pennsylvania Press, June 1997).

THE UNFINISHED REVOLUTION: VOICES FROM THE GLOBAL FIGHT FOR WOMEN'S RIGHTS (Minky Worden Ed. Seven Stories Press, March 2012).

THIS BRIDGE CALL MY BACK: WRITINGS BY RADICAL WOMEN OF COLOR (Cherrie Moraga and Gloria Anzaldua Eds. Kitchen Table/Women of Color Press, March 1984).

TRANSCENDING THE BOUNDARIES OF LAW: GENERATIONS OF FEMINIST AND LEGAL THEORY (Martha Albertson Fineman Ed. Routledge Cavendish, August 2010).

UNLINKING CITIZENSHIP (Amanda Gouws Ed. Ashgate, January 2005).

VIOLENCE AGAINST WOMEN UNDER INTERNATIONAL HUMAN RIGHTS LAW (Alice Edwards Ed. Cambridge University Press, February 2011).

VOICES OF AFRICAN WOMEN: WOMEN'S RIGHTS IN GHANA, UGANDA AND TANZANIA (Johanna Bond Ed. Carolina Academic Press, April 2005).

WOMEN AND ISLAMIZATION: CONTEMPORARY DIMENSIONS OF DISCOURSE ON GENDER RELATIONS (Karin Ask and Marit Tjomsland Eds. Berg Publishers, September 1998).

WOMEN AND LAND IN AFRICA: CULTURE, RELIGION AND REALIZING WOMEN'S RIGHTS (L. Muthoni Wanyeki Ed. Zed Books, May 2003).

WOMEN AND THE LAW: STORIES (Elizabeth M. Schneider and Stephanie M. Wildman Eds. Foundation Press, October 2010).

WOMEN, CULTURE AND SOCIETY (M.Z. Rosaldo and L. Lamphere Eds. Stanford University Press, June 1974).

WOMEN, GENDER AND HUMAN RIGHTS: A GLOBAL PERSPECTIVE (Marjorie Agosin Ed. Rutgers University Press, September 2001).

WOMEN MAKING CONSTITUTIONS (Alexandra Dobowolsky and Vivian Hart Eds. Palgrave Macmillan, January 2004).

WOMEN'S ACTIVISM AND GLOBALIZATION: LINKING LOCAL STRUGGLES AND TRANSNATIONAL POLITICS (Nancy A. Naples and Manisha Desai Eds. Routledge, February 2002).

WOMEN'S MOVEMENTS IN THE GLOBAL ERA: THE POWER OF LOCAL FEMINISMS (Amrita Basu Ed. Westview Press, February 2010).

WOMEN'S RIGHTS AND TRADITIONAL LAW: A CONFLICT?, THIRD WORLD LEGAL STUDIES 1994–95 (Guest Editor, Penelope E. Andrews International Third World Legal Studies Association, 1994 95).

WOMEN'S RIGHTS, HUMAN RIGHTS: INTERNATIONAL FEMINIST PERSPECTIVES (Julie Peters and Andrea Wolper Eds. Routledge, December 1994).

Chapters in Books

Haleh Afshar, *Islam and Feminism: An Analysis of Political Strategies*, in FEMINISM AND ISLAM: LEGAL AND LITERARY PERSPECTIVES (Mai Yamani Ed. NYU Press, December 1996) 197.

Penelope E. Andrews, *Imagine All the Women: Power, Gender, and the Transformative Possibilities of the South African Constitution*, in Power, Gender, and Social Change in Africa and the Diaspora (Muna Ndulo Ed. Cambridge Scholars Publishing, June 2009) 213.

Penelope Andrews, *The Step-Child of National Liberation: Women and Rights in the New South Africa*, in THE POST-APARTHEID CONSTITUTIONS: REFLECTIONS ON SOUTH AFRICA'S BASIC LAW (Penelope E. Andrews and Stephen Ellmann Eds. Ohio University Press, December 2001) 326.

Denise D. Bielby, *Gender and Family Relations*, in HANDBOOK OF THE SOCIOLOGY OF GENDER (Janet Saltzman Ed. Kluwer Academic/Plenum Publishers, May 1999) 391.

D. Brand, *The Politics of Need Interpretation and the Adjudication of Socio-Economic Rights Claims in South Africa*, in THEORIES OF SOCIAL AND ECONOMIC JUSTICE (A.J. Van der Walt Ed. Sun Press 2005) 17.

Andrew Byrnes, *Toward More Effective Enforcement of Women's Human Rights Through the Use of International Human Rights Law and Procedures*, in HUMAN RIGHTS OF WOMEN: NATIONAL AND INTERNATIONAL PERSPECTIVES (Rebecca J. Cook Ed. University of Pennsylvania Press, January 1994) 189.

Martin Chanock, *Cutting and Sewing: Goals and Means in the Constitutionalist Project in Africa*, in LAW AND RIGHTS: GLOBAL PERSPECTIVES ON CONSTITUTIONALISM AND GOVERNANCE (Penelope Andrews and Susan Bazilli Eds. Vandeplas Publishing, July 2008) 47.

Helene Combrinck, *The Dark Side of the Rainbow: Violence against Women in South Africa after 10 Years of Democracy*, in ADVANCING WOMEN'S RIGHTS: THE FIRST DECADE OF DEMOCRACY (Christina Murray and Michelle O'Sullivan Eds. Juta, 2005) 171.

Megan Davis, *The Globalisation of International Human Rights Law: Aboriginal Women and the Practice of Aboriginal Customary Law*, in WOMEN, CRIME AND SOCIAL HARM: TOWARDS A CRIMINOLOGY FOR THE GLOBAL ERA (Maureen Cain and Adrian Howe Eds. Hart, 2008) 137.

Richard Falk, *Cultural Foundations for the International Protection of Human Rights*, in HUMAN RIGHTS IN CROSS-CULTURAL PERSPECTIVES: A

QUEST FOR CONSENSUS (Abdullah Ahmed An-Na'im Ed. University of Pennsylvania Press, March 1995) 44.

Rhoda Howard, *Women's Rights in English-speaking Sub-Saharan Africa*, in HUMAN RIGHTS AND DEVELOPMENT IN AFRICA (Claude E. Welch, Jr. and Ronald I. Meltzer Eds. State University of New York Press, July 1984) 46.

Indira Jaising, *The Convention on the Elimination of All Forms of Discrimination Against Women (CEDAW) and Realisation of Rights: Reflections on Standard Settings and Culture*, in WITHOUT PREJUDICE: CEDAW AND THE DETERMINATION IN A LEGAL AND CULTURAL CONTEXT (Meena Shivdas and Sarah Coleman Eds. Commonwealth Secretariat, July 2010) 9.

Amanda Kemp *et al.*, *The Dawn of a New Day: Redefining South African Feminism*, in THE CHALLENGE OF LOCAL FEMINISMS: WOMEN'S MOVEMENTS IN GLOBAL PERSPECTIVE (Amrita Basu Ed. Westview Press, February 1995) 131.

David Kennedy, *Losing Faith in the Secular: Law, Religion, and the Culture of International Governance*, in RELIGION AND INTERNATIONAL LAW (Mark W. Janis and Carolyn Evans Eds. Martinus Nijhoff, February 2004) 309.

A. Krog, *Locked into Loss and Silence: Testimonies of Gender and Violence at the South African Truth Commission*, in VICTIMS, PERPETRATORS, OR ACTORS?: GENDER, ARMED CONFLICT AND POLITICAL VIOLENCE (C. Moser and F. Clark Eds. Zed Boks, July 2001) 203.

Gail Linsenbard, *Women's Rights as Human Rights: An Ontological Grounding*, in WOMEN'S RIGHTS AS HUMAN RIGHTS: ACTIVISM AND SOCIAL CHANGE IN AFRICA (Diana J. Fox and Naima Hasci Eds. Edwin Mellen Press, 2000) 65.

Mary Maboreke, *Women and Law in Post-Independence Zimbabwe*, in PUTTING WOMEN ON THE AGENDA (Susan Bazilli Ed. Ravan Press, July 1992) 227

Joseph McLaren, *Alice Walker and the Legacy of African-American Discourse on Africa*, in THE AFRICAN DIASPORA: AFRICAN ORIGINS AND NEW WORLD IDENTITIES (Isadore Okpewhu *et al.* Eds. Indiana University Press, November 2001) 525.

Kathryn Pauly Morgan, *Women and the Knife: Cosmetic Surgery and the Colonization of Women's Bodies*, in NAGGING QUESTIONS: FEMINIST ETHICS IN EVERYDAY LIFE (Dana E. Bushnell Ed. Rowman & Littlefield Publishers 1995) 305.

Siobhan Mullally, *Migrant Women Destabilizing Borders: Citizenship Debates in Ireland*, in INTERSECTIONALITY AND BEYOND: LAW, POWER AND THE POLITICS OF LOCATION (Emily Grabham, Davina Cooper, Jane Krishnadas and Didi Herman Eds. Routledge-Cavendish, October 2008) 251.

Thandabantu Nhlapo, *African Customary Law in the Interim Constitution*, in THE CONSTITUTION OF SOUTH AFRICA FROM A GENDER PERSPECTIVE (Sandra Liebenberg Ed. David Philip 1995). 157.

Katha Pollitt, *Whose Culture?*, in IS MULTICULTURALISM BAD FOR WOMEN? (Joshua Cohen *et al.* Eds. Princeton University Press, August 1999) 27.

Laura Reanda, *The Commission on the Status of Women*, in THE UNITED NATIONS AND HUMAN RIGHTS: A CRITICAL APPRAISAL (Philip Alston Ed. Oxford University Press, July 1995) 265.

Ruthann Robson, *Convictions: Theorizing Lesbians and Criminal Justice*, in LEGAL INVERSIONS (Didi Herman and Carl Stychin Eds. Temple University Press, December 1995) 180.

Boaventura de Sousa Santos, *Toward a Multicultural Conception of Human Rights*, in *INTERNATIONAL HUMAN RIGHTS LAW IN A GLOBAL CONTEXT* (Felipe Gómez Isa and Koen Feyter Eds. University of Deusto Press, June 2009) 97.

Articles

Brooke Ackerly and Jacqui True, *Back to the Future: Feminist Theory, Activism, and Doing Feminist Research in an Age of Globalization*, 33 WOMEN'S STUDIES INTERNATIONAL FORUM (2010) 464.

Adeno Addis, *Constitutionalizing Deliberative Democracy in Multilingual Societies*, 25 BERKELEY JOURNAL OF INTERNATIONAL LAW (2007) 117.

Afghan Apartheid, 2 THE WOMEN'S WATCH 2, International Women's Rights Action Watch (Spring 1997).

Afra Afsharipour, *Empowering Ourselves: The Role of Women's NGOs in the Enforcement of the Women's Convention*, 99 COLUMBIA LAW REVIEW (1999) 129.

Rina Agarwal and Scott M. Lynch, *Refining the Measurement of Women's Autonomy: An International Application of a Multi-dimensional Construct*, 84 SOCIAL FORCES (2006) 2077.

Meredith Aherne, *Olowo v Ashcroft: Granting Parental Asylum Based on Child's Refugee Status*, 18 PACE INTERNATIONAL LAW REVIEW (2006) 317.

Huma Ahmed-Ghosh, *A History of Women in Afghanistan: Lessons Learnt for the Future or Yesterdays and Tomorrow: Women in Afghanistan*, 4 JOURNAL OF INTERNATIONAL WOMEN'S STUDIES (2003) 1.

Cathi Albertyn and Beth Goldblatt, *Facing the Challenge of Transformation: Difficulties in the Development of an Indigenous Jurisprudence of Equality*, 14 SOUTH AFRICA JOURNAL OF HUMAN RIGHTS (1998) 248.

Aziz al-Hibri, Who Defines Women's Rights? A Third World Woman's Response, HUMAN RIGHTS BRIEF (1994) at: *http://www.wcl.american.edu/hrbrief/ v2i1/alhibr21.htm.*

Jean Allan and Andreas O'Shea, *African Disunity: Comparing Human Rights Law and Practice of North and South African States*, 24 HUMAN RIGHTS QUARTERLY (2002) 86.

Philip Alston, *The Myopia of the Handmaidens: International Lawyers and Globalization*, 8 EUROPEAN JOURNAL OF INTERNATIONAL LAW (1998) 435.

Michelle J. Anderson, *Marital Immunity, Intimate Relationships, and Improper Inferences: A New Law on Sexual Offenses by Intimates*, 54 HASTINGS LAW JOURNAL (2003) 1465.

Penelope E. Andrews, *Who's Afraid of Polygamy? Exploring the Boundaries of Family, Equality and Custom in South Africa*, 2 UNIVERSITY OF UTAH LAW REVIEW (2009) 351.

Penelope E. Andrews, *Democracy Stops at My Front Door: Obstacles to Gender Equality in South Africa*, 5 LOYOLA UNIVERSITY OF CHICAGO INTERNATIONAL LAW REVIEW (2007) 15.

Penelope E. Andrews, *Learning to Love after Learning to Harm: Post-Conflict Reconstruction, Gender Equality and Cultural Values*, 15 MICHIGAN STATE JOURNAL OF INTERNATIONAL LAW (2007) 41.

Penelope E. Andrews, *Reparations for Apartheid's Victims: The Path to Reconciliation?*, 53 DE PAUL LAW REVIEW (2004) 1155.

Penelope E. Andrews, *Women's Human Rights and the Conversation Across Cultures*, 67 ALBANY LAW REVIEW (2003) 609.

Penelope Andrews, *From Gender Apartheid to Non-Sexism: The Pursuit of Women's Rights in South Africa*, 26 NORTH CAROLINA JOURNAL OF INTERNATIONAL LAW AND COMMERCIAL REGULATION (2001) 693.

Penelope E. Andrews, *Globalization, Human Rights and Critical Race Feminism: Voices from the Margins*, 3 JOURNAL OF GENDER, RACE AND JUSTICE (2000) 373.

Penelope E. Andrews, *Violence against Women in South Africa: The Role of Culture and the Limitations of the Law*, 8 TEMPLE POLITICAL AND CIVIL RIGHTS LAW REVIEW (1999) 425.

Penelope E. Andrews, *Striking the Rock: Confronting Gender Equality in South Africa*, 3 MICHIGAN JOURNAL OF RACE AND LAW (1998) 307.

Penelope E. Andrews, *Violence against Aboriginal Women in Australia: Redress from the International Human Rights Framework*, 60 ALBANY LAW REVIEW (1997) 917.

Penelope Andrews, *The Legal Underpinnings of Gender Oppression in Apartheid South Africa*, 3 AUSTRALIAN JOURNAL OF LAW AND SOCIETY (1986) 92.

Deborah E. Anker, *Refugee Law, Gender, and the Human Rights Paradigm*, 15 HARVARD HUMAN RIGHTS JOURNAL (2002) 133.

Lisa M. Ayoub, *The Crisis in Afghanistan: When Will Gender Apartheid End?* 7 TULSA JOURNAL OF COMPARATIVE AND INTERNATIONAL LAW (2000) 513.

Scott Baldauf, *Letter from Afghanistan*, THE NATION, April 28, 2003 at 24.

Taunya Banks, *Toward a Global Critical Feminist Vision: Domestic Work and the Nanny Tax Debate*, 3 JOURNAL OF GENDER, RACE AND JUSTICE (1999) 1.

K. Barron, *The Bumpy Road to Womanhood*, 12 DISABILITY AND SOCIETY (1997) 223.

Shannon V. Barrow, *Nigerian Justice: Death-by-Stoning Sentence Reveals Empty Promises to the State and the International Community*, 17 EMORY INTERNATIONAL LAW REVIEW (2003) 1203.

Upendra Baxi, *Voices of Suffering and the Future of Human Rights*, 8 TRANSNATIONAL LAW AND CONTEMPORARY PROBLEMS (1998) 125.

Mary Becker, *Patriarchy and Inequality: Towards A Substantive Feminism*, UNIVERSITY OF CHICAGO LEGAL FORUM (1999) 21.

Andra Nahal Behrouz, *Transforming Islamic Family Law: State Responsibility and the Role of the Internal Initiative*, 103 COLUMBIA LAW REVIEW (2003) 1136.

M. Bell, *Re/Forming the Anorexic "Prisoner": Inpatient Medical Treatment as the Return to Panoptic Femininity*, 6 CULTURAL STUDIES AND CRITICAL METHODOLOGIES (2006) 282.

Leslie Bender, *An Overview of Feminist Torts Scholarship*, 78 CORNELL LAW REVIEW (1993) 575.

T.W. Bennett, *The Equality Clause and Customary Law*, 10 SOUTH AFRICAN JOURNAL OF HUMAN RIGHTS (1994) 122.

Karima Bennoune, *Secularism and Human Rights: A Contextual Analysis of Headscarves, Religious Expression, and Women's Equality under International Law*, 45 COLUMBIA JOURNAL OF TRANSNATIONAL LAW (2007) 367.

G. Binder, *Cultural Relativism and Cultural Imperialism in Human Rights Law*, 5 BUFFALO HUMAN RIGHTS LAW REVIEW (1999) 211.

Benjamin D. Bleiberg, *Unveiling the Real Issue: Evaluating the European Court of Human Rights' Decision to Enforce the Turkish Headscarf Ban in Leyla Sahin v Turkey*, 91 CORNELL LAW REVIEW (2003) 130.

Elsje Bonthuys, *Accommodating Gender, Race, Culture and Religion: Outside Legal Subjectivity*, 18 SOUTH AFRICAN JOURNAL OF HUMAN RIGHTS (2002) 41.

Robert Booth, *Human Trafficking Victims Will Not Be Treated as Criminals*, THE GUARDIAN, July 3, 2011.

Gwen Brodsky and Shelagh Day, *Beyond the Social and Economic Rights Debate: Substantive Equality Speaks to Poverty*, 14 CANADIAN JOURNAL OF WOMEN AND THE LAW (2002) 184.

Victoria Bronstein, *Confronting Custom in the New South African State: An Analysis of the Recognition of Customary Marriages Act 120 of 1998*, 16 SOUTH AFRICAN JOURNAL ON HUMAN RIGHTS (2000) 558.

Janelle Brown, *A Coalition of Hope*, 12 MS. MAGAZINE 2 (Spring 2002) 65.

Debbie Budlender, *South Africa: The Women's Budget*, 12 SOUTHERN AFRICA REPORT (1996) 16.

Charlotte Bunch, *Women's Rights as Human Rights: Toward a Re-Vision of Human Rights*, 12 HUMAN RIGHTS QUARTERLY (1990) 486.

Catherine Campbell, *Learning to Kill? Masculinity, the Family and Violence in Natal*, 18 JOURNAL OF SOUTHERN AFRICAN STUDIES (1992) 614.

Mary Anne Case, *Feminist Fundamentalism on the Frontier between Government and Family Responsibility for Children*, UTAH LAW REVIEW (2009) 382.

M. Chanock, *Law, State and Culture: Thinking about Customary Law after Apartheid*, ACTA JURIDICA (1991) 53.

Martin Chanock, *Neither Customary nor Legal: African Customary Law in an Era of Family Law Reform*, 3 INTERNATIONAL JOURNAL OF LAW, POLICY AND THE FAMILY (1989) 72.

Hilary Charlesworth *et al.*, *Feminist Approaches to Law*, 85 AMERICAN JOURNAL OF INTERNATIONAL LAW (1991) 613.

Sarah Chayes, *Afghanistan's Future, Lost in the Shuffle*, NEW YORK TIMES, July 1, 2003 at A23.

Daina C. Chiu, *The Cultural Defense: Beyond Exclusion, Assimilation and Guilty Liberalism*, 82 CALIFORNIA LAW REVIEW (1994) 1053.

Janie A. Chuang, *Rescuing Trafficking from Ideological Capture: Prostitution Reform and Anti-Trafficking Law and Policy*, 158 UNIVERSITY OF PENNSYLVANIA LAW REVIEW (2010) 1655.

J. Church, *Constitutional Equality and the Position of Women in a Multi-Cultural Society*, 28 COMPARATIVE AND INTERNATIONAL LAW OF SOUTHERN AFRICA (1995) 289.

Aninka Claasens, *Who Told Them We Want This Bill? The Traditional Courts Bill and Rural Women*, 82 AGENDA (2009) 9.

Aninka Claasens and Sindiso Mnisi, *Rural Women Redefining Land Rights in the Context of Living Customary Law*, 25 SOUTH AFRICAN JOURNAL ON HUMAN RIGHTS (2009) 491.

Kerith Cohen, *Truth, Beauty and Deception: A Feminist Analysis of Breast Implant Litigation*, 1 WILLIAM AND MARY JOURNAL OF WOMEN AND LAW (1994) 149.

Rebecca J. Cook, *The Elimination of Sexual Apartheid: Prospects for the Fourth World Conference on Women*, 5 ASIL ISSUE PAPERS ON WORLD CONFERENCES (1995) 3.

Rebecca J. Cook and Charles Ngwena, *Women's Access to Health Care: The Legal Framework*, 94 INTERNATIONAL JOURNAL OF GYNECOLOGY AND OBSTETRICS (2006) 216.

Radhika Coomaraswamy, *Identity Within: Cultural Relativism, Minority Rights and the Empowerment of Women*, 34 GEORGE WASHINGTON INTERNATIONAL LAW REVIEW (2002) 483.

Kenneth J. Cooper, *Kabul Women under Virtual House Arrest*, WASHINGTON POST, October 7, 1996: CNN, March 9, 1997.

I. Currie, *The Future of Customary Law: Lessons from the Lobolo Debate*, ACTA JURIDICA (1994) 156.

Mary Daly, *Gender Mainstreaming in Theory and Practice*, 12 SOCIAL POLITICS (2005) 433.

D.M. Davis, *Adjudicating the Socio-Economic Rights in the South African Constitution: Towards "Deference Lite"?*, 22 SOUTH AFRICAN JOURNAL OF HUMAN RIGHTS (2006) 301.

D.M. Davis, *Constitutional Borrowing: The Influence of Legal Culture and Local History in the Reconstitution of Comparative Influence: The South African Experience*, INTERNATIONAL JOURNAL OF CONSTITUTIONAL LAW (2003) 181.

D.M. Davis, *Equality: The Majesty of Legoland Jurisprudence*, 116 SOUTH AFRICAN LAW JOURNAL (1999) 398.

Seble Dawit and Salem Mekuria, *The West Just Doesn't Get It*, NEW YORK TIMES, December 7, 1993 at A27.

Maneesha Deckha, *Is Culture Taboo? Feminism, Intersectionality, and Culture Talk in Law*, 16 CANADIAN JOURNAL OF WOMEN AND LAW (2004) 106.

Shefali Desai, *Hearing Afghan Women's Voices: Feminist Theory's Re-Conceptualization of Women's Human Rights*, 16 ARIZONA JOURNAL OF INTERNATIONAL AND COMPARATIVE LAW (1999) 805.

Lorenzo Di Silvio, *Correcting Corrective Rape: Carmichele and Developing South Africa's Affirmative Obligations to Prevent Violence against Women*, 99 GEORGIA LAW JOURNAL (2011) 1469.

Douglas Lee Donoho, *Autonomy, Self-Governance, and the Margins of Appreciation: Developing a Jurisprudence of Diversity within Universal Human Rights*, 15 EMORY INTERNATIONAL LAW REVIEW (2001) 391.

Mark Drumbl, *Rights, Culture and Crime: The Role of the Rule of Law for the Women of Afghanistan*, WASHINGTON AND LEE PUBLIC LAW AND LEGAL THEORY RESEARCH PAPER SERIES, January 2004 at: *http://ssrn.com/abstract=452440*.

Celia Duggar, *Senegal Curbs a Bloody Rite for Girls and Women*, NEW YORK TIMES, October 15, 2011 at: *http://www.nytimes.com/2011/10/16/world/africa/movement-to-end-genital-cutting-spreads-in-senegal.html?_r=2*.

Tim Dyson and Mick Moore, *On Kinship Structure, Female Autonomy, and Demographic Behavior in India*, 9 POPULATION AND DEVELOPMENT REVIEW (1983) 35.

Buthaina Ahmed Elnaiem, *Human Rights of Women and Islamic Identity in Africa*, RECHT IN AFRICA (2002) 1.

Melissa Evan, *Bay Area Women's Group Visits Afghanistan*, OAKLAND TRIBUNE, March 3, 2003.

Dexter Filkins, *Afghan Women Protest New Restrictive Law*, NEW YORK TIMES, April 15, 2009 at: *http://www.nytimes.com/2009/04/16/world/asia/16afghan.html?_r=1&emc=eta1*.

Lucinda Finley, *Feminist Jurisprudence*, 1 COLUMBIA JOURNAL OF GENDER AND LAW (1991) 5.

Lisa Fishbayn, *Litigating the Right to Culture: Family Law in the New South Africa*, 13 INTERNATIONAL JOURNAL OF LAW, POLICY AND THE FAMILY (1999) 147.

Catherine A. Fitzpatrick, *Afghanistan Women: Progress and Unmet Promises*, RADIO FREE EUROPE/RADIO LIBERTY AFGHAN REPORT, 27 March 2003.

Katherine M. Franke, *Gendered Subjects of Transitional Justice*, 15 COLUMBIA JOURNAL OF GENDER AND LAW (2006) 813.

Bruce P. Frohnen, *Multicultural Rights? Natural Law and the Reconciliation of Universal Norms with Particular Cultures*, 52 CATHOLIC UNIVERSITY LAW REVIEW (2002) 39.

Carlotta Gall, *Afghan Women in Political Spotlight*, NEW YORK TIMES, June 28, 2002.

Ruth L. Gana, *Which "Self"? Race and Gender in the Right to Self-Determination as a Prerequisite to the Right to Development*, 14 WISCONSIN INTERNATIONAL LAW JOURNAL (1995) 133.

Randall Garrison, *Rebuilding Justice? The Challenges of Accountability in Policing in Post-Conflict Afghanistan*, PAPER PRESENTED AT THE CONFERENCE OF THE INTERNATIONAL SOCIETY FOR THE REFORM OF CRIMINAL LAW, August 8–12, 2004 at: *www.isrcl.org/Papers/2004/Garrison.pdf*.

Y. Ghai, *Universalism and Relativism: Human Rights as a Framework for Negotiating Interethnic Claims*, 21 CARDOZO LAW REVIEW (2000) 1095.

Marjon E. Ghasemi, *Islam, International Human Rights and Women's Equality: Afghan Women under Taliban Rule*, 88 SOUTHERN CALIFORNIA LAW REVIEW AND WOMEN'S STUDIES (1999) 445.

Paula Ruth Gilbert, *Discourses of Female Violence and Societal Gender Stereotypes*, 8 VIOLENCE AGAINST WOMEN (2002) 1271.

Nils Peter Gleditsch *et al.*, *Armed Conflict 1946–2001: A New Dataset*, 39 JOURNAL OF PEACE RESEARCH (2002) 615.

Julie Goldscheid, *Gender-Motivated Violence: Developing a Meaningful Paradigm for Civil Rights Enforcement*, 22 HARVARD WOMEN'S LAW JOURNAL (1999) 123.

Jenna Goudreau, *The Hidden Dangers of Cosmetic Surgery*, FORBES, June 16, 2011 at: *http://www.forbes.com/sites/jennagoudreau/2011/06/16/hidden-dangers-of-cosmetic-surgery/*.

Karthy Govender, *The Developing Equality Jurisprudence in South Africa*, 107 MICHIGAN LAW REVIEW FIRST IMPRESSIONS (2009) 120.

Denise Grady, *In War and Isolation: A Fighter for Afghan Women*, NEW YORK TIMES, July 28, 2009.

Lynn Graybill, *The Contribution of the Truth and Reconciliation Commission toward the Promotion of Women's Rights in South Africa*, 24 WOMEN'S STUDIES INTERNATIONAL FORUM (2001) 1.

Reg Graycar and Jenny Jane Morgan, *Examining Understandings of Equality: One Step Forward, Two Steps Back?*, 20 AUSTRALIAN FEMINIST LAW JOURNAL (2004) 23.

Jamal Greene, *Selling Originalism*, 97 THE GEORGETOWN LAW JOURNAL (2009) 657.

Isabelle R. Gunning, *Global Feminism at the Local Level: Criminal and Asylum Laws Regarding Female Genital Surgeries*, 3 JOURNAL OF GENDER, RACE AND JUSTICE (1999–2000) 45.

Isabelle Gunning, *Arrogant Perception: World Travelling and Multi-Cultural Feminism: The Case of Female Genital Surgeries*, 23 COLUMBIA HUMAN RIGHTS LAW REVIEW (1992) 189.

Helen Habila, *Justice, Nigeria's Way*, NEW YORK TIMES, October 4, 2003 at A13.

Louise Halper, *Law and Women's Agency in Post-Revolutionary Iran*, 28 HARVARD JOURNAL OF LAW AND GENDER (2005) 85.

Catharine Hantzis, *Is Gender Justice a Completed Agenda*, 100 HARVARD LAW REVIEW (1987) 690.

Audrey E. Haroz, *South Africa's 1996 Choice on Termination of Pregnancy Act: Expanding Choice and International Human Rights to Black South African Women*, 30 VANDERBILT JOURNAL OF TRANSNATIONAL LAW (1997) 863.

Angela Harris, *Race and Essentialism in Feminist Theory*, 42 STANFORD LAW REVIEW (1990) 581.

Meri Melissi Hartley-Blecic, *The Invisible Women: The Taliban's Oppression of Women in Afghanistan*, 7 ILSA JOURNAL OF INTERNATIONAL AND COMPARATIVE LAW (2001) 553.

Berta Esperanza Hernandez-Truyol, *Building Bridges V – Cubans without Borders*, 55 FLORIDA LAW REVIEW (2003) 225.

Berta Esperanza Hernandez-Truyol and Sharon Elizabeth Rush, *Culture, Nationhood, and the Human Rights Ideal*, 33 UNIVERSITY OF MICHIGAN JOURNAL OF LAW REFORM (2000) 234.

Constance Hilliard, *Feminists Abroad: Ugly Americans?*, USA TODAY, April 12, 2002 at 15A.

Tracy E. Higgins, *Anti-Essentialism, Relativism, and Human Rights*, 19 HARVARD WOMEN'S LAW JOURNAL (1996) 89.

Charles Hirschkind and Saba Mahmood, *Feminism, the Taliban, and Politics of Counter-Insurgency*, 75 ANTHROPOLOGICAL QUARTERLY (2002) 339.

Ran Hirschl, *The Political Origins of the New Constitutionalism*, 11 INDIANA JOURNAL OF GLOBAL LEGAL STUDIES (2004) 71.

Cindy Holder, *Are Patriarchal Cultures Really a Problem? Rethinking Objections from Cultural Viciousness*, JOURNAL OF CONTEMPORARY LEGAL ISSUES (2002) 727.

Khaled Hosseini, *Desperation in Kabul*, NEW YORK TIMES, July 1, 2003 at A23.

Courtney W. Howland, *The Challenge of Religious Fundamentalism to the Liberty and Equality Rights of Women: An Analysis under the Nations Charter*, COLUMBIA JOURNAL OF TRANSNATIONAL LAW (1997) 271.

Rana Husseini, *Enforcing Laws against "Honor" Killings in Jordan*, 14 INTERIGHTS BULLETIN (2004) 157.

Michael Ignatieff, *Human Rights: The Midlife Crisis*, NEW YORK REVIEW OF BOOKS, May 20, 1999, 58.

Shireen J. Jejeebhoy and Zeba A. Sathar, *Women's Autonomy in India and Pakistan: The Influence of Religion and Region*, 27 POPULATION AND DEVELOPMENT REVIEW (December 2001) 687.

Jennifer Jewett, *The Recommendations of the International Conference on Population and Development: The Possibility of the Empowerment of Women in Egypt*, 29 CORNELL INTERNATIONAL LAW JOURNAL (1996) 191.

Ann Jones, *Remember the Women?*, THE NATION, November 9, 2009.

Rhoda Kadalie, *Constitutional Equality: The Implications for Women in South Africa*, 2 SOCIAL POLITICS (1995) 208.

Ratna Kapur, *The Tragedy of Victimization Rhetoric: Resurrecting the "Native" Subject in International Post-Global Feminist Legal Politics*, 15 HARVARD HUMAN RIGHTS JOURNAL (2002) 1.

Johanna Kehler, *Women and Poverty in South Africa*, JOURNAL OF INTERNATIONAL WOMEN'S STUDIES (2001) at: *http://www.bridgew. edu/soas/jiws/fall01/index.htm*.

Suzanne A. Kim, *Betraying Women in the Name of Revolution: Violence against Women as an Obstacle to Nation-Building in South Africa*, 8 CARDOZO WOMEN'S LAW JOURNAL (2001) 1.

Michael S. Kimmel, *Why Men Should Support Gender Equality*, WOMEN'S STUDIES REVIEW (Fall 2005) 102.

Karl Klare, *Legal Culture and Transformative Constitutionalism*, SOUTH AFRICAN JOURNAL OF HUMAN RIGHTS (1998) 146.

Karen Knop, *Examining the Complex Role of Women*, 15 EUROPEAN JOURNAL OF INTERNATIONAL LAW (2004) 395.

Nicholas Kristof, *The Women's Crusade*, NEW YORK TIMES, August 17, 2009 at: *http://www.nytimes.com/2009/08/23/magazine/23Women-t.html?pagewanted=all*.

Marc Lacey, *African Women Gather to Denounce Genital Cutting*, NEW YORK TIMES, February 6, 2003 at: *http://www.nytimes.com/2003/02/06/world/african-women-gather-to-denounce-genital-cutting.html*.

Monica Laganparsad and Yasantha Naidoo, *Four Better or for Worse*, SUNDAY TIMES (Johannesburg), January 6, 2008 at: *http://www.thetimes.co.za/PrintEdition/Article.aspx?id=673124*.

Paul Lansing and Julie C. King, *South Africa's Truth and Reconciliation Commission: The Conflict between Individual Justice and National Healing in the Post-Apartheid Age*, 15 ARIZONA JOURNAL OF INTERNATIONAL AND COMPARATIVE LAW (1998) 753.

Charles Lawrence III, *The Id, the Ego and Equal Protection: Reckoning with Unconscious Racism*, 1987 STANFORD LAW REVIEW 317.

Jennifer Kristen Lee, *Legal Reform to Advance the Rights of Women in Afghanistan within the Framework of Islam*, 49 SANTA CLARA LAW REVIEW (2009) 531.

Nancy Levit, *A Different Kind of Sameness: Beyond Formal Equality and Antisubordination Principles in Gay Legal Theory and Constitutional Doctrine*, 61 OHIO STATE LAW JOURNAL (2000) 867.

Hope Lewis, *Embracing Complexity: Human Rights in Critical Race Feminist Perspective*, 12 COLUMBIA JOURNAL OF GENDER AND LAW (2003) 510.

Hope Lewis and Isabelle R. Gunning, *Cleaning Our Own House: "Exotic" and Familial Human Rights Violations*, 4 BUFFALO HUMAN RIGHTS LAW REVIEW (1998) 123.

Magda Lewis, *Interrupting Patriarchy: Politics, Resistance, and Transformation in the Feminist Classroom*, 60 HARVARD EDUCATIONAL REVIEW (1990) 467.

Sandra Liebenberg, *The Value of Freedom in Interpreting Socio-Economic Rights*, 1 ACTA JURIDICA (2008) 149.

Sandra Liebenberg, *Needs, Rights and Social Transformation: Adjudicating Social Rights*, CENTER FOR HUMAN RIGHTS AND GLOBAL JUSTICE WORKING PAPER, No. 8 (2005).

Antoinette Sedillo Lopez, *Women's Rights as Human Rights: Intersectional Issues of Race and Gender Facing Women of Color*, 28 SOUTHERN UNIVERSITY LAW REVIEW (2001) 279.

Audrey Macklin, *Cross-Border Shopping for Ideas: A Critical Review of United States, Canadian, and Australian Approaches to Gender-Related Asylum Claims*, 13 GEORGIA IMMIGRATION LAW JOURNAL (Fall 1998) 25.

Kathleen Mahoney, *Theoretical Perspectives on Women's Human Rights and Strategies for Their Implementation*, 21 BROOKLYN JOURNAL OF INTERNATIONAL LAW (1996) 799.

Margaret (Peggy) Maisel, *Have Truth and Reconciliation Commissions Helped Remediate Human Rights Violations against Women? A Feminist Analysis of the Past and Formula for the Future*, 20 CARDOZO JOURNAL OF INTERNATIONAL AND COMPARATIVE LAW (2011) 143.

Holly Maquigan, *Cultural Evidence and Male Violence: Are Feminist and Multiculturalist Reformers on a Collision Course in Criminal Courts?*, 70 NEW YORK UNIVERSITY LAW REVIEW (1995) 36.

Meredith Marshall, *United Nations Conference on Population and Development: The Road to a New Reality for Reproductive Health*, 10 EMORY INTERNATIONAL LAW REVIEW (1996) 441.

Serena Mayeri, *Constitutional Choices: Legal Feminism and the Historical Dynamics of Change*, 92 CALIFORNIA LAW REVIEW (2004) 755.

Nomtuse Mbere, *The Beijing Conference: A South African Perspective*, 16 SAIS REVIEW 1 (1996) 167.

Eve McCabe, *The Inadequacy of International Human Rights Law to Protect the Rights of Women as Illustrated by the Crisis in Afghanistan*, 5 UCLA JOURNAL OF INTERNATIONAL LAW AND FOREIGN AFFAIRS (2001) 419.

Anne McClintock, *"No Longer in a Future Heaven": Women and Nationalism in South Africa*, 51 TRANSITION (1991) 104.

Joyce McConnell, *Beyond Metaphor: Battered Women, Involuntary Servitude and the Thirteenth Amendment*, 4 YALE JOURNAL OF LAW AND FEMINISM (1992) 207.

C. Alison McIntosh and Jason Finkle, *The Cairo Conference on Population and Development: A New Paradigm?*, 21 POPULATION AND DEVELOPMENT REVIEW (1995) 223.

Euserbius McKaiser, *When Mandela Goes*, NEW YORK TIMES, January 4, 2012 at: *http://latitude.blogs.nytimes.com/2012/01/04/when-mandela-goes/? ref=nelsonmandela.*

Sheila Meintjies, *The Women's Struggle for Equality during South Africa's Transition to Democracy*, 30 TRANSFORMATION (1996) 47.

Sally Engle Merry, *Constructing a Global Law: Violence against Women and the Human Rights System*, 28 LAW AND SOCIAL INQUIRY (FALL 2003) 941.

Diana Tietjens Meyers, *Feminism and Women's Autonomy: The Challenge of Female Genital Cutting*, 31 METAPHILOSOPHY (2000) 469.

Shannon A. Middleton, *Women's Rights Unveiled: Taliban's Treatment of Women in Afghanistan*, 11 INDIANA INTERNATIONAL AND COMPARATIVE LAW REVIEW (2001) 421.

Valentine Moghadam, *Meeting Practical Needs and Strategic Gender Interests: Women and Development in Afghanistan*, PAPER PRESENTED TO FULBRIGHT CONFERENCE ON WOMEN IN THE GLOBAL COMMUNITY, Bogazici University, Istanbul, September 18–21, 2002.

Valentine M. Moghadam, *Patriarchy, the Taleban, and Politics of Public Space in Afghanistan*, 25 WOMEN'S STUDIES INTERNATIONAL FORUM (2002) 19.

Valentine M. Moghadam, *Revolution, the State, Islam and Women: Sexual Politics in Iran and Afghanistan*, 22 SOCIAL TEXT (1989) 40.

Justice Yvonne Mokgoro, *Constitutional Claims for Gender Equality in South Africa: A Judicial Response*, 67 ALBANY LAW REVIEW (2003) 565.

Kathryn Pauly Morgan, *Women and the Knife: Cosmetic Surgery and the Colonization of Women's Bodies*, 6 HYPATIA 3, FEMINISM AND THE BODY (1991) 25.

Martha I. Morgan, *Founding Mothers: Women's Voices and Stories in the 1987 Nicaraguan Constitution*, BOSTON UNIVERSITY LAW REVIEW (1990) 1.

Justice Dikgang Moseneke, *Transformative Constitutionalism: Its Implications for the Law of Contract*, ANNUAL PUBLIC LECTURE, UNIVERSITY OF STELLENBOSCH, October 22, 2008.

D. Moseneke, *Transformative Adjudication*, SOUTH AFRICAN JOURNAL OF HUMAN RIGHTS (2002) 309.

Christina Murray and Felicity Kaganis, *The Contest between Culture and Gender Equality under South Africa's Interim Constitution*, 5 OXFORD INTERNATIONAL LAW REVIEW (1994) 17.

Makau Mutua, *Savages, Victims, and Saviors: The Metaphor of Human Rights*, 42 HARVARD INTERNATIONAL LAW JOURNAL (2001) 201.

Makau Mutua, *Hope and Despair for a New South Africa: The Limits of Rights Discourse*, 10 HARVARD HUMAN RIGHTS LAW JOURNAL (1997) 63.

Makau Mutua, *The Ideology of Human Rights*, 36 VIRGINIA JOURNAL OF INTERNATIONAL LAW (1996) 589.

Makau Mutua, *The Banjul Charter and the African Cultural Fingerprint: An Evaluation of the Language of Duties*, 35 VIRGINIA JOURNAL OF INTERNATIONAL LAW (1995) 344.

Stephen Lee Myers *et al.*, *Against Odds, Path Opens up for US-Taliban Talks*, NEW YORK TIMES, January 11, 2012 at: *http://www.nytimes. com/2012/01/12/world/asia/quest-for-taliban-peace-talks-at-key-juncture. html?pagewanted=all.*

Laura Nader, *Tracing the Dynamic Components of Power*, 38 CURRENT ANTHROPOLOGY (1997) 711.

Gemma Tang Nain, *Black Women, Sexism and Racism: Black or Antiracist Feminism?*, 37 FEMINIST REVIEW (1991) 1.

Sibongile Ndashe, *Challenges to Litigating Women's Right to Inheritance*, 14 INTERIGHTS BULLETIN (2004) 154.

Muna Ndulo, *African Customary Law, Customs, and Women's Rights*, 18 INDIANA JOURNAL OF GLOBAL LEGAL STUDIES (2011) 87.

David L. Neal, *Women as a Social Group: Recognizing Sex-Based Persecution as Grounds for Asylum*, 20 COLUMBIA HUMAN RIGHTS LAW REVIEW (1988) 203.

Vasuki Nesiah, *Toward a Feminist Intersectionality: A Critique of U.S. Feminist Legal Scholarship*, 16 HARVARD WOMEN'S LAW JOURNAL (1993) 189.

Thandabantu Nhlapo, *Cultural Diversity, Human Rights and the Family in Contemporary Africa: Lessons from the South African Constitutional Debate*, 9 INTERNATIONAL JOURNAL OF LAW AND THE FAMILY (1995) 208.

Ronald Thandabantu Nhlapo, *International Protection of Human Rights and the Family: African Variations on a Common Theme*, 3 INTERNATIONAL JOURNAL OF LAW AND FAMILY (1989) 1.

Rod Nordland, *For a Women's Soccer Team, Competing Is a Victory*, NEW YORK TIMES, December 8, 2010 at: *http://www.nytimes.com/2010/12/09/world/ asia/09kabul.html.*

Barbara Nussbaum, *Ubuntu: Reflections of a South African on Our Common Humanity*, 4 REFLECTIONS (2003) 21.

Celestine I. Nyamu, *How Should Human Rights and Development Respond to Cultural Legitimization of Gender Hierarchy in Developing Countries*, 41 HARVARD INTERNATIONAL LAW JOURNAL (2000) 381.

L. Amede Obiora, *Bridges and Barricades: Rethinking Polemics and Intransigence in the Campaign against Female Circumcision*, CASE WESTERN RESERVE LAW REVIEW (1997) 275.

L. Amede Obiora, *Feminism, Globalization, and Culture: After Beijing*, 4 INDIANA JOURNAL OF GLOBAL LEGAL STUDIES (1997) 355.

Leslye Amede Obiora, *New Skin, Old Wine: (En)gaging Nationalism, Traditionalism, and Gender Relations*, 28 INDIANA LAW REVIEW (1995) 575.

Chineze J. Onyejekwe, *The Interrelationship between Gender Based Violence and HIV/AIDS in South Africa*, 6 JOURNAL OF INTERNATIONAL WOMEN'S STUDIES (2004) 34.

Wiktor Osiatynski, *Human Rights for the 21st Century*, SAINT LOUIS-WARSAW
TRANSATLANTIC LAW JOURNAL (2000) 29.

Dianne Otto, *Rethinking the Universality of Human Rights Law*, 29 COLUMBIA
HUMAN RIGHTS LAW REVIEW (1997) 1.

Dianne Otto, *Holding up Half the Sky: But for Whose Benefit?: A Critical Analysis
of the Fourth World Conference on Women*, 6 AUSTRALIAN FEMINIST
LAW JOURNAL (1996) 9.

Susan Page, *Poll: Half of Americans Back Faster Pullout from Afghanistan*, USA
TODAY, March 14, 2012 at: *http://www.usatoday.com/news/washington/
story/2012-03-14/poll-afghanistan-pullout/53529896/1.*

E. Diane Pask, *Canadian Family Law and Social Policy: A New Generation*, 31
HOUSTON LAW REVIEW (1994) 499.

Denis Patterson, *Postmodernism/Feminism/Law*, 77 CORNELL LAW REVIEW
(1991–1992) 254.

Marius Pieterse, *Resuscitating Socio-Economic Rights: Constitutional Entitlement
to Health Care Service*, 22 SOUTH AFRICAN JOURNAL ON HUMAN
RIGHTS (2006) 473.

Nekima Levy Pounds, *Beaten by the System and Down for the Count: Why Poor
Women of Color and Children Don't Stand a Chance Against U.S. Drug Sentencing
Policy*, 3 UNIVERSITY OF ST. THOMAS LAW JOURNAL (2006) 464.

Catherine Powell and Jennifer Lee, *Recognizing the Interdependence of Rights
in the Anti-Discrimination Context through the World Conference against
Racism*, 34 COLUMBIA HUMAN RIGHTS LAW REVIEW (2002) 235.

Carla Power, *The Politics of Women's Head Coverings*, TIME MAGAZINE, July 13,
2009 at: *http://www.time.com/time/magazine/article/0,9171,1908306,00.html.*

R. Christopher Preston and Ronald Z. Ahrens, *United Nations Convention
Documents in Light of Feminist Theory*, 8 MICHIGAN JOURNAL OF
GENDER AND LAW (2001) 1.

Lisa R. Pruitt and Marta R. Vanegas, *CEDAW and Rural Development:
Empowering Women with Law from the Top Down, Activism from the Bottom
Up*, 41 BALTIMORE LAW REVIEW (2011) 263.

Questions, Answers and Comments, *Reluctant National Building: Promoting the
Rule of Law in Post-Taliban Afghanistan*, 17 CONNECTICUT JOURNAL OF
INTERNATIONAL LAW (2002) 461.

Jaya Ramji-Nogales, *Designing Bespoke Transitional Justice: A Pluralist Process
Approach*, 32 MICHIGAN JOURNAL OF INTERNATIONAL LAW (2010) 1.

Christa Rautenbach, *Gender Equality, Constitutional Values and Religious Family
Laws in South Africa*, INTERNATIONAL JOURNAL OF DISCRIMINATION
AND LAW (2001) 103.

Judith Resnick, *Reconstructing Equality: Of Justice, Justicia, and the Gender of
Jurisdiction*, 14 YALE JOURNAL OF LAW AND FEMINISM (2002) 393.

Jenny Rivera, *The Violence Against Women Act and the Construction of Multiple
Consciousness in the Civil Rights and Feminist Movements*, 4 JOURNAL OF
LAW AND POLICY (1996) 463.

Ruthann Robson, *Assimilation, Marriage, and Lesbian Liberation,* 75 TEMPLE LAW REVIEW (Winter 2002) 710.

Ruthann Robson, *Making Mothers: Lesbian Legal Theory and the Judicial Construction of Lesbian Mothers,* 22 WOMEN'S RIGHTS LAW REPORTER (2000) 15.

Ruthann Robson, *To Market, to Market: Considering Class in the Context of Lesbian Legal Theories and Reforms,* 5 UNIVERSITY OF SOUTHERN CALIFORNIA JOURNAL OF LAW AND WOMEN'S STUDIES (1995) 173.

Christopher Roederer, *Negotiating the Jurisprudential Terrain: A Model Theoretic Approach to Legal Theory,* 27 SEATTLE UNIVERSITY LAW REVIEW (2003) 385.

Cesare P.R. Romano, *The Proliferation of International Judicial Bodies: The Pieces of the Puzzle,* 31 NEW YORK UNIVERSITY JOURNAL OF INTERNATIONAL LAW AND POLICY (1999) 709.

Celina Romany, *Black Women and Gender Equality in a New South Africa: Human Rights Law and the Intersection of Race and Gender,* 21 BROOKLYN JOURNAL OF INTERNATIONAL LAW (1996) 857.

Albie Sachs, *Judges and Gender: The Constitutional Rights of Women in a Post-Apartheid South Africa,* 7 AGENDA (1990) 1.

Jeremy J. Sarkin and Erin Daly, *Too Many Questions, Too Few Answers: Reconciliation in Transitional Societies,* 35 COLUMBIA HUMAN RIGHTS LAW REVIEW (2004) 101.

Leila P. Sayeh and Adriaen M. Morse, Jr., *Islam and the Treatment of Women: An Incomplete Understanding of Gradualism,* 30 TEXAS INTERNATIONAL LAW JOURNAL (1999) 311.

Cornelia Schneider, *Striking a Balance in Post-Conflict Constitution Making: Lessons from Afghanistan for the International Community,* 7 PEACE, CONFLICT AND DEVELOPMENT: AN INTERDISCIPLINARY JOURNAL (2005) 174.

Ofelia Schutte, *Indigenous Issues and the Ethics of Dialogue in Latcrit Theory,* 54 RUTGERS LAW REVIEW (2002) 1021.

Stephanie Seguino, *Gender Inequality and Economic Growth: A Cross-Country Analysis,* 28 WORLD DEVELOPMENT (2000) 1211.

B. Seidman, *Law and Development: A General Model,* 6 LAW AND SOCIETY (1972) 311.

Gay Seidman, *Feminist Interventions: The South African Gender Commission and "Strategic" Challenges to Gender Inequality,* 2 ETHNOGRAPHY (2001) 219.

Kirk Semple, *Afghan Women Slowly Gaining Protection,* NEW YORK TIMES, March 3, 2009.

Kim Sengupta, *Women Who Took on the Taliban and Lost,* INDEPENDENT (UK), October 3, 2008.

Liz Sly, *Afghan Women Wage Own War,* CHICAGO TRIBUNE, October 22, 2001.

David Smith, *South Africa Rights Groups Condemn Jacob Zuma's Choice of Top Judge,* THE GUARDIAN, August 25, 2011 at: *http://www.guardian.co.uk/world/2011/aug/25/south-africa-jacob-zuma-choice-top-judge.*

Diana-Marie Strydom, *Zackie Achmat to Tie the Knot*, DIE BURGER, March 12, 2007 at *http://www.news24.com/News24/Entertainment/Celebrities/0,2-1225-2108_223218000.html*.

Jennifer T. Sudduth, *CEDAW's Flaws: A Critical Analysis of Why CEDAW Is Failing to Protect a Woman's Right to Education in Pakistan*, 38 JOURNAL OF LAW AND EDUCATION (2009) 563.

Anastasia Telesetsky, *In the Shadows and Behind the Veil: Women in Afghanistan under Taliban Rule*, 13 BERKELEY WOMEN'S LAW JOURNAL (1998) 293.

Robin Toner, *A Call to Arms by Abortion Rights Groups*, NEW YORK TIMES, April 22, 2004 at: *http://www.nytimes.com/2004/04/22/politics/22MARC.html?pagewanted=all*.

Hannibal Travis, *Freedom or Theocracy? Constitutionalism in Afghanistan and Iraq*, 3 NORTHWESTERN JOURNAL OF INTERNATIONAL HUMAN RIGHTS (2005) 1.

David Trubek and Marc Galanter, *Scholars in Self-Estrangement: Some Reflections on the Crisis in Law and Development Studies in the United States*, 1974 WISCONSIN LAW JOURNAL REVIEW (1974) 1062.

Esther Vicente, *Feminist Legal Theories: My Own View from a Window in the Caribbean*, 66 REVISTA JURIDICA UNIVERSIDAD DE PUERTO RICO (1997) 211.

Leti Volpp, *The Culture of Citizenship*, 8 THEORETICAL INQUIRIES IN LAW (2007) 571.

Leti Volpp, *Feminism v Multiculturalism*, 101 COLUMBIA LAW REVIEW (2001) 1181.

Scott Walker and Steven C. Poe, *Does Cultural Diversity Affect Countries Respect for Human Rights?*, 24 HUMAN RIGHTS QUARTERLY (2002) 237.

Christine J. Walley, *Searching for "Voices": Feminism, Anthropology and the Global Debate over Female Genital Operations*, 12 CULTURAL ANTHROPOLOGY (1997) 403.

Natasha Walte, *Comment and Analysis: The US and Britain Used the Oppression of Afghan Women to Justify Their Intervention*, THE GUARDIAN (London), October 12, 2004.

Stephanie Walterick, *The Prohibition of Muslim Headscarves from French Public Schools and Controversies Surrounding the Hijab in the Western World*, 20 TEMPLE INTERNATIONAL AND COMPARATIVE LAW JOURNAL (2006) 251.

Kathryn J. Webber, *The Economic Future of Afghan Women: The Interaction between Islamic Law and Muslim Culture*, 18 UNIVERSITY OF PENNSYLVANIA JOURNAL OF INTERNATIONAL ECONOMIC LAW (1997) 1049.

Deborah M. Weissman, *The Human Rights Dilemma: Rethinking the Humanitarian Project*, 35 COLUMBIA HUMAN RIGHTS LAW REVIEW (2004) 259.

Lucy A. Williams, *Issues and Challenges in Addressing Poverty and Legal Rights: A Comparative United States/South African Analysis*, 21 SOUTH AFRICAN JOURNAL ON HUMAN RIGHTS (2005) 436.

Stuart Wilson and Jackie Dugard, *Taking Poverty Seriously: The South African Constitutional Court and Socio-Economic Rights*, 22 STELLENBOSCH LAW REVIEW (2011) 664.

Adrien K. Wing and Samuel P. Nielson, *An Agenda for the Obama Administration on Gender Equality: Lessons from Abroad*, 107 MICHIGAN LAW REVIEW (2009) 124.

Adrien Katherine Wing, *The South African Constitution as a Role Model for the United States*, 74 HARVARD BLACK LETTER LAW JOURNAL (2008) 24.

Adrien Katherine Wing and Tyler Murray Smith, *The New African Union and Women's Rights*, 13 TRANSNATIONAL LAW AND CONTEMPORARY PROBLEMS (2003) 33.

Adrien Katherine Wing and Eunice P. de Carvalho, *Black South African Women: Toward Equal Rights*, 8 HARVARD HUMAN RIGHTS JOURNAL (1995) 57.

Miriam Koktvedgaard Zeitzen, *The Many Wives of Jacob Zuma*, FOREIGN POLICY MAGAZINE, March 12, 2010 at: *http://www.foreignpolicy.com/articles/2010/03/12/the_many_wives_of_jacob_zuma.*

Gintautas Zenkevicius, *Post-Conflict Reconstruction: Rebuilding Afghanistan – Is That Post-Conflict Reconstruction?*, 9 BALTIC SECURITY AND DEFENCE REVIEW (2007) 28.

Jean C. Zorn, *Lawyers, Anthropologists and the Study of Law: Encounters in the New Guinea Highlands*, 15 LAW AND SOCIAL INQUIRY (1990) 271.

Websites

Afghan Anti-Women Law Attacked, BBC NEWS, April 1, 2009 at: *http://news.bbc.co.uk/2/hi/south_asia/7977293.stm.*

Afghan Force to Fight Corruption, BBC NEWS, November 16, 2009 at: *http://news.bbc.co.uk/2/hi/americas/8363148.stm.*

Afghan Widows Find Employment, USAID/AFGHANISTAN, March 7, 2012 at: *http://afghanistan.usaid.gov/en/USAID/Article/2581/Afghan_Widows_Find_Employment.*

Afghan Women and Their Newborns Immunized for Tetanus, UNICEF, January 31, 2003 at: *http://www.unicef.org/media/media_7353.html.*

Afghan Women's Bill of Rights Presented to President Hamid Karzai by Women's Rights Groups, WOMEN FOR AFGHAN WOMEN at: *http://www.womenforafghanwomen.org/publications.php?ID=pubs.html* [accessed July 1, 2012].

Afghanistan: Judicial Reform and Transitional Justice, THE INTERNATIONAL CRISIS GROUP (2003) at: *http://unpan1.un.org/intradoc/groups/public/documents/apcity/unpan016653.pdf.*

Afghanistan: The Worst Place in the World to Give Birth, OXFAM at: *http://www.oxfam.org/en/campaigns/health-education/afghanistan-worst-place-world-give-birth* [accessed July 1, 2012].

Noorjahan Akbar, *Despite Widening Opportunities, Schooling Is Still the Preserve of the Few*, ALJAZEERA.NET, 28 July 2011 at: *http://english.aljazeera.net/indepth/opinion/profile/2011726102930470716.html*.

ALIA FOUNDATION at: *www.aliafoundation.com*.

All South Africans Must Act against Corrective Rape, WEEKLY MAIL AND GUARDIAN, May 11, 2011 at: *http://mg.co.za/article/2011-05-11-all-south-africans-must-act-against-corrective-rape*.

Amina Lawal's Death Sentence Quashed at Last but Questions Remain about Discriminatory Legislation, AMNESTY INTERNATIONAL, September 25, 2003 at: *http://www.amnesty.org/en/library/asset/AFR44/032/2003/en/bfab7b16-d68a-11dd-ab95-a13b602c0642/afr440322003en.html*.

AMNESTY INTERNATIONAL, AFGHANISTAN: "NO ONE LISTENS TO US AND NO ONE TREATS US AS HUMAN BEINGS": JUSTICE DENIED TO WOMEN (October 2003) at: *http://amnesty.org/en/library/asset/ASA11/023/2003/en/39a4c8fd-d693-11dd-ab95-a13b602c0642/asa110232003en.pdf*.

AMNESTY INTERNATIONAL, ANNUAL REPORT 2011: THE STATE OF THE WORLD'S HUMAN RIGHTS at: *http://www.amnesty.org/en/region/afghanistan/report-2011#page*.

BEYOND THE 11TH at: *www.beyondthe11th.org*.

Bibi Aisha, Disfigured Afghan Woman Featured on "Time" Cover, Visits US, NPR NEWSBLOG, October 13, 2010 at: *http://www.npr.org/blogs/thetwo-way/2010/10/13/130527903/bibi-aisha-disfigured-afghan-woman-featured-on-time-cover-visits-u-s*.

BRITISH MUSEUM, *What's on*, at: *http://www.britishmuseum.org/whats_on/exhibitions/afghanistan.aspx* [accessed July 1, 2012] and *http://blog.britishmuseum.org/category/exhibitions/afghanistan-crossroads-of-the-ancient-world/* [accessed July 1, 2012].

President George W. Bush, State of the Union Address (January 29, 2002), at: *allpolitics/01/29/bush.speech.txt/index.html*.

Cambodia: Young Trafficking Victims Treated as Criminals, HUMAN RIGHTS WATCH, June 22, 2002 at: *http://www.hrw.org/news/2002/06/22/cambodia-young-trafficking-victims-treated-criminals*.

CAMPAIGN FOR AFGHAN WOMEN AND GIRLS, at: *http://www.feminist.org/afghan/facts.html*.

Candidate List Outburst a Reminder of ANC's Gender Equality Policy, SABC NEWS.COM, April 24, 2011 at: *http://www.sabc.co.za/news/a1/d4948ee662 88f210VgnVCM10000077d4ea9bRCRD/'Candidate-list-outburst-a-reminder-of-ANC's-gender-equality-policy'-20110424*.

THE CIA WORLD FACTBOOK at: *https://www.cia.gov/library/publications/the-world-factbook/geos/sf.html* (South Africa) [accessed July 1, 2012] and *https://www.cia.gov/library/publications/the-world-factbook/geos/af.html* (Afghanistan) [accessed July 1, 2012].

Congo Mass Rape Comprises 170 Female Victims: U.N. Report, THE HUFFINGTON POST, August 27, 2011 at: *http//www.huffigntonpost.com/2011/06/24/congo-mass-rape-female-victims-united-nations-_N_883836*.

Mikaela Conley, *Toddlers, Tiaras, and Thigh-High Boots: 3-Year-Old Hooker's Outfit*, ABCNEWS.COM, September 8, 2011 at: *http://abcnews.go.com/blogs/health/2011/09/08/toddlers-tiaras-and-thigh-high-boots-3-year-olds-hooker-outfit/*.

COPERMA at: *http://www.crosiersincongo.com/1/cic/around_the_country.asp?artid=7218*.

Vexen Crabtree, *Which Countries Set the Best Examples?* (2005) at: *http://www.vexen.co.uk/countries/best.html*.

CRIMINAL JUSTICE: VIOLENCE AGAINST WOMEN IN SOUTH AFRICA, SHADOW REPORT ON BEIJING + 15 (POWA and others, March 2010) at: *www.powa.co.za/files/SouthAfricaShadowReportMarch2010.pdf*.

Demand for Surgery Rebounds by almost 9%, AMERICAN SOCIETY FOR AESTHETIC PLASTIC SURGERY, April 4, 2011 at: *http://www.surgery.org/media/news-releases/demand-for-plastic-surgery-rebounds-by-almost-9%25*.

ENGAGING MEN AND BOYS IN GENDER EQUALITY (United Nations Population Fund, 2011) available at: *https://www.unfpa.org/public/cache/offonce/home/publications/pid/8050;jsessionid=FAFE50AF624F5B8B7948E5AF01F31556.jahia01*.

FIGHTING CORRUPTION IN AFGHANISTAN: A ROADMAP FOR STRATEGY AND ACTION (Asian Development Bank and others, February 16, 2007) at: *http://www.unodc.org/pdf/afg/anti_corruption_roadmap.pdf*.

FINAL REPORT OF THE TRUTH AND RECONCILIATION COMMISSION, Vol. 6 (2003) at: *http://www.info.gov.za/otherdocs/2003/trc/*.

FIVE-YEAR REVIEW OF THE IMPLEMENTATION OF THE BEIJING DECLARATION AND PLATFORM FOR ACTION (BEIJING + 5) HELD IN THE GENERAL ASSEMBLY, 5–9 JUNE 2000 at: *http://www.un.org/womenwatch/daw/followup/beijing+5.htm*.

Diana J. Fox, *Women's Human Rights in Africa: Beyond the Debate over the Universality or Relativity of Human Rights*, AFRICAN STUDIES QUARTERLY (1998) at: *http://www.africa.ufl.edu/asq/v2/v2i3a2.htm*.

Alan Gelb, *Gender and Growth: Africa's Missed Potential*, WORLD BANK INSTITUTE (2001) at: *http://www.devoutreach.com/spring01/SpecialReport/tabid/1067/Default.aspx*.

Katy Glassboro, *Forced Marriage Appeal May Influence ICC*, INTERNATIONAL JUSTICE – ICC ACR ISSUE 123, August 6, 2007 at: *http://iwpr.net/report-news/forced-marriage-appeal-may-influence-icc*.

Pumla Gobodo-Madikizela, *Women's Contributions to South Africa's Truth and Reconciliation Commission*, WOMEN WAGING PEACE POLICY COMMISSION, vii (2005) at: *http://www.womenwagingpeace.net/content/articles/SouthAfrica/TJFullCaseStudy.pdf*.

BETH GOLDBLATT AND SHIELA MEINTJES, GENDER AND THE TRUTH AND RECONCILIATION COMMISSION: A SUBMISSION TO THE TRUTH AND RECONCILIATION COMMISSION (1996), available at http://*www.justice.gov.za/trc/hrvtrans/submit/gender.htm*.

KRISTIAN BERG HARPVIKEN, ANNE STRAND AND KARIN ASK, AFGHANISTAN AND CIVIL SOCIETY (2002) at: *http://www.prio.no/ sptrans/461921303/Harpviken%20et%20al%2002%20Afghanistan%20 and%20Civil%20Society.pdf*.

HOW COULD THE CONVENTION ON THE ELIMINATION OF ALL FORMS OF DISCRIMINATION AGAINST WOMEN BE IMPLEMENTED IN THE EU LEGAL FRAMEWORK? (2011) at: *http://www.europarl.europa.eu/ document/activities/cont/201107/20110725ATT24656/20110725ATT24656 EN.pdf*.

How the TRC Failed Women in South Africa: A Failure That Has Proved Fertile Ground for the Gender Violence Women in South Africa Face Today, KHULUMANI.NET, October 3, 2011 at: *http://khulumani.net/truth-a-memory/item/527-how-the-trc-failed-women-in-south-africa-a-failure-that-has-proved-fertile-ground-for-the-gender-violence-women-in-south-africa-face-today.html*.

JGLS and Cornell Law School Jointly Organize the Second Annual Women and Justice Conference, BAR & BENCH NEWS NETWORK, October 20, 2011 at: *http://barandbench.com/brief/9/1800/jgls-and-cornell-law-school-jointly-organize-the-second-annual-women-and-justice-conference*.

Peter Juul, *Advancing Women's Rights Is Progressive Foreign Policy*, CENTER FOR AMERICAN PROGRESS, June 19, 2011 at: *http://www. americanprogress.org/issues/2011/06/hillary_womens_rights.html*.

Judie Kaberia, *Meru Elders on the Spot over FGM*, CAPITAL FM NEWS, August 13, 2011 at: *http://fgcdailynews.blogspot.com/2011/08/meru-elders-on-spot-over-fgm.html*.

Hamid Karzai, Afghanistan President, Welcomes Taliban Office in Qatar, THE HUFFINGTON POST, January 4, 2012 at: *http://www.huffingtonpost. com/2012/01/04/hamid-karzai-taliban-office-qatar_n_1183089.html*.

Lack of Female Judges Worries JSC, WEEKLY MAIL AND GUARDIAN, October 25, 2011 at: *http://mg.co.za/article/2011-10-25-lack-of-female-judges-worries-jsc/*.

Bernard Makhosezwe Magubane, *Reflections on the Challenges Confronting Post-Apartheid South Africa*, UNESCO (1994) at: *http://www.unesco.org/ most/magu.htm*.

Mavivi Manzini Mayakayaka, *Political Party-Quotas in South Africa*, in THE IMPLEMENTATION OF QUOTAS: AFRICAN EXPERIENCES (Julie Ballington ed. 2004) 58, at: *http://www.idea.int/loader.cfm?url=/commonspot/ security/getfile.cfm&pageid=7841*.

ANDY MCKAY AND POLLY VIZARD, HUMAN RIGHTS AND POVERTY REDUCTION (March 2005) at: *http://www.odi org.uk/resources/docs/4355.pdf*.

MENSWORK: ELIMINATING VIOLENCE AGAINST WOMEN at: *http://menswperkinc.com/*.

Marianne Mollman, *The Deeply Rooted Parallels between Female Genital Mutilation and Breast Implantation*, RH REALITY CHECK, January 10, 2012 at: *http://www.rhrealitycheck.org/article/2012/01/04/female-genital-mutilation-breast-implantation-why-do-they-happen-and-how-do-we-st*.

Mavivi Myakayaka-Manzini, *Women Empowered: Women in Parliament in South Africa*, WOMEN IN PARLIAMENT: BEYOND NUMBERS (International IDEA, 1998) at: *http://archive.idea.int/women/parl/studies5a.htm*.

Nigerian Woman Facing Death Seeks Leniency, NEW YORK TIMES, August 27, 2003 at: *http://www.nytimes.com/2003/08/28/world/nigerian-woman-facing-death-seeks-leniency.html?ref=aminalawal*.

NEAMAT NOJUMI, DYAN MAZURANA AND ELIZABETH STITES, AFGHANISTAN'S SYSTEM OF JUSTICE: FORMAL, TRADITIONAL AND CUSTOMARY (June 2004) at: *www.gmu.edu/depts/crdc/neamat1.pdf*.

JUSTICE KATHERINE O'REGAN, HELEN SUZMAN MEMORIAL LECTURE, November 22, 2011 at: *http://writingrights.nu.org.za/2011/11/24/justice-kate-oregans-helen-suzman-memorial-lecture/*.

Obama Administration: Health Insurers Must Cover Birth Control with No Co-Pays, AP/HUFFINGTON POST, October 1, 2011 at: *http://www.huffingtonpost.com/2011/08/01/obama-birth-control-health-insurance_n_914818.html*.

OFFICE OF THE HIGH COMMISSIONER FOR HUMAN RIGHTS, INTEGRATING THE RIGHTS OF WOMEN INTO THE HUMAN RIGHTS MECHANISMS OF THE UNITED NATIONS (March 8, 1993) at: *www.amun.org/undocs/chr_1993_46.pdf*.

OFFICE OF THE UNITED NATIONS HIGH COMMISSIONER FOR HUMAN RIGHTS, GOOD GOVERNANCE PRACTICES FOR THE PROTECTION OF HUMAN RIGHTS (2007), 1 at: *www.ohchr.org/Documents/Publications/GoodGovernance.pdf*.

Nonso Okafo, *Law Enforcement in Postcolonial Africa: Interfacing Indigenous and English Policing in Nigeria*, IPES WORKING PAPER No. 7, May 2007 at: *www.ipes.info/WPS/WPS%20No%207.pdf*.

PHYSICIANS FOR HUMAN RIGHTS REPORT (2002) at: *https://s3.amazonaws.com/PHR_Reports/afghanistan-herat-maternal-mortality-2002.pdf*.

Powell and Dobriansky on Afghan Women's Crucial Role, RELIEFWEB, November 19, 2001, at: *http://reliefweb.int/node-90366.pdf*.

Malik Steven Reeves, *Alternative Rite to Female Circumcision Spreading in Kenya*, AFRICA NEWS SERVICE, November 1997 at: *http://www.hartford-hwp.com/archives/36/041.html*.

Callie Marie Rennison, *Intimate Partner Violence, 1993–2001*, UNITED STATES DEPARTMENT OF JUSTICE, BUREAU OF JUSTICE STATISTICS, CRIME DATA BRIEF (February 2003) at: *http://www1.umn.edu/aurora/pdf/Rennison%20BJS.pdf*.

REPORT OF THE INTERNATIONAL CONFERENCE ON POPULATION AND DEVELOPMENT (October 18, 1994) at: *http://www.un.org/popin/icpd/ conference/offeng/poa.html.*

REPORT OF THE SECRETARY-GENERAL, REVIEW OF THE IMPLEMENTATION OF THE BEIJING DECLARATION AND PLATFORM FOR ACTION, THE OUTCOMES OF THE 23RD SPECIAL SESSION OF THE GENERAL ASSEMBLY AND ITS CONTRIBUTION TO SHAPING A GENDER PERSPECTIVE TOWARDS THE FULL REALIZATION OF THE MILLENNIUM DEVELOPMENT GOALS (February 8, 2010) at: *http://daccess-dds-ny.un.org/doc/UNDOC/GEN/N09/637/20/PDF/N0963720. pdf?OpenElement.*

REPORT OF THE SPECIAL RAPPORTEUR ON EXTRAJUDICIAL, SUMMARY OR ARBITRARY EXECUTIONS, CHRISTOF HEYNS (May 27, 2011) at: *http://www2.ohchr.org/english/bodies/hrcouncil/docs/17session/A. HRC.17.28.Add.6_en.pdf.*

REPRODUCTIVE HEALTH RESEARCH UNIT, HIV AND SEXUAL BEHAVIOR AMONG YOUNG SOUTH AFRICANS: A NATIONAL SURVEY OF 15–24 YEAR OLDS (April 6, 2004), at: *http://ww.health08. org/southafrica/upload/HIV-and-Sexual-Behaviour-Among-Young-South-Africans-A-National-Survey-of-15-24-Year-Olds.pdf.*

Cecile Richards, *Birth Control Coverage a Victory for Women's Health*, January 21, 2012 at: *http://mustafashen.com/2012/01/21/cecile-richards-birth-control-coverage-a-victory-for-womens-health/.*

Hanna Rosin, *The End of Men*, THE ATLANTIC, July/August 2010 at: *http:// www.theatlantic.com/magazine/archive/2010/07/the-end-of-men/8135/.*

SADC PROTOCOL ON GENDER AND DEVELOPMENT (2008), at: *http://www. sadc.int/key-documents/protocols/protocol-on-gender-and-development/.*

AMBER SCHNEEWEIS, GENDER APARTHEID IN AFGHANISTAN at: *http:// www.public.iastate.edu/~rhetoric/105H17/aschneeweis/cof.html* [accessed July 1, 2012].

Jim Sciutto, *Afghanistan President Hamid Karzai Passes Controversial Law Limiting Women's Rights*, ABC NEWS, August 14, 2009 at: *http://abcnews. go.com/International/story?id=8327666#.T1J8TZjleJo.*

HELEN SCOTT, THE LIABILITY OF POLICE FOR FAILING TO PREVENT CRIMES IN ENGLISH AND SOUTH AFRICAN LAW, PAPER DELIVERED AT ST. ANNE'S COLLEGE, OXFORD, July 14, 2010 at: *http://www. privatelaw.uct.ac.za/usr/private_law/attachments/Police%20Liability.pdf.*

Geraldine Sealey, *Erections Get Insurance: Why Not the Pill?*, ABC NEWS, June 9, 2002 at: *http://abcnews.go.com/US/story?id=91538#.Ty74HiOQ324.*

INDIRA SINHA, GLOBAL FINANCIAL MELTDOWN AND WORKING WOMEN'S RIGHTS – WITH SPECIAL REFERENCE TO DEVELOPING COUNTRIES, PAPER PRESENTED AT 2010 ANNUAL MEETING OF AMERICAN POLITICAL SCIENCE ASSOCIATION at: *http://papers.ssrn. com/sol3/papers.cfm?abstract_id=1642054*

Serra Sippel, *Women's Health and Rights: Why US Foreign Policy Matters*, THE HUFFINGTON POST, November 22, 2010 at: *http://www.huffingtonpost. com/serra-sippel/womens-health-and-rights_b_786804.html*.

SONKE GENDER JUSTICE NETWORK at: *http://www.genderjustice.org.za/*.

SONKE GENDER JUSTICE NETWORK, STORIES OF COURAGE AND LEADERSHIP: SOUTH AFRICAN TRADITIONAL LEADERS SPEAK OUT TO ENGAGE MEN IN CREATING HEALTHY COMMUNITIES (February 2010), at: *http://www.genderjustice.org.za/*.

SOUTHAFRICA.INFO at: *http://www.southafrica.info/about/people/population. htm#religions*.

STATEMENT BY SIMA WALI, PRESIDENT, REFUGEE WOMEN IN DEVELOPMENT ON THE OCCASION OF INTERNATIONAL WOMEN'S DAY, NEW YORK, 8 MARCH, 2002 at: *http://www.un.org/events/ women/2002/wali.htm*.

STOP GENDER APARTHEID IN AFGHANISTAN, at *http://www.feminist.org/ afghan/facts.html*.

Dr. Paul Sullivan, *Who Are the Shia?*, HISTORY NEWS NETWORK, April 12, 2004 at: *http://hnn.us/articles/1455.html*.

Masuda Sultan, *From Rhetoric to Reality: Afghan Women on the Agenda for Peace*, WOMEN WAGING PEACE POLICY COMMISSION (2005) at: *http://www. iiav.nl/epublications/2005/from_rhetoric_to_reality.pdf*.

Khalid Tanver, *Family Suspected of Electrocuting Pakistani Bride*, MSNBC. COM, January 23, 2011, at: *http://www.msnbc.msn.com/id/41220289/ns/ world_news-south_and_central_asia/t/family-suspected-electrocuting- pakistani-bride/#.tybxncoq324*.

TATE MODERN at: *http://www.tate.org.uk/whats-on/tate-modern/exhibition/ level-2-gallery-burke-norfolk* [accessed July 1, 2012].

TEN-YEAR REVIEW AND APPRAISAL OF THE IMPLEMENTATION OF THE BEIJING DECLARATION AND PLATFORM FOR ACTION AND THE OUTCOME OF THE TWENTY-THIRD SPECIAL SESSION OF THE GENERAL ASSEMBLY HELD DURING THE FORTY-NINTH SESSION OF THE CSW, FROM 28 FEBRUARY TO 11 MARCH 2005, at: *http://www. un.org/womenwatch/daw/review/english/49sess.htm*.

THE SITUATION OF WOMEN AND CHILDREN IN AFGHANISTAN at: *http://reliefweb.int/node/120295* [accessed July 1, 2012].

The Ten Worst Countries for Women, FEMINIST EZINE, at: *http://www. feministezine.com/feminist/international/Ten-Worst-Countries-for-Women. html* [accessed July 1, 2012].

The War on Women, NY TIMES EDITORIAL, February 25, 2011 at: *http://www. nytimes.com/2011/02/26/opinion/26sat1.html*.

Patricia Tjaden and Nancy Thoennes, *Extent, Nature, and Consequence of Intimate Partner Violence*, FINDINGS FROM THE NATIONAL VIOLENCE AGAINST WOMEN SURVEY (2000) at: *https://www.ncjrs.gov/pdffiles1/ nij/181867.pdf*.

TRUTH AND RECONCILIATION COMMISSION, *INTERIM REPORT* (June 1996), Section 4: Committee Reports available at: *http://www.justice.gov.za/ trc/report/finalreport/Volume%205.pdf*.

2003 ASAPS Statistics — 8.3 Million Cosmetic Procedures: American Society for Aesthetic Plastic Surgery Reports 20 Percent Increase, AMERICAN SOCIETY FOR AESTHETIC PLASTIC SURGERY, February 18, 2004 at *http://www. surgery.org/media/statistics*.

UNAIDS, VIOLENCE AGAINST WOMEN AND GIRLS IN THE ERA OF HIV/ AIDS A SITUATION AND RESPONSE ANALYSIS IN KENYA (June 2006) at: *http://data.unaids.org/pub/report/2006/20060630_gcwa_re_violence_ women_girls_kenya_en.pdf*.

UNITED NATIONS CHILDREN'S FUND STATISTICS REPORT: SOUTH AFRICA at: *http://www.unicef.org/infobycountry/southafrica_statistics.html* [accessed July 1, 2012].

UNITED NATION'S COMMISSION ON THE STATUS OF WOMEN at: *http:// www.un.org/womenwatch/daw/csw/index.html* [accessed July 1, 2012].

UN WOMEN, IN PURSUIT OF JUSTICE: PROGRESS OF THE WORLD'S WOMEN 2011–2012 at: *http://progress.unwomen.org/wp-content/uploads/ 2011/06/EN-Summary-Progress-of-the-Worlds-Women1.pdf*.

UN WOMEN 2012 WORLD DEVELOPMENT REPORT ON GENDER EQUALITY AND DEVELOPMENT, at: *http://go.worldbank.org/ CQCTMSFI40*.

UNWOMEN.ORG, EXECUTIVE DIRECTOR at: *http://www.unwomen.org/ about-us/directorate/executive-director//*.

UN Women's First Chief Voices Optimism after Being Named to New Post, UN NEWS, September 15, 2010 at: *http://www.unwomen.org/2010/09/un-womens-first-chief-voices-optimism-after-being-named-to-new-post/*.

US AID, WOMEN AND CONFLICT AN INTRODUCTORY GUIDE FOR PROGRAMMING (2007) at: *pdf.usaid.gov/pdf_docs/PNADJ133.pdf*.

US AID'S WEBSITE FOR GENDER EQUALITY AND WOMEN'S EMPOWERMENT at: *http://www.usaid.gov/our_work/cross-cutting_ programs/wid/*.

Sher Verick, *Who Is Hit Hardest during a Financial Crisis? The Vulnerability of Young Men and Women to Unemployment in an Economic Downturn*, ILO/ IZA DISCUSSION PAPER NO. 4359 (2009) at: *http://papers.ssrn.com/sol3/ papers.cfm?abstract_id=1455521*.

NJOKI WAINANA, THE ROLE OF AFRICAN MEN IN THE FIGHT AGAINST HIV/AIDS (2005) at: *http://www.ww05.org/english3/speech/5.3. NjokiWainana.pdf*.

WHITE RIBBON CAMPAIGN, *http://www.whiteribboncampaign.co.uk/*.

WOMEN AND THE LAW CONFERENCE, REPRODUCTIVE JUSTICE: EXAMINING CHOICE AND AUTONOMY IN THE NEW MILLENNIUM (2012), at: *http://www.tjsl.edu/conferences/wlc*.

WOMEN AND THE LAW STORIES CONFERENCE, *The Power of Women's Stories II: Examining Women's Role in Law and the Legal System*, April 16, 2010 at: *http://law.scu.edu/womenlawstories/*.

WOMEN FOR WOMEN INTERNATIONAL'S CAMPAIGN IN THE DEMOCRATIC REPUBLIC OF CONGO, at: *http://www.womenforwomen. org/global-initiatives-helping-women/help-women-congo.php*.

Women in Face Veils Detained as France Enforces Ban, BBC NEWS EUROPE, April 11, 2011 at: *http://www.bbc.co.uk/news/world-europe-13031397*.

WOMEN'S HUMAN RIGHT'S RESOURCES PROGRAMME, BORA LASKIN LAW LIBRARY at: *http://www.law lib.utoronto.ca/diana/*.

http://fxreflects.blogspot.com/2011/06/burke-norfolk-photographs-from-war-in. html [accessed July 1, 2012].

http://womensenews.org/story/the-world/051021/constitutions-give-slow-birth-female-blocs [accessed July 1, 2012].

http://www.afghanwomensmission.org.

http://www.afghanwomensnetwork.org.

http://www.amnestyusa.org/our-work/issues/women-s-rights.

http://www.bbc.co.uk/religion/religions/islam/subdivisions/sunnishia_1.shtml [accessed July 1, 2012].

http://www.equalitynow.org.

http://www.feminist.org/afghan/facts.html [accessed July 1, 2012].

http://www.globalfundforwomen.org.

http://www.hrw.org/category/topic/women.

http://www.iol.co.za/blogs/carmel-rickard-1.2528 [accessed July 1, 2012].

http://www.law.syr.edu/deans-faculty-staff/profile.aspx?fac=72 [accessed July 1, 2012].

http://www.mifumi.org/.

http://www.un.org/en/documents/udhr/.

http://www.un.org/en/globalissues/women/.

http://www.womenforafghanwomen.org.

http://www.womenforwomen.org.

http://www2.ohchr.org/english/law/ccpr.htm.

http://www2.ohchr.org/english/law/cescr.htm.

Documents

AFRICAN CHARTER OF HUMAN AND PEOPLES RIGHTS (1981).

AGREEMENT ON PROVISIONAL ARRANGEMENTS IN AFGHANISTAN PENDING THE RE-ESTABLISHMENT OF PERMANENT GOVERNMENT INSTITUTIONS (2001) at: *http://www.afghangovernment.com/Afghan AgreementBonn.htm*.

BEIJING DECLARATION AND PLATFORM FOR ACTION, FOURTH WORLD CONFERENCE ON WOMEN, 15 SEPTEMBER 1995, A/CONF.177/20 (1995) AND A/CONF.177/20/ADD.1 (1995).

CONSTITUTION OF AFGHANISTAN (2004).

CONSTITUTION OF SOUTH AFRICA (1996).

CONVENTION AGAINST TORTURE AND OTHER CRUEL, INHUMAN AND DEGRADING TREATMENT OR PUNISHMENT.

CONVENTION RELATING TO THE STATUS OF REFUGEES.

DECLARATION OF VIOLENCE AGAINST WOMEN IN THE ASEAN REGION (June 30, 2004) at: *http://www.asean.org/16189.htm.*

DECLARATION ON THE ELIMINATION OF VIOLENCE AGAINST WOMEN, G.A. Res. 48/104, U.N. Doc. A/RES/48/104 (December 20, 1993).

FINAL REPORT ON THE SITUATION OF HUMAN RIGHTS IN AFGHANISTAN, U.N. ESCOR, 51st Sess., Agenda Item 12, No. 17, U.N. Doc. E/CN.4/1995/64 (1995).

INTERNATIONAL CONVENTION ON THE ELIMINATION OF ALL FORMS OF DISCRIMINATION AGAINST WOMEN.

INTERNATIONAL CONVENTION ON THE SUPPRESSION AND PUNISHMENT OF THE CRIME OF APARTHEID (1973). G.A. res. 3068 (XXVIII), 28 U.N. GAOR Supp. (No. 30) at 75, U.N. Doc. A/9030 (1974), 1015 U.N.T.S. 243, *entered into force* July 18, 1976.

INTERNATIONAL COVENANT ON CIVIL AND POLITICAL RIGHTS.

INTERNATIONAL COVENANT ON ECONOMIC, SOCIAL AND CULTURAL RIGHTS.

RESOLUTION ADOPTED BY THE GENERAL ASSEMBLY 55/2, UNITED NATIONS MILLENNIUM DECLARATION at: *http://www.un.org/millennium/declaration/ares552e.htm.*

RESOLUTION 1325 (2000) Adopted by the Security Council at its 4213th meeting, on October 31, 2000 at: *http://www.un.org/events/res_1325e.pdf.*

ROME STATUTE OF THE INTERNATIONAL CRIMINAL COURT, UN Doc. A/Conf. 183/9 entered into force July 1, 2002 at: *http://untreaty.un.org/cod/icc/statute/romefra.htm.*

SEX DISCRIMINATION ACT OF 1984 (Australia).

TRANSITIONAL EXECUTIVE COUNCIL ACT No. 151 of 1993 (South Africa).

UNITED NATIONS REPORT OF THE FOURTH WORLD CONFERENCE ON WOMEN BEIJING, 4–15 SEPTEMBER 1995 (1996).

UN PERMANENT FORUM OF INDIGENOUS PEOPLES, REPORT ON THE STATE OF THE WORLD'S INDIGENOUS PEOPLES, 2009 U.N. Doc ST/ESA/328.

VIENNA DECLARATION AND PROGRAMME OF ACTION, 1993.

Cases

Alexkor Ltd & Another v The Richtersveld Community & Others 2004 (5) SA 460 (CC).

Bhe & Others v The Magistrate, Khayelitsha, 2005 (1) SA 581 (CC).

Carmichele v Minister of Safety and Security and Others 2001 (1) SA 489 (CC).

Fraser v The Children's Court, Pretoria North and Others 1997 (2) BCLR 153 (CC).

Government of the Republic of South Africa v Grootboom and Others (2001) (1) 46 (CC).

Gumede (Born Shange) v President of the Republic of South Africa & Others 2009 (3) BCLR 243 (CC).

Gundwana v Steko Development CC and Others 2011 (3) SA 608 (CC).

Hoffmann v South African Airways 2001 (1) SA 1.

In re Alvarado No. A73753922 (United States Board of Immigration Appeals, 20 September 1996) at: *http://www.unhcr.org/refworld/docid/3f8fb4774.html.*

Larbi-Odam and Others v MEC for Education (Northwest Province) and Another (1998) 1 SA 745 (CC).

Minister of Health and Others v Treatment Action Campaign and Others 2002 (5) SA 721 (CC).

Minister of Home Affairs v National Institute for Crime Prevention (2004) 5 BCLR 445 (CC).

Minister of Safety and Security and Another v Carmichele 2004 (3) SA 305 (SCA).

Mojekwu v Mojekwu [1997] 7 N.W.L.R. 305 (C.A.) (Nigeria).

Nel v Le Roux and Others 1996 (3) SA 562 (CC).

President of the Republic of South Africa and Another v Hugo 1997 (6) BCLR 708.

Reina Izabel Garcia-Martinez v John Ashcroft, Attorney General 371 F.3d 1066 (9th Cir. 2004).

S v Baloyi and Others 2000 (1) BCLR 86.

Shibi v Sithole & Others 2005 (1) SA 580 (CC) (S. Afr.).

Soobramoney v Minister of Health, Kwa Zulu-Natal (1998) 1 (SA) 765 (CC).

South African Human Rights Commission and Women's Legal Center Trust v President of the Republic of South Africa and Minister for Justice and Constitutional Development 2005 (1) SA 580 (CC) (S. Afr.).

The National Coalition for Gay and Lesbian Equality and Another v The Minister of Justice and Others, 1999 (1) SA 6 (CC).

The Prosecutor v Jean-Paul Akaysu (Trial Judgment) ICTR-96-4-T, September 2, 1998.

Index

For Product Safety Concerns and Information please contact our EU
representative GPSR@taylorandfrancis.com
Taylor & Francis Verlag GmbH, Kaufingerstraße 24, 80331 München, Germany